AIRBORNE WARFARE 1918-1945

The face of Blitzkrieg. Oberst Bräuer, victor of Moerdijk, Dordrecht and Heráklion.

AIRBORNE WARFARE 1918-1945

Barry Gregory and John Batchelor

Phoebus

Men of the 503rd Parachute Infantry (Regimental Combat Team) landing as reinforcements at Noemfoor Island, in the Pacific, 3 July 1944.

Introduction

The parachute is not a new invention but the idea of dropping fighting men into action was not fully realised until the end of the First World War. It was during the Twenties and Thirties that Italy, Poland and Russia conducted experiments which showed the enormous potential of this new dimension. By 1938, Germany, too, had its fledgling parachute and glider force.

In 1940 these men were the spearhead of the *Blitzkrieg* lance and opened the way into Norway and Denmark. They bridged Holland's water defences for the Panzer and glider troops, knocked out the mighty fortress of Eban-Emael and were about to spring across the English Channel in the van of Operation Sealion.

The embattled British were quick to learn the hard lesson and Winston Churchill urged the formation of airborne forces while the trucks of the British Expeditionary Force still burned on the Dunkirk beaches. The climax of German victory came, however, in May 1941, when 6000 *Fallschirmtrüppen* dropped into Crete to seize the island after an epic week-long battle.

As the tide of victory turned, the British and American airborne forces became a powerful fighting machine. From the invasion of Sicily and the Italian campaign, through 'D'-Day and the tragically heroic battle of Arnhem, they opened the doors of Hitler's Europe.

This book is a fascinating history of the rise of airborne forces up to the climax of the Second World War. It encompasses operations from the Arctic to the Burmese jungle. Barry Gregory's well-researched text charts the fortunes of the men and the action. John Batchelor's full colour illustrations complete the record of the special planes, the equipment, the uniforms and the insignia.

BARRY GREGORY made his first parachute jump with the airborne gunners in 1951. He was commissioned in the Special Air Service Regiment (Artists' Rifles) and was associated with airborne forces for over ten years. He has

worked as a publisher's executive in London, Nigeria and Dorset.

JOHN BATCHELOR, after serving in the RAF, worked in the technical publications departments of several British aircraft firms before

becoming a freelance artist. His work, which has appeared in a wide range of books and magazines, and most notably in Purnell's History of the World War Specials, has established him as one of the leading artists in his field.

Soviet paratroops lined up before boarding their planes, PS-84 troop transports.

Imperial War Museum

Contents

AIRBORNE TO BATTLE

The fortunes of Bellerophon, the first airborne warrior, were spiced with both triumph and disaster. Greek legend tells us that the erring son of Glaucus captured and tamed the winged horse Pegasus and as an act of atonement took off on his loyal steed to slay the fire-breathing dragon Chimera. Bellerophon's mission was successful: the monstrous creature was destroyed by aerial attack with bow and arrows; and the Prince of Corinth was all set for a brief spell of military glory. Not long after killing the Chimera, however, Bellerophon, was made to fall to earth from his winged mount, and he spent the rest of his life as a pathetic cripple.

Whether General 'Boy' Browning ever read on to the end of the story of Bellerophon when he approved of the choice of Pegasus as the proud emblem of Britain's airborne forces has never been recorded but there was a strangely prophetic ring to the legend. Airborne troops in the service of modern armies similarly knew both victory and defeat.

The idea of airborne warfare has occupied the minds of men since artists first sketched on paper the imaginary means of non-controlled flight. But it was the Montgolfier brothers, Jacques Etienne and Joseph, who in the Parisian summer of 1783 first devised a method of air transportation when they launched a hot-air balloon. Benjamin Franklin, America's versatile commissioner in Paris, was so enthused by the success of hot-air and hydrogen-filled balloons that he posed ahead of his time in 1784 an interesting military question. 'Where is the prince who can so afford to cover his country with troops for its defence as that ten thousand men descending from the clouds might not in many places do an infinite deal of mischief?'

The air transport dream was further defined by illustrators of warlike themes during the Napoleonic Wars. By this time Captain Coutelle had already made an ascent in a military observation balloon at Fleurus on June 20, 1794. Captive balloons were used in the American Civil War (1861–65) for observation by both the Union and Confederate armies; the Northerners proudly boasting a 'Balloon Corps of the Army of the Potomac'. In the Franco-Prussian War of 1870–71, during the siege of Paris, balloons regularly lifted important people out of the city and carried many tons of mail. Pigeons conveyed in the balloon baskets later brought back military information and news to the metropolis.

Parachutes pre-dated the Montgolfier hot-air balloon but were still unproven in the late nineteenth century. Many daring jumps were made with ill-contrived parachute equipment until stunt parachuting after the introduction of powered flight by Orville and Wilbur Wright at Kittyhawk, North Carolina, in 1903, became a common event.

During the First World War, the static nature of the confrontation in the trenches, made captive 'kite' balloons invaluable for observation by artillery spotters. Several kinds of hydrogen-filled balloons were widely used by the opposing forces on the Western and Italian fronts. These huge gasbags, which were made of rubberized cloth and controlled by windlass and cable from trucks, supported either one or two observation baskets. Depending on weather conditions, balloons were raised to an altitude of 5000 ft and on a fine day the observation post officers could survey the terrain over a radius of ten miles or more. Communication with the ground was made by wireless telegraphy or by telephone line.

Captive balloons, however, were sitting targets for marauding aircraft and were regularly assigned as objectives for offensive patrols. The operational life of these aerial look-out posts was reckoned to be a mere 15 days, and German airmen rated balloon-busting as being worth $1\frac{1}{2}$ planes per balloon for the record. The only means of escape for the spotters was by parachute; a terrifying experience with the rudimentary gear then available; more especially as hesitation in leaping from the basket with a blazing mass of hydrogen above you could be fatal.

The prewar fairground parachutes were of simple design. The parachutist fell away from the aircraft and pulled out his parachute and rigging lines from a crude pack. Canopies were also often spread out below balloon baskets held by cords which snapped under the weight of the falling body. The jumper then fell freely for the benefit of the excited onlookers.

Everard Calthorp's Guardian Angel parachute was a typical successful wartime Army model. The equipment, apart from a simple body harness, was stowed in an aluminium sleeve on the outside of the basket. On making his exit the escaper grabbed a rope that led out of the sleeve and hitched it to his harness. The man then jumped drawing out the parachute after him.

Surprisingly the Air Board in Britain rejected the idea of issuing parachutes to Royal Flying Corps pilots. These life-saving umbrellas 'invited cowardice in action', an obdurate

Left: The winged Pegasus – legendary flying steed and symbol of Britain's airborne forces. Below: Leonardo da Vinci's prophetic notebooks contained this sketch of a parachute c 1500. Right: A fantastic vision of the aerial warfare of the future seen in a German drawing of the 1880s. In substance it is not far off the attack on the Belgian fortress of Eban-Emael in 1940

*An Italian **Tenente** of engineers ready for an ascent in an observation balloon c 1918, equipped with a British Guardian Angel Calthorp parachute*

attitude that probably led to the loss of more than 6000 lives. German pilots by now were already using a static line-operated parachute packed into a sack. In September 1917 the uses of the Guardian Angel were demonstrated to service observers in London. Major T Orde-Lees and Lieutenant the Hon A E Bowen jumped from the top of Tower Bridge into the river Thames. But the Air Board were not persuaded to authorize the issue of the Guardian Angel to RAF pilots until September 1918.

The first significant development in airborne tactics during the First World War came with the secret missions carried out by parachutists on the Western Front, in the Italian theatre and by the Russians in Eastern Europe. Winston Churchill had a scheme for dropping troops to blow up bridges; an idea that was to be reversed in the Second World War when the object was to secure them intact! A French sabotage team dropped in the Ardennes in 1918; but it was the Italians who were the most active in the clandestine rôle. Parachute spies were successfully infiltrated behind the Austrian lines and Italian Intelligence was well rewarded for its initiative.

The first recorded instance in British service flying of supplies being dropped from the air was one day in March 1916 during the Turkish siege of the British garrison at Kut-el-Amara in Mesopotamia. On this historic occasion the pilot of a lone aircraft of the Royal Naval Air Service dropped a millstone weighing 70 lb to the beleaguered troops. During the following month a resourceful RNAS detachment dropped more than seven tons of food and other supplies into Kut before the ill-fated garrison surrendered to the Turkish Army. This inaugural contribution to the logistics of airborne warfare may also be said to be the first quasi-combined operation in which the naval and aviation elements of the armed services went to the aid of their military comrades.

By the beginning of 1917 air supply was commonly practised in Europe and the flyers were increasingly becoming the eyes of the armies stranded in deadlock in the mud and detritus of the battlefields of northern France. The Italians, as will again be demonstrated in these pages, had a special zest for flying and during the great offensive towards the Vittorio Veneto in October 1918 succeeded in dropping large quantities of ammunition to the advancing Italian troops and their allies.

Airborne warfare as it was to develop in the Second World War was *per se* a demonstration of air power. The transportation of men and equipment by air to battle demanded reliable aircraft handled by superior crews; complete control of the air routes by fighter escorts was moreover mandatory. The military plan based on forming a stronghold in enemy-held territory in the onward path of advancing ground troops called for swiftness of coordinated command decision and instant air mobility. It was only the air force that could provide the means, the skill and determination of the airmen in no small measure preordaining the fate of the airborne troops in their charge.

It is surprising that the essential strategy of airborne manoeuvre should have been so firmly grasped – at least by one man – before 1918. A full analysis of General William Mitchell's career is not relevant to this text but firstly it should be mentioned that he was the outstanding United States air-combat commander of the war.

John Fraser

Below: Testing a dummy parachutist with static line attached to an Avro 504 – Croydon Airport near London, April 1922. Bottom: Early US Marine Corps experiments over San Diego harbour in 1926. The aircraft is a Martin MB-2

In September 1918, in the Battle of the St Mihiel Bulge, Billy Mitchell, as he was known throughout the American Expeditionary Force, commanded a French-US air fleet of almost 1500 aircraft, the largest concentration of air power up to that time. He was promoted one star general during the ensuing Argonne-Meuse offensive and he frequently used formations of up to 200 aircraft for mass bombing of enemy targets. His views on the use of air power as a vital element of land warfare were shared by Britain's Major-General Hugh Trenchard, the father of the Royal Air Force, and the war's foremost advocate of strategic air bombardment.

Mitchell added an extra dimension by suggesting the mass use of parachute troops to envelop and capture the fortress city of Metz. At this time the American First Army was fighting its way yard by yard through the Argonne Valley; 117,000 First Army casualties were suffered for a final advance of no more than 32 miles. Here was an opportunity to leapfrog the still strongly resisting German Army in the Argonne and destroy a bastion of the German defensive system, which served also as the main depot in the enemy lifeline by rail from Germany to the front-line in north-western France.

The plan to drop the US 1st Division from Handley-Page 0/400 bombers on Metz, actually devised by another young officer called Lewis H Brereton, was shelved by General 'Black Jack' Pershing, Commander-in-Chief of the AEF, until 1919. Perhaps Mitchell at least kept faith with his distinguished fellow countryman, Benjamin Franklin, by posing his most princely proposition. It was left to Lieutenant-General Lewis H Brereton, commanding the First Allied Airborne Army during Operation Market-Garden on 17 September 1944 to see the airborne dream come true.

In the years immediately after the First World War the parachute was relegated to its prewar status as stunt apparatus. In the United States, Mitchell ardently pursued his maverick theories on the unified control of air power; the efficacy of bombing aircraft; and 'vertical envelopment' by parachute troops. As Assistant Chief of the Air Service, Mitchell in the mid-1920s became increasingly critical of the military hierarchy that did not accept his views. His contention that the Navy no longer provided the first line of defence; his inspired prophecy of Japanese imperialism; and finally his outspoken criticism of the War and Navy Departments over the loss of the US Navy dirigible *Shenandoah*, resulted in his court martial in December 1925 and loss of privileges as an officer. He resigned from the Army and devoted the remaining ten years of his life to propagating his philosophy of air power.

The end of the Mitchell story was enacted in 1946 when Congress as a result of the events of the Second World War posthumously reinstated him as a general in the United States Army. A medal, struck in his honour, was presented to his son by the Chief of Staff of the newly formed United States Air Force.

The Guardian Angels that had saved so many British soldiers' lives during the war were taken into RAF service as escape parachutes but were soon superseded by a new aircrew parachute opened by a rip-cord. First introduced in 1919, this latest development was designed and perfected by one, Leslie Leroy Irvin, an American, whose A-type parachute with a 28 ft (8400 mm) canopy was in 1925 formally adopted by the RAF. Irvin, who already enjoyed a colourful reputation as a

VICKERS VIRGINIA

The RAF's main heavy night-bomber from 1924 to the mid-thirties, the Virginia was developed through several versions during its long service career. A few Virginias retired from front-line duties were used for parachute training by the Home Aircraft Depot (HAD) at RAF Henlow

(Virginia Mk X)

Engines: 2 x Napier Lion

Max speed: 108 mph

Span: 87 ft 8 in

Length: 62 ft 3 in

Max take-off weight: 17,600 lb

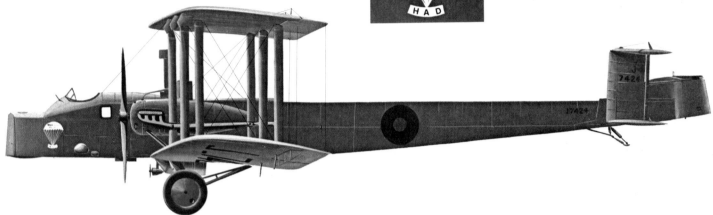

Radio Times Hulton

Vickers Vimys from RAF
Henlow practise a formation
drop sometime in the late 1920s

Below: The Italians were among
the very first to see the
potential of airborne warfare.
Here parachute pupils pose at
the Aeroporto di Centocelle
near Rome in 1931. Right:
Italian parachutists practise
a formation drop from Caproni
bombers at Littorio, 1931

parachute pioneer and stuntman in the United States, emigrated to Britain in 1926 and set up his now famous parachute factory at Letchworth in Hertfordshire. Later his 24-ft (7200 mm) escape parachute was carried by pilots but the 28-ft version was retained for training purposes.

Although there was still no talk in Britain of involving the Army in parachuting, a parachute training unit was set up at Henlow in Bedfordshire and airmen were taught to pack their own parachutes and jump from biplanes flying at 500 ft (152 m). (The Vickers Vimy was the usual trainer but the Virginia and several others were used for this purpose.) The first jumps of the course were performed by the 'pull-off' method: the trainee braced himself on a platform erected on one of the lower wings; pulled his rip-cord; and trusted to providence as the wind inflated his canopy and his body was dragged into the slipstream. The qualifying jump was made from the more realistic height of 3000 ft (913 m). The existence of RAF Henlow was, as will be seen later, vital to the establishment of Britain's parachute forces in 1940.

Mention should be made here, however, of Britain's early

if spasmodic contribution to the history of air trooping. In 1922 the RAF accepted the twin-engined Vickers Vernon as a troop carrier and the following year Nos 45 and 70 Squadrons flew troops into Iraq to apprehend dissidents in a long-forgotten quarrel with HM Government. Ten years later the 1st Northamptons were lifted in 21 Vickers Victoria troop carriers on another air-policing mission in the same country.

The Americans, like the British, did not take airborne warfare seriously until they entered the Second World War. Parachuting, like tight-rope walking, was a crowd-puller; the all-American genius for showmanship did not include airborne military manoeuvres; after all Uncle Sam had let Leslie Irvin go to Britain! The United States Marine Corps did use air transport nevertheless in the 1920s for minor expeditionary missions in South and Central America, and before his demise, General Mitchell's influence resulted in six men debouching in quick succession from an aircraft over Kelly Field in Texas. Then in 1932, a Captain Kenney startled the umpires on an exercise in Delaware by flying in a surprise package in the form of a fully-armed infantry section.

CAPRONI Ca 73

The Ca 73 appeared in the mid 1920s as a medium bomber but gave extensive service as a transport to Italy's fledgeling parachute arm

Engines: 2 x Lorraine, 400 hp	
Max speed: 109 mph	
Span: 82 ft	
Length: 49 ft 6½ in	

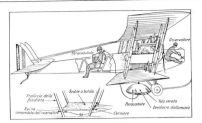

Left: The extraordinary system used by the Italians in 1917 to drop their informatori behind the Austrian lines. The parachutists' trapdoor seat in the Savoia-Pomilio SP 4 is under the control of the observer

Perhaps the real portent of things to come was the 250 ft (76 m) parachute tower erected at the 1939 New York World Fair; this was the model used for two simulated training towers erected by the US Army in New Jersey in 1940 when they heard about the German invasion of the Low Countries.

In Italy, the advent of Mussolini's dictatorship and his Fascist creed in the aftermath of the First World War, and the political strife that was endemic in Europe after the end of hostilities, played no special part in the development of the fast-growing *Regia Aeronautica*, the Italian Air Force. The Italians had a natural talent for flying and as fast as they took to the air in aeroplanes so they took immense pleasure in jumping out of them! Italian airfields were littered with deflated canopies! Military experiments with paratroops began in 1927 with a drop at Cinisello, near Milan. The Italians used the Salvatore parachute operated by hand grip on the belt or static line.

The Salvatore was a development of the Guardian Angel but the man carried his parachute on his back rather than on a balloon basket or an aircraft. The static line was hooked to a strong point in the aircraft. The basic principle was that the jumper was suspended from the back of his harness by a single piece of cord leading to his rigging lines. Hence the crouching pose adopted also by German paratroopers their RZ models derived from the Salvatore parachute.

Many military experiments followed the Cinisello parachute exercise but General Allesandro Guidoni, the founder of Italian airborne forces, was to plunge to his death in 1928 at the Campo di Montecelio. The *Storia del Paracutismo Militare Italiano* never quite recovered from this event. Colonial conquest in 1937 induced the Italians to make lamentable use of donkeys, sheep and goats air-dropped in support of their mountain troops in the Ethiopian campaign. Marshal Balbo, the suave Governor of Libya, formed in March 1938 the 300-strong 1st Battalion of the Air recruited from Italian officers and native colonial volunteers. A parachute training school was established at Castel Benito, near Tripoli, and a 'home-grown' 2nd Battalion made its debut in Italy at the same time based on the parachute training school in existence since 1925 at Tarquinia.

THE SILENT WEAPON

In spring 1920 the German Air Force was formally dissolved as a result of the Treaty of Versailles and the Allied Control Commission set about breaking up the German armaments industry. In the sphere of military aviation the defeated nation was denied the privilege of maintaining an air force and no fewer than 14,000 aircraft and 25,000 aero engines were destroyed. But Germany was allowed an army of 100,000 men and General Hans von Seeckt, the new *Chef der Heeresleitung*, devised an efficient method of training that gave scope for expansion. Illegal volunteer military units such as the *Freikorps* also existed and experienced cadres of NCOs were hidden in the ranks of the Prussian police and the security police. The Prussian police force at the time of the creation of the *Reichswehr* numbered 85,000 men, and were equipped with armoured cars, machine-guns, rifles, pistols and rubber truncheons. But Germany had to look beyond her frontiers for the clandestine means of training aircrew and rebuilding an air force.

Russia was not a signatory to the Treaty of Versailles, nor had the new Communist state been invited to join the League

Gliding clubs kept young German pilots in the air during the time of the Versailles Treaty's ban on a German air force. After the Luftwaffe came into the open, gliding continued to have a direct military function – as primary training and developing assault gliders

of Nations. The vastness of Russia and limitless open spaces, remote from Western interference, offered factory sites, proving grounds, and tactical training areas for an air force as large as Germany could afford. Germany and the Soviet Union had much in common: the government of the former was ruled by a Socialist majority; both nations in the eyes of the rest of the world were outcasts. In 1921 Lenin asked Seeckt for the *Reichswehr*'s help in training the new Red Army; on May 6 the 'German-Russian Commercial Agreement' was signed; and German agents in civilian clothes were given access to Red Army and Red Air Force training centres. The understanding with Russia augured well for the future of German military aviation.

The longing of German flyers to rise phoenix-like from the disillusionment of defeat and spread their wings became obsessional and another scheme for beating the ban on military flying was to indulge in the seemingly harmless sport of gliding. It was a German, Otto Lilienthal, who had pioneered man-carrying gliders, and zealous would-be pilots throughout the land scrounged wood, wire and fabric to make crude-looking gliders in abandoned sheds. In the early twenties a man named Steiner launched in his home-made glider from a lofty perch on the Wasserkuppe mountains, near Gersfeld, set up a German record for remaining airborne for two hours. Horsepower and manpower were used in those early days to haul the tow ropes.

Among the many onlookers to visit the valley near Gersfeld was *Hauptmann* Kurt Student, an Imperial military cadet at Potsdam at the tender age of 11 and since 1913 at 23 a military pilot. Student, who at first had not been too keen on flying, after the outbreak of hostilities in 1914 flew combat missions during the battles of Tannenberg and Augustovo and rose to command a Fokker biplane squadron (*Jasta 9*) based on the Champagne sector of the Western Front. Student's appointment in 1920 to Seeckt's Central Flying Office (*Fliegerzentrale*) was concerned with the technological aspects of equipping a non-existent military flying arm of the *Reichswehr* and that is why he was often to be seen in the vicinity of the Wasserkuppe mountains. Student was himself a glider pilot, although he very nearly

Smithsonian

This sequence of stills from a pre-war training film shot at the Stendal parachute school shows the thoroughness of German airborne training from parachute packing to the combat jump

Right: The backwash from the spinning prop of a wingless 1918-vintage Junkers CL 1 is used to inflate parachutes during ground training

met his end after fracturing his skull in a glider crash in the winter of 1921. He made a good recovery, and in 1923, as director in charge of air technology, he visited the German Air Force mission training secretly with Russian airmen at Lipetsk, near Voronezh, in the Soviet Union. In 1928 Student reverted to the infantry but the concept of airborne warfare had already formed in his mind; the acknowledged father of parachute and glider troops had to wait for Hitler's rise to power before he could put his ideas into practice.

Another seasoned air warrior, Hermann Wilhelm Göring, who unlike Student, was inclined towards politics, had not succeeded in obtaining an appointment in the Seeckt regime. His position as Commander of the Richthofen *Jasta* – shortly after the master's death in action – and his Blue Max, Iron Cross and numerous other decorations and awards were, if anything, an embarrassment in the political climate of the immediate postwar years. Much given to violent explosions of temper over the Versailles Treaty and the outrageous conduct of the 'November criminals', Göring was sufficiently stung by the German government's ingratitude for his distinguished services to go to Denmark, where he worked as a Fokker demonstration pilot and part-time stunt man. He then moved to Stockholm and managed to land a job with *Svensk Lufttrafik* as a charter pilot and again ran a sideline as an agent for Heinicken, manufacturer of an automatically opening parachute.

Göring soon returned to Germany where in Munich he became one of Hitler's disciples but was obliged to leave the country again as a result of the 1923 *Putsch*. He returned in 1926 after a spell in a lunatic asylum and after four years of idleness obtained the job of sales manager of Tornblad Parachutes Ltd; he worked on commission with German territorial rights only. Still an ardent Nazi and one of the few with the right connexions, Göring's career received a dramatic uplift when on 30 August 1932, he was elected

Junkers JU 52/3m: Workhorse of the German Airborne Forces

One of the truly important aircraft of the Second World War, and indeed of aviation history, the Ju 52/3m was from the beginning the backbone of the German airborne forces. Derived from the single-engined Ju 52, the first trimotor prototype with Pratt & Whitney engines flew in April 1931 and was in airline service a year later. When the *Luftwaffe* came into the open, its first bomber squadrons were equipped with Ju 52/3m g3e 'auxiliary bombers' but it was as a transport that the trimotor saw its first important action, ferrying Moroccan troops to Seville in 1936 at the beginning of Franco's Nationalist revolt in Spain.

When *Fliegerdivision* 7 was formed in the autumn of 1937, the Ju 52/3m began its intimate connexion with the German airborne forces. The occupation of Austria proved a dress rehearsal but proof of the aircraft's qualities came in April 1940 during the invasion of Norway in which Ju 52/3ms flew 3018 sorties. On May 10, 1940 this force was committed to its second major airborne operation – in the skies above the Low Countries, where the German *Fallschirmtruppen* achieved perhaps their greatest successes.

In 1941 the Ju 52/3m *Transportverbande* were committed to their most ambitious operation – the invasion of Crete. From May 1, the Ju 52s were flown to bases in Germany and an enormous overhaul operation was successfully completed – then on May 20 the Aegean skies were filled with the droning trimotors as Operation *Merkur* was launched. In Crete more than 270 Ju 52/3ms were lost but the attrition rate in Russia was much higher.

Obsolescent in 1939, the qualities of the Junkers trimotor kept it in production until 1944 and in the front line of the German war effort to the very end, long after the time of victory for the German airborne forces had passed

Engines: 3 x BMW 132A–3, 830 hp	
Max speed: 172 mph	
Range: 620 miles	
Span: 95 ft 11 in	
Length: 62 ft 0 in	
Max take-off weight: 24,250 lb	
Armament: 2 x 7.9-mm MG 15	

Smithsonian Insitution

JUNKERS Ju 52/3m

Crew: 2/3

Load: 18 fully-equipped paratroops

Smithsonian Institution

JUNKERS-JUMO 5

JU 52/3m

SCHWERÖL FLUGMOTOREN

Smithsonian Institution

Far left: Ju 52s in Spanish nationalist markings but with German pilots prepare to transport battle-hardened Moroccan troops to southern Spain. Their arrival secured the south for Franco's Nationalist revolt in 1936 and the operation was an early example of the effectiveness of air-transportation. Left: Junkers promotional brochure of 1937 included this picture of a world air-route spanning Ju 52/3m equipped with Jumo diesel in-line engines

Above: The Ju 52 was already proven in airline service. Wilhelm Cuno, a Ju 52/3m of Deutsche Lufthansa takes on passengers at a Baltic airfield sometime in the late 1930s

GERMAN RZ 16 PARACHUTE HARNESS

Unlike British and American parachutes the RZ 16 could not be steered by its lift webs. The soldier hung forward and upon landing absorbed the shock with his knees and elbows

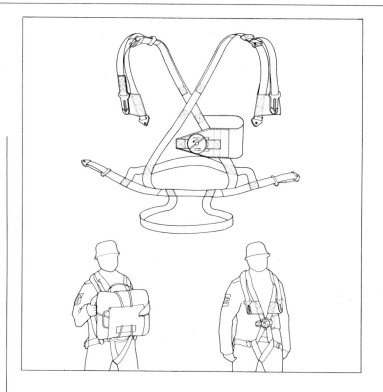

President of the *Reichstag*. Under Hitler the following year Göring among other appointments was named *Reichs* Air Commissioner and he enlisted as his principal aide Erhard Milch, the man who had been responsible for the development of *Lufthansa*, the airline that had also played a secret rôle in testing transport aircraft and providing flying experience for future military pilots.

In 1932 now *Oberst* Kurt Student was reassigned as Director of Air Technical Training Schools. Göring's new *Luftwaffe* was born in 1935 with the immediate aim of deploying 1000 aircraft. Student thought that parachutists would ideally implement Seeckt's concept of lightning wars. *Reichswehr* generals had witnessed, in 1931, the first publicized drop by armed infantrymen of the Red Army near Voronezh and reported favourably on the idea. Student's job embraced all aspects of military aircraft technology, including equipment, weaponry and parachutes. In September 1936, Student was one of many observers, who in the Minsk area witnessed a Red Army demonstration drop by no fewer than 1500 infantrymen free-falling from ANT-6 bombers. During the same exercise light trucks, 3-ton trucks, light armoured-cars and light guns slung between the wheels of the bombers were parachuted safely to the ground. At this time too the Red Army was already experimenting with gliders towed both singly and in tandem. Britain's General Wavell, who was also present at the demonstration, was impressed but saw no future in airborne troops; Student on the other hand was tremendously excited by the prospect. His strategy was to be based on the superiority of air power preached more than ten years previously by Mitchell, Douhet and Trenchard.

On January 20 1936, Hermann Göring issued orders for the raising of a parachute battalion based on a parachute training school to be established at Stendal, in North-West Germany. This was the first of the three battalions of *Fallschirmjäger-Regiment 1*. The first volunteers were recruited from the Hermann Göring Regiment, formerly the Prussian state police. Bruno Bräuer, their Colonel, had been a battalion commander of the Hermann Göring state police-group; he became a general during the war and at the end of it was executed in Athens by a Greek firing squad. In the same year a parachute infantry company was formed from Army volunteers. Its commander was Richard Heidrich, also to be a general and who is best remembered for his leadership of the *Fallschirmkorps I* in the defence of Monte Cassino, in Italy, in 1943. The school at Stendal was at first commanded by *Major* F W Immans, followed in 1937 by *Oberst* Bassenge.

The Germans decided that the rip-cord idea for releasing a parachute canopy and rigging lines that they had seen in operation in Russia was useless for military operations. At this stage technical development of the German parachute was focused on the state-line operated, single-point suspension Salvatore type developed by the Italian Air Force. An operational jumping height of 300 ft (91 m) was considered necessary and even at the training level of twice that height manually operated parachutes could not always be relied on to develop fully before the parachutist hit the ground. The *Rückenpackung Zwangauslösung* (RZ) 1, as the first German type was called, had a 28-panel, 28-ft (8400 mm) diameter canopy and was far from safe. This model was followed by the RZ 16 and in 1941 by the RZ 20, the standard

German parachute for the rest of the war. The RZ 36 also appeared in 1943.

A study of photographs of the *Fallschirmjäger* in flight clearly reveals that the rigging lines descending from the canopy converged on a strop, which was attached to the back of his harness. The jumper had no means as was the case with the more efficient Irvin X-type in British wartime service – and later – of manipulating lift webs, attached to groups of rigging lines to control oscillation. The German paratrooper fell suspended from his back, face and body downwards in a crouching position; a swimming motion with all four limbs explaining his efforts to control his line of flight. The characteristic method of making an exit from the aircraft door was head first in the manner of a diver but with arms and legs outstretched; a risky experience as there was a high incidence of fouling the static line. The Germans, who packed their own parachutes before take-off, wore knee-pads to absorb the shock of a forward roll on reaching the ground.

Milch in the meantime had not been idle in building up the *Luftwaffe*. In 1934, the former *Lufthansa* director, who had controlled the largest civil air fleet in Europe, projected the production of more than 4000 military aircraft, including primary trainers, over a period of 21 months. The total quantity envisaged included 450 Junkers Ju 52/3M transports, which flew at 150 mph (241 kmph). The Ju 52/3M was then the mainstay of *Lufthansa* and had enjoyed thousands of hours' successful flying before the first military version (a bomber) was delivered in 1934. The Ju 52, or Auntie Annie or Judula as the German airborne troops called it, was the ideal aircraft for dropping parachutists as well as lifting air-landing troops into battle.

In spite of its fame as one of the greatest transport aircraft of all time the Ju 52 was a rather ugly-looking beast. Its corrugated surfaces and square-cut wings gave the machine an appearance all of its own. The aircraft was nevertheless very strong and could take off from improvised air strips. Freight was loaded through a door on the port side and extra supplies could be carried on bomb racks under the fuselage and wings. Alternatively these external points could be loaded with weapons containers for dropping to parachute troops on the ground. This new breed of the Hugo Junkers long line of all-metal aircraft could be loaded with up to 10,000 lb (4500

German para insignia. Left to right: *Luftwaffe* **cloth, Army breast badge,** *Luftwaffe* **breast badge**

kg) of cargo, or 18 troops as passengers, or 13 jumpers. The speed of the Ju 52 reached 182 mph (293 kmph) with a range of 800 miles (1287 km) in later models.

The Ju 52 first gained operational experience with the *Legion Kondor* in Spain, although it was not used during the Civil War as a paratroop aircraft. But apart from carrying supplies, Junkers transport aircraft did figure with some Italian Savoia-Marchetti transports of the *Regia Aeronautica* in the first major airlift of reinforcements to the battle zone. The period was July-September 1936, when 9000 colonial troops of Franco's Army of Africa were transported from Spanish Morocco to Tetuan, in Seville. These airborne reinforcements probably saved the nationalists from defeat right at the inception of the revolt.

As the war developed, at least six schools were opened at different times in Germany for parachute training but it was the first at Stendal that was the best known, because of its early associations with airborne warfare. Volunteers were subjected to three months' military training, including the handling of enemy weapons before the 16-day jump course began. Parachuting following the simulated training in Ju 52 fuselages on the ground and tumbling from platforms on to matting then became a reality. Six jumps, including participation in a company descent, were necessary to obtain the parachutist's badge.

For parachuting the Ju 52 was stripped of all fitments except canvas seats and a strong point for the static line. On approaching the dropping zone the *Absetzer* (despatcher) on a signal from the pilot, shouted the order: 'Make ready' and sounded a horn as a warning to prepare for action. No further orders were now given as the parachute troops clipped their static lines or pull-out cords to a metal cable and sliding their hooks along with them as they shuffled through the fuselage made their exits from the port door. Once into the slip stream the static line broke open the parachute pack and was left trailing from the aircraft.

Student first visited Stendal as inspector general of *Luftwaffe* flying schools. He was then a major-general and on 1 July 1938 he assumed command of all airborne units. The German paratroopers were *Luftwaffe* personnel and not infantry soldiers; airborne operations 1939–45 were with a few exceptions an air force responsibility. By September, Student had established the main elements of the 7th Air Division, which included a small glider unit and an auxiliary force of Junkers transports assigned to the airlifting rôle. The 16th Infantry Regiment had been flown into the Sudetenland and during the main invasion of Czechoslovakia Student's 7th and 22nd (Air-Landing) Divisions gave a demonstration of air power if nothing else by flying into Freudenthal, in Moravia.

One problem facing all airborne forces at their inception over the next few years was that the paratrooper could carry little in the way of weapons and equipment during the descent. The *Fallschirmjäger's* webbing equipment was worn beneath a gabardine overall but he relied on the weapons containers dropped into action at the same time as the troops for his fire-power and essential supplies. Another method had to be found of supporting parachute troops by flying both men and *matériel* to the scene of battle.

The small glider force referred to above had originated from the *Deutsche Forschungsanstalt für Segelflug* who had developed a military glider from a sailplane used for high-altitude meteorological research. The DFS-230, as the new glider was known for short, could be used for freight or accommodating ten men, including two pilots seated in tandem. The DFS-230s were in full-scale production in 1937 at the Gothaer vehicle factory but the fuller development of the glider arm of the *Luftwaffe* awaited the introduction of the Messerschmitt 321 – *Gigant* – in 1941 and Gotha 242 in 1942. More about these gliders, the tow aircraft and their methods and the deployment of German gliders follows later. Whereas General von Kluge was impressed by the new parachute element of the *Luftwaffe* and promised Student all the help he needed in developing the airborne method, General von Brauchitsch, who witnessed a display drop at Munsterlage in June 1939, formed a less favourable opinion of the proposed spearhead of the German lance. The first time the *Luftlandetruppen* were exposed to the public was at the Berlin military parade of the same year when *Oberst* Bräuer led a goose-stepping detachment wearing airborne apparel and parachute bags past Hitler's saluting base. But whereas the pride of the German armed forces were the Panzers, the airborne warriors clearly had their uses in capturing key positions behind the enemy lines. It remained to be seen however, if it was worth training an expendable *corps d'élite*. *Generalleutnant* Student – described by Brauchitsch as an 'optimist' – was nevertheless ready for war. Three parachute regiments (*FJR 1, 2* and *3*) with airborne support units were in existence when *Fliegerdivision 7* in September 1939 moved as ground troops into Poland with a view to exploiting air-landing opportunities. The campaign was over before the *Fallschirmjäger* had a chance to buckle their seat-straps.

DFS 230

The *Deutsches Forschungs-institut für Segelflug* (DFS), nominally the German Research Institute for Gliding, was responsible for much innovatory work within the German aero industry on projects as diverse as the Me 163 *Komet* and the DFS 230 assault glider.
The DFS 230 was developed in great secrecy as an arm of the *Luftwaffe's* fledgling parachute forces, and began flight tests late in 1937. Production gathered pace and *Fliegerdivision 7* began developing glider assault techniques before 1939.

Max speed: (under tow Ju 52/3m) 130 mph	
Span: 72 ft 1⅓ in	
Length: 36 ft 10½ in	
Max take-off weight: 4630 lb	

Russian para badges. Left to right: 500 jumps, instructor, basic, 10 and 30 jumps

In Russia in the 1930s parachuting was a national sport. People's Commissar for Defence, Comrade Voroshilov, warmly praised the Soviet citizens said to number over a million men and women of all ages who jumped purely for fun! The Red Air Force was also enthusiastic about airborne warfare and as the German visitors at Lipetsk had discovered, Russian pilots and their fitters were adept at trying out new techniques. Nine men were dropped with success on an exercise in 1930 and over five hundred parachute descents were made during the course of the year. The following year fifteen paratroops carried out a punitive raid against bandits at Basmach in Central Asia. Test jumps by aviators mounted and during the course of 1932 four airborne motorized units were mustered. Some thirty parachute battalions forming three brigades were in being within the next four years.

The Russians, who in 1942 went over to using a parachute with a square-shaped canopy operated by static-line and wore a second rip-cord type as a reserve on the chest, at first used a manually operated copy of the Irvin version with a circular canopy. As was noted by the foreign observers who witnessed the large-scale Soviet airborne manoeuvres in 1935 and 1936, the huge, rather ponderous ANT-6 bombers flew in at about 2000 ft (610 m) and the parachutists clambered in quick succession through hatches in the tops of the fuselages and descended earthwards by free-fall after rolling off the starboard wings. The dropping height was unrealistic

operationally as wide dispersal of the troops on the ground prevented swift assembly. The slow-flying carrier aircraft would be vulnerable moreover to anti-aircraft fire.

Even during the war the Russians had no standard method of dropping equipment and supplies and much use was made of improvization. Consideration was actually given, as it was indeed by the British, to drop troops in containers mounted on platforms suspended from clusters of parachutes; a lunatic scheme that hardly merits evaluation! The Russians from early on, however, did succeed in dropping a considerable variety of light ordnance, tanks and transport both with and without parachutes, but again the chances of speedy deployment on the ground were remote. Limited experiments were made with gliders but it was not until 1941 that the Antonov A-7, a straight copy of the German DFS 230, put in an appearance after many prototypes had been rejected. The A-7 was mainly used for supplying partisan groups.

Marshal Tuchachevski, the guiding spirit of Russian armoured warfare policy, was also responsible for the swift build-up of the Red Army airborne brigades but did not survive the Stalin purges of 1937–38. In 1939 small groups of parachutists were dropped in action near Summa and Petsamo in Finland and the build-up of airborne forces continued until in mid-1941 the Red Army boasted five Airborne Corps, each consisting of three brigades; a grand total of approximately 50,000 men. This was a formidable

A Russian parachutist hits the ground. Luftwaffe intelligence watched Russian developments with interest

Imperial War Museum

TUPOLEV TB–3 (ANT–6)

Designed as a bomber, and like the Ju 52 skinned in corrugated metal, the first TB–3 flew in 1932. In 1937 an improved version appeared with smooth skin covering. Both versions served the fledgling Russian airborne forces extensively as a transport, the paratroops exiting through a hatch in the upper rear fuselage

Engines: 4 x M–17, 730 hp	
Max speed: 143 mph	
Span: 132 ft 10$\frac{3}{8}$ in	
Length: 82 ft 8$\frac{1}{4}$ in	
Max take–off weight: 41,021 lb	

Polish para badges

establishment but the Russians throughout the war never grasped the potential of parachute troops. The air-lifting of whole divisions, on the other hand, became common practice and was crucial to the successful outcome of a number of major battles.

Although Rumania opened a parachute school in 1937 at Pantelimon, near Bucharest, the only other countries apart from Russia, Germany and Italy to possess organised parachute units before the outbreak of the Second World War were Spain, Poland and France.

In 1938 during the Spanish Civil War *Luftwaffe* instructors trained a small group of Nationalists as parachutists at Barbastro. Similarly a small group of Republicans received instruction from Russian teachers at Las Rosas. Neither unit jumped in action.

Although largely unmechanized, the Polish Army in 1939 was powerful; that at least was the opinion of the Polish leaders who – as the Nazi menace mounted on their western borders – talked confidently of a 'cavalry ride to Berlin'. Parachute training had been undertaken since 1936 and the Polish Air Force had suitable transport planes. Jumping instructors were trained at Jablonna, near Warsaw; descents being made from towers and balloons. Demonstration jumps from aircraft followed at Wieliszew in 1937 and at Lwow in 1938. A Military Parachute Centre was established at Bydgoszc in May 1939 when the first Army cadre began a

two-month parachute course. A second course was in being when on 1 September the Germans advanced across the Polish frontier. Some Polish parachutists were among General Sikorski's Army in Exile in France and they later escaped to Britain. In mid-1940, Poles were among the earliest recruits to volunteer for training at the newly-opened Parachute Training School at Manchester's Ringway airport and Polish officers went on to make a distinguished contribution to the development of the RAF's parachute training methods.

A parachute school was opened in France at Avignon-Pujaut in November 1935. A French Air Force mission had visited Russia earlier that year and had reported favourably on the concept of airborne forces. The French school was an Air Force responsibility and the training methods Russian. Two companies, 601 and 602, of *L'Infanterie de l'Air* were formed. This was in January 1937 though the first parachute wings were not awarded until 12 months later. Both companies were sent to North Africa but recalled to France as soon as war was declared. An operation against the Dutch island of Walcheren was proposed in November 1939 but was never performed and the parachutists were used on the Western Front in a commando/reconnaissance ground rôle. *L'Infanterie de l'Air* was disbanded on 27 July 1940; the Vichy government's decision to break up the regiment being announced in the words of the para commander with 'regrettable indifference'.

PZL 4

This high-wing trimotor transport was designed and built at the Polish government aircraft factory and was the mainstay of Poland's pre-war parachute experiments

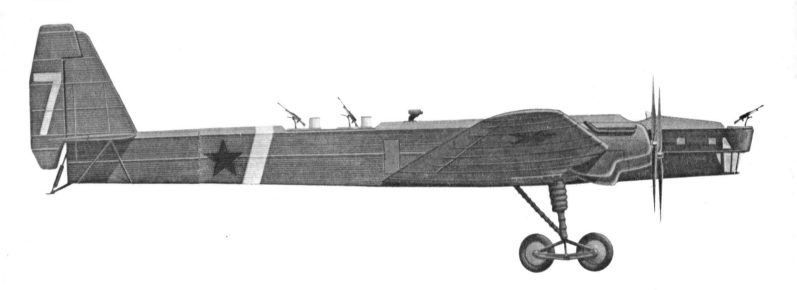

THE TIP OF THE LANCE

After the collapse of Poland, *Fliegerdivision 7* was stationed at the German garrison towns of Braunschweig, Hildesheim, Gardelegen and Tangermünde. *Infanterie-Division 22* at this time was already committed to an air-landing rôle alongside *Fliegerdivision 7* as part of German airborne forces. Kurt Student, who had narrowly missed capture in Poland after his staff car had strayed into a Polish defensive position, was in overall control and retained personal command of the parachute division. Parachute training was continued at Stendal and highly secret glider experiments were conducted at Hildesheim.

The six months' deceptive calm that followed the conquest of Poland ended with thunder and lightning when on 9 April 1940 the Germans invaded Norway and Denmark. The landings in Norway were almost entirely a naval matter with every serviceable warship of the *Kriegsmarine* protecting convoys carrying two mountain and five infantry divisions (*XXI Korps*) to various points of disembarkation on the Norwegian coast. Student's parachute and air-landing troops played their part in the invasion by securing airfields at Oslo and Stavanger.

Bad weather on 9 April prevented a drop

*German paratroops drop
near Narvik, silhouetted against
the Norwegian snows*

by *FJR 1* on Oslo's Fornebu airport and so the 1st and 2nd Companies of the 1st Battalion of that regiment followed by *Infanterie-Regiment (IR)324* were air-landed from Ju 52/3m transport planes. The seizure of Oslo the same day by a German infantry division storming ashore from transport ships berthed in the Oslo Fjord was greatly assisted by the assault from the sky and the airborne troops participated in the capture of the city.

The 3rd Company of 1st Battalion *FJR 1* made a successful drop at Sola airfield, near Stavanger; *IR 193* flying in to participate with the paratroopers in the capture of the port – facilitating the entry of the seaborne invaders at this point. On 14 April, 1st Battalion *FJR 1* was redeployed to intervene in the fighting further north. At Dombas the battalion was parachuted in with an assignment to cut a road and so prevent Norwegian troops linking up with British forces that had just landed from the sea at Andalsnes. The *Fallschirm-jäger* received bloody noses for their initiative in a four-day battle and were obliged to surrender to the Norwegians when an air resupply of ammunition failed to arrive because of the adverse weather conditions. The battalion could not have remained in captivity for long as between 18–29 May further airborne operations were mounted by *FJR 1* in the Narvik area in support of General Dietl's forces locked in combat with Allied troops. Norway was finally evacuated by the British and French on 9 June.

Meanwhile in Denmark, King Christian X and his Government had yielded to Hitler's ultimatum on 9 April; the Germans occupied the country to the sound of marching jackboots and military music before nightfall. In the early hours of the 9th two minuscule groups of paratroopers from the 4th Company *FJR 1*, were dropped, one at Aalborg, on the northern tip of Jutland, and the other at both ends of the 3500-metre long Vordingborg bridge connecting the islands of Falster and Zeeland. The seizure of the bridge enabled motorized infantry disembarking at the ferry-port of Gedser to advance immediately on Copenhagen.

Neither Hitler nor the British Government made special account of the involvement of German airborne troops in the invasions of Norway and Denmark. Hitler, however, immediately summoned Student and informed him that the time had come to commit the full strength of the two air divisions to battle. Britain was still not ready for war nor still indeed inclined to take it seriously; but on 10 May came a dramatic change in the nation's attitude with the arrival of Winston Churchill as Prime Minister; he was greeted on the first morning of his arrival in office with the news that two German army groups had launched full-scale offensives into the Low Countries and France.

When *Blitzkrieg West* began in the dark hours before dawn on 10 May, the attack by von Bock's Army Group B on Holland and Belgium was largely a manoeuvre to deflect the attention of the Anglo-French forces in northern France from the main thrust by von Rundstedt's Army Group A through the Ardennes to the English Channel. Although credit for the downfall of France has been given to General Heinz Guderian's superior Panzer tactics based on outflanking the Maginot Line to the north by driving his tanks through the difficult terrain of the Ardennes, the battle on the Western Front was won by the *Luftwaffe*'s superior air power.

Overall, the *Luftwaffe* for the two offensives assembled two air fleets numbering 4500 first-line aircraft, including more than 1000 Messerschmitt 109s and some 400 JuBf 52 troop carriers. The RAF could offer no effective defence and the *Armée de l'Air*, Dutch and Belgian air forces were largely decimated on the ground before take-off. With absolute air superiority these were favourable conditions for the deployment of airborne troops.

The idea to use *Fliegerdivision 7* and *Luftland-Division 22* to secure important strategic bridges and airfields in Holland and a fortress in Holland was Hitler's own but Student devised the operational plans. More than 16,000 men of *FJR 1* and *FJR 2* and Graf von Sponeck's air-landing division with full-scale light artillery and other support and service units were integrated as two formations under Kesselring's *Luftflotte II* for the assault on Holland. Student as commanding general of the *Luftlandekorps* was personally to lead *Fliegerdivision 7* on the ground. The seizure by *coup de main* of the modern fortress of Eban-Emael and nearby bridges over the Albert Canal in Belgium was assigned to *Hauptmann Koch*'s single company of paratroopers from 1st Company *FJR 1* accompanied by *Oberleutnant* Witzig's parachute engineer platoon. Assault Group Koch was to be landed in DFS 230 gliders inside the fortress walls.

As we have learned gliding as a sport had been actively encouraged in the days of the Weimar Republic. The German Glider Flying Association was said to have as many as 50,000 members as early as 1932. Sport gliding centres such as the one near Fulda, in the Wasserkuppe Mountains attracted both weekend enthusiasts and others sufficiently dedicated to take jobs in local factories to enable them to pursue their hobby. At *Fliegerkorps* training centres such as Rhön pilots

FOCKE-WULF Fw 200

Originally designed as an airliner, the Fw 200 *Kondor* was to achieve notoriety as a long-range commerce-raider. Civil Fw 200s in Lufthansa markings however had already seen action in April 1940

flying troops into Norwegian airports seized by parachute and air-landing troops

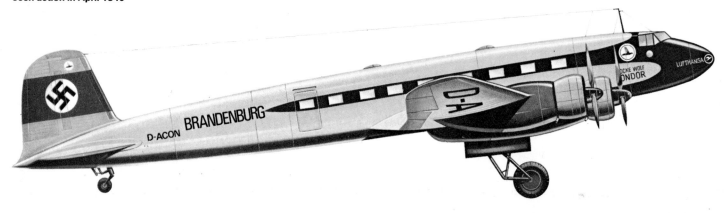

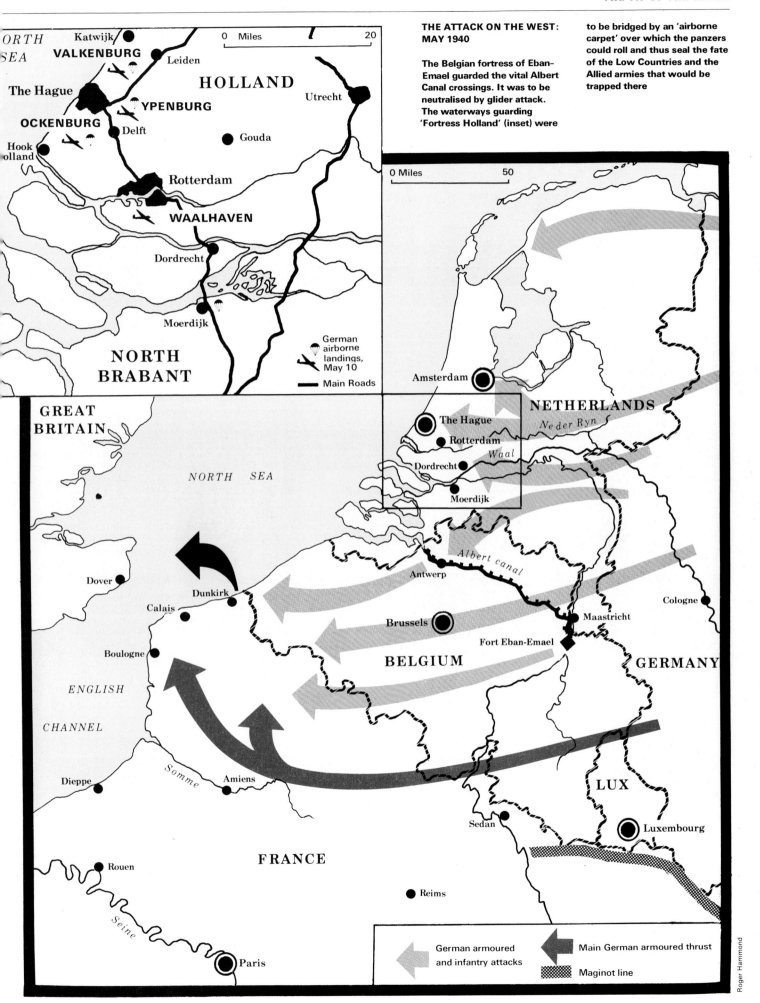

THE ATTACK ON THE WEST: MAY 1940

The Belgian fortress of Eban-Emael guarded the vital Albert Canal crossings. It was to be neutralised by glider attack. The waterways guarding 'Fortress Holland' (inset) were to be bridged by an 'airborne carpet' over which the panzers could roll and thus seal the fate of the Low Countries and the Allied armies that would be trapped there

Katwijk
VALKENBURG
Leiden
HOLLAND
0 Miles 20
The Hague
YPENBURG
Utrecht
OCKENBURG
Delft
Gouda
Hook Holland
Rotterdam
WAALHAVEN
Dordrecht
Moerdijk
NORTH BRABANT

German airborne landings, May 10
Main Roads

0 Miles 50

Amsterdam
NETHERLANDS
Neder Ryn
The Hague
Rotterdam
Waal
Dordrecht
Moerdijk

GREAT BRITAIN

NORTH SEA

Dover
Dunkirk
Calais
Boulogne

ENGLISH CHANNEL

Dieppe

Antwerp
Albert canal
Brussels
Fort Eban-Emael
BELGIUM
Maastricht
Cologne
GERMANY

Somme
Amiens

FRANCE

Rouen

Sedan

LUX
Luxembourg

Seine

Reims

Paris

German armoured and infantry attacks
Main German armoured thrust
Maginot line

Roger Hammond

EBAN-EMAEL: DAWN MAY 10, 1940

Built between 1932 and 1935, the Belgian fortress of Eban-Emael guarded the Albert Canal crossings at the towns of Visé and Maastricht. The central batteries of triple 75-mm guns were trained on these town's exits and provided the strategic function of the fort. All the rest was to guard the fort itself. The fort was triangular in shape, surrounded by an anti-tank ditch and to the east by the formidable barrier of the Albert Canal itself. Blockhouses provided with 60-mm anti-tank guns and machine-guns punctuated the outer ramparts while within the interior of the fort, Mitrailleuse (machine-gun) NORD and Mi SUD provided further anti-infantry defence backed up by twin 75-mm weapons in disappearing cupolas and a central 120-mm twin

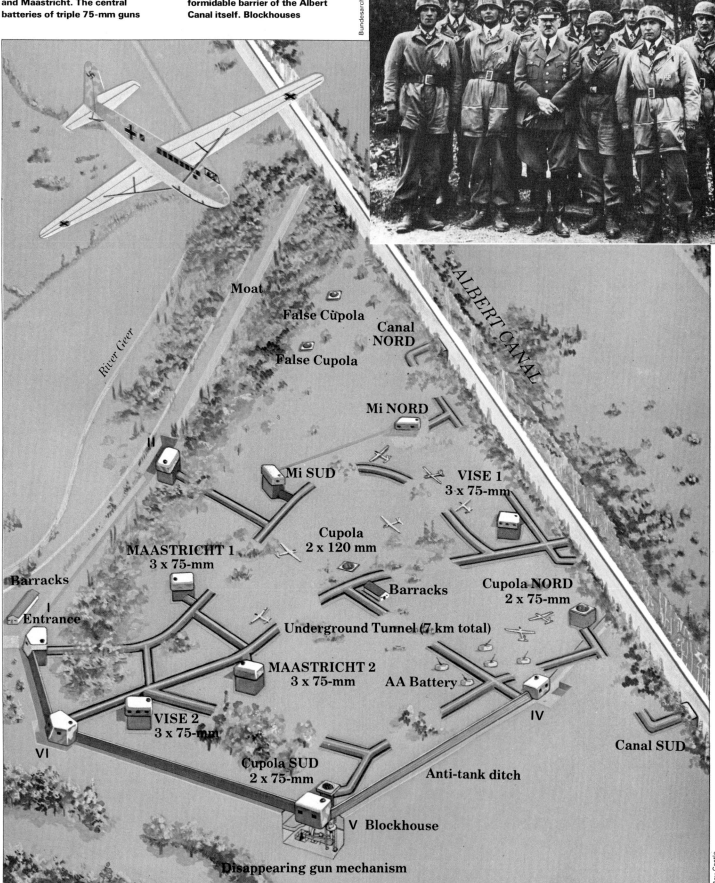

Bundesarchiv

Moat

False Cupola

Canal NORD

False Cupola

River Geer

ALBERT CANAL

Mi NORD

II

Mi SUD

VISE 1
3 x 75-mm

MAASTRICHT 1
3 x 75-mm

Cupola
2 x 120 mm

Barracks

I

Entrance

Barracks

Cupola NORD
2 x 75-mm

Underground Tunnel (7 km total)

MAASTRICHT 2
3 x 75-mm

AA Battery

IV

Canal SUD

VISE 2
3 x 75-mm

VI

Cupola SUD
2 x 75-mm

Anti-tank ditch

V Blockhouse

Disappearing gun mechanism

Roy Castle

cupola mounting. 7 km of tunnels burrowed beneath the fort's gently undulating surface and the garrison of 1200 were amply provided with gas-tight underground barrack facilities.

Anti-aircraft defence was light and the installations within the fort were not protected by mines, wire or trenches.

It was a fatal weakness and the 55 glider-borne troops of assault force Granite who landed within the fort's outer defences armed with concrete busting hollow-charge weapons found it. (inset) Hitler congratulates the leaders of the glider attack on

Fort Eban-Emael. (left to right) *Leutnant* Delica, *Oberleutnant* Witzig, *Hauptmann* Koch, *Oberleutnant* Zierach, *Leutnant* Ringler, *Leutnant* Messner, *Oberleutnant* Kies, *Oberleutnant* Altmann, *Oberarzt* Dr Jäger

could take A and B tests on gliders and when the Nazis were actively rearming, schools were established at Rossiten, in East Prussia, Dörnberg, near Kassel, and Syat, in Westerland.

'Assault Group [*Sturmabteilung*] Koch' had been in training at Hildesheim, near Hanover, since November 1939. Walter Koch, who had joined *FJR 1* from the Hermann Göring Regiment, set about the formation of Experimental Section Friedrichshafen, the code name for the Eban-Emael operation, with great energy. The most important feature of the training with DFS 230 gliders was the perfecting of spot landings; blind flying too was taught at another glider school at Braunschweig-Weggum. Hanna Reitsch, the German Women's Champion Glider Pilot, had told Hitler that properly handled, troop-carrying gliders were capable of swooping down almost silently on to defensive positions. It seemed the ideal method of immobilizing a fortress system that lay in the path of an advancing army.

In Belgium, General van Overstraeten's Belgian 7th Division defended the line of the Albert Canal. Reputedly the strongest fort of its time in the world, Eban-Emael stood at the northern end of the Liège fortress system. Its machine-guns covered the adjacent crossings of the canal, including the nearest bridge at Canne. Two 120-mm and sixteen 75-mm guns housed in armoured turrets and casemates covered the roads converging on Maastricht and two key canal bridges north-west of Eban-Emael near Vroenhoven and Veldwezelt. Koch's objectives were the capture of the fortress complex as well as the bridges at Canne, Vroenhoven and Veldwezelt. The fortress had only just been completed. Six outer walls of reinforced concrete – the longest abutted the canal – enclosed an area of 800,000 sq yd (668,901 sq m). The other walls concealed flood gates and were protected by entrenchments and barbed wire. Besides the artillery and machine-guns, anti-aircraft guns and searchlights were positioned inside the walls. In the tradition of classic siege warfare, the garrison numbering 1000 infantrymen and gunners possessed enough food and water to hold out for two months.

All the objectives were to be taken by glider-borne troops. The bridges were the responsibility of Koch's party split up into three sections: Veldwezelt – 'Steel' (Altmann); Vroenhoven – 'Concrete' (Schacht); and Canne – 'Iron' (Schächter). (What the *Fallschirmjäger* lacked in the way of armour-plate in their flimsy gliders was substituted in their operational code-names). Koch's HQ was to be centred on the Vroenhoven bridge. *Oberleutnant* Rudolf Witzig's party of parachute engineers were assigned to the main target, code-named 'Granite'.

On the early morning of 10 May, 42 DFS 230 gliders were towed in darkness into the air above Cologne by their Ju 52 tugs. One glider had already crash-landed when the glider force was released before crossing the frontier in the neighbourhood of Aachen. It was a raw morning and the men huddled in blankets could see little through the small windows of the gliders; 35 minutes after take-off the gliders swooped down into the battle zone.

Of Witzig's 11 gliders, seven landed as was intended inside the fortress walls; two crash-landed outside the operational area and the other two through faulty observation chose the wrong targets. The garrison was not awake when 55 combat engineers debouching from the fuselages of the gliders blew in the fortress exits and destroyed 14 of the guns by shoving short-fused explosives with hollow charges into the barrels. The alerted Belgian troops were kept down with submachine-gun fire and quickly surrendered. The German sappers' situation inside the sealed walls of Eban-Emael might well have turned into a predicament but for the timely arrival of German motorized troops later that day. The 'world's most powerful fortress' had fallen for the loss of six German dead.

Koch's gliders landed west of the canal astride the southern road into Maastricht. Belgians who saw the gliders landing mistook them for aircraft in trouble and were alarmed to see armed troops clambering out of the dismembered fuselages. The *Luftwaffe* had dropped dummy parachutists at several spots nearby and confusion reigned as the Belgian defenders were aroused. Plans had already been made by General van Overstraeten to blow up all three bridge objectives in the event of invasion, but after capturing the bridges at Veldwezelt and Vroenhoven, the Germans cut the cables to the demolition charges fixed to the bridges and threw the explosives into the canal. Schächter's section at Canne, however, were delayed in their approach march because of the widespread dispersal of their gliders on the landing zone. Belgian troops succeeded in demolishing the bridge and then turned their weapons on 'Iron' section, which was virtually annihilated.

In the meantime Kesselring's *Luftflotte II* droned over the peaceful Dutch countryside. Student's *Luftlandekorps* objectives were to capture The Hague and Rotterdam, and a few other vital communications centres. Graf von Sponeck's *Infanterie-Division 22* was assigned to The Hague with the specific mission of capturing the Dutch Government offices and, on personal orders from Hitler, to arrest the Royal Family. *FJR 2* had first to drop to secure airfields along the coast on either side of the capital to allow the transport aircraft to land, but in the event the Junkers pilots flew into any convenient field they could find and even on to beaches and roadways. The assigned landing zones north of the Lek (Rhine) were – from the north – Valkenburg, west of Leiden, Ypenburg, on the highway from The Hague to Rotterdam near Delft, and Loosduinen, just south-west of The Hague. In each case the jump zones were situated some distance from the actual landing zones.

In the Rotterdam area, Student's 4500 paratroopers were to pounce on the city airport at Waalhaven and to hold bridges to the south-east across the Waal at Dordrecht and at Moerdijk, on the Maas estuary. The successful capture of these bridges would facilitate the advance of the 9th Panzer Division spearheading the 18th Army moving up from the south. *Fliegerdivision 7* was reinforced by *IR 16* and *IR 65*.

The invasion of Holland was heralded by devastating *Luftwaffe* bomber raids on key targets. Heinkels flew in from the sea to deceive the Dutch Air Force and anti-aircraft batteries, but the Dutch fighters quickly detected the ruse and went out to meet them. Thirty-seven transport planes out of 55 belonging to *Kampfgruppe zb V9* alone were shot out of the sky. Crippled Ju 52s, some of them on fire, tried to make emergency landings but were torn to pieces by obstacles.

On The Hague sector, *FJR 2* encountering defiant resistance from Dutch troops, took their objectives but the air-landed infantry were unable to exploit bridgeheads won by the paratroopers to converge on the capital. A furious battle ensued in which the infantry lost the airfields, and by late

A parachute delivered machine-gun section in action on the Dutch polders with an MG 34. Section weapons were dropped separately in containers

evening more than a thousand of them had been taken prisoner. General Graf von Sponeck, mindful of his unsolicited appointment with Queen Wilhelmina, arrived in full-dress uniform, only to be removed from the field of battle as the best-dressed casualty in Holland.

Further south Student's men were enjoying more success. Waalhaven was captured by the third battalion of *FJR 1*, and *IR 16* deplaning at the airport moved off to the east to hold the banks of the Lek. The Dordrecht and Moerdijk bridges were surprised and held by the second battalion of *FJR 1*, personally led by their regimental commander, Oberst Bräuer. These positions were retained in spite of Dutch counter-attacks thanks to the support of the aircraft of *Luftflotte II*. The Germans quickly consolidated their grip on this area but now the French 7th Army was racing north to intercept the German 18th Army. The success of the invasion depended on the result of the fighting around The Hague.

The paratroopers fought their way into Rotterdam on the first day of the battle for Holland, but the smooth passage of the armour to the city from the south over the next few days made the surrender of the city and its port inevitable. During the street fighting Student was hit in the head by a sniper's bullet; his life was saved on an operating table by the skill of a Dutch surgeon. On the afternoon of the 14th the notorious 'horror raid' on Rotterdam took place during which almost a thousand Dutch civilians died and 25,000 homes were destroyed. *Luftflotte II* was unaware that General Schmidt, commanding *XXXXIX Panzer Korps*, was then negotiating for the surrender of the city.

At The Hague, German troops were in the suburbs when the Dutch General Winkelman ordered the cease-fire. The Royal Family and the Dutch Government had already made the decision to continue the fight in exile and were evacuated in two destroyers. The instrument of surrender was signed on 15 May, five short days after the Ju 52 transport planes had left their emplaning airfields in Germany.

While Student fought for his life in a Berlin clinic, the Führer inundated his airborne warriors with praise. Although

their deployment had been tactical in concept, their success on the southern sector had been almost strategic in importance. The *Luftlandekorps* losses had nevertheless been heavy and the air transport fleet had been ravaged both in the air and on the landing grounds. Time was needed for rehabilitation. In spite of his elation, Hitler surprisingly for the most evil warlord of all time, felt almost fatherly concern for the vulnerability of airborne troops. How often in the First World War had commanding generals had their ceremonial finery bespattered with blood or been hit in the head with a sniper's bullet? Airborne warfare was a new dimension that demanded the strictest evaluation of the chances of success as compared with the risks involved.

Meanwhile, in London, Service chiefs were examining samples of long, loose-fitting jump smocks, side-lacing boots and steel helmets conveyed from Holland. This unusual military attire was quite unlike any apparel worn by any known arm of the Wehrmacht. Who were these men who jumped from the sky?

The Great Invasion Scare: Britain 1940

The parachute scare that undoubtedly reigned in Britain throughout the summer of 1940 may seem exaggerated with benefit of hindsight but the threat of airborne invasion of the southern counties of England seemed a very real threat at the time. Newspaper reports from Holland during the *Luft-lande-korps'* assault were certainly enough to create widespread alarm and despondency. German paratroopers – it was rumoured – jumped in action disguised as English policemen, tradesmen and it was even suggested that suitably attired their shaven faces would pass off as nuns. Contrary to the belief at that time, the *Fallschirmjäger* fought strictly in combat dress at all times. The rumour, however, did have some substance in fact, as *Abwehr* agents, who operated in civilian clothes were active in Holland. These men belonged to the Special-Purpose Brandenburg Regiment *abV*, which was raised in 1938 for sabotage and counter-intelligence work, and did possess a small glider unit.

The Local Defence Volunteers, (LDV) later designated by Winston Churchill as the Home Guard, were raised in May 1940 primarily to counter the parachute menace. A watchful eye was kept on all possible landing grounds and in remote country areas horse patrols of 'parashots' armed with shotguns and pikes searched for suspicious vagrants lurking in copse and hedgerow. An instruction manual circulating to the LDV at the time stated that the German paratroopers' boots were fitted with spring devices that absorbed the shock of the body's impact on landing. Marksmen were advised to take aim and fire on the first bounce, but it was a gymnastic exercise that would have almost certainly broken the paratrooper's back without any help from a bullet. Thousands of square miles in Britain were covered with obstacles to impede airborne invasion and in London's Whitehall spikes were erected to impale descending assassination squads.

In July 1940, the Führer ordered the preliminary staff studies for Operation *Seelöwe*. In August, *OKH* the German Army Supreme Command, discussed plans for the use of *Fliegerdivision 7* in forming bridgeheads on the south coast of Britain. The intention was for Student, who returned to active duty in September, to establish airheads on the South Downs and northwards from Dover. The Luftwaffe raised objections to this operational scheme and the initial airborne objective was finally chosen as the Royal Military Canal, which extends from Kent via Romney Marsh into Sussex. The military significance of this obscure waterway in the dark days of 1940 will have escaped all but the most ardent military pedant; perhaps even Hitler was so overawed at the prospect of thrashing the British that even he could not take Operation *Seelöwe* seriously!

Although the Me 321 – *Gigant*, a mammoth glider capable of lifting a small tank, or 7.5-cm gun, or 200 men, which was expressly manufactured for the invasion of Britain, was stockpiled together with DFS 230s and miscellaneous airborne equipment in northern France, Student himself showed no personal interest in Sealion. In autumn 1940 the ad hoc *Luftlandekorps* formed for the invasion of Holland, was replaced officially by *Fliegerkorps XI*. The newly titled formation still comprised *Fliegerdivision 7* and *Luftlande-Division 22*. Student now gave consideration to daring plans for the capture of Gibraltar, the Cape Verde Islands, Malta and certain of the Greek islands.

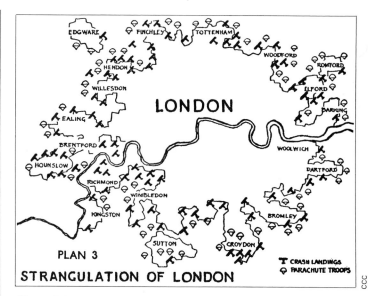

PLAN 3

STRANGULATION OF LONDON

T CRASH LANDINGS
Q PARACHUTE TROOPS

Above: A Local Defence Volunteers manual of 1940 shows one projected method of the airborne invaders' arrival.
Right: A Punch *cartoon of June 1940 demonstrates a suitably phlegmatic way of greeting a German parachute landing.*
Below: Priority targets for German parachutists in Holland had been bridges and communications centres. These two 1940 pictures show pill-boxes guarding such sites in London disguised as a coal-merchant's office (top) and a municipal lavatory (bottom)

'Would you mind not rustling that parachute'

MESSERSCHMITT ME 321 *GIGANT*

Whereas the Junkers giant glider programme proved disastrous, Messerschmitt produced their wood and tubular metal *Gigant* in a remarkably short time, the prototype taking the air in February 1941. Meanwhile the chance to send an airborne armada against Britain had slipped away and the Me 321 *Staffeln* went to Russia in the transport role, where, with the ponderous *Troikaschlepp* towing procedure and limited range, they were of limited usefulness

Max speed: (under tow, He IIIZ) 137 mph	
Span: 180 ft 5⅓ in	
Length: 92 ft 4¼ in	
Max take-off weight: 86,860 lb	
Armament: 2 x 7·9-mm MG 15, 4 x 7·9-mm MG 34	

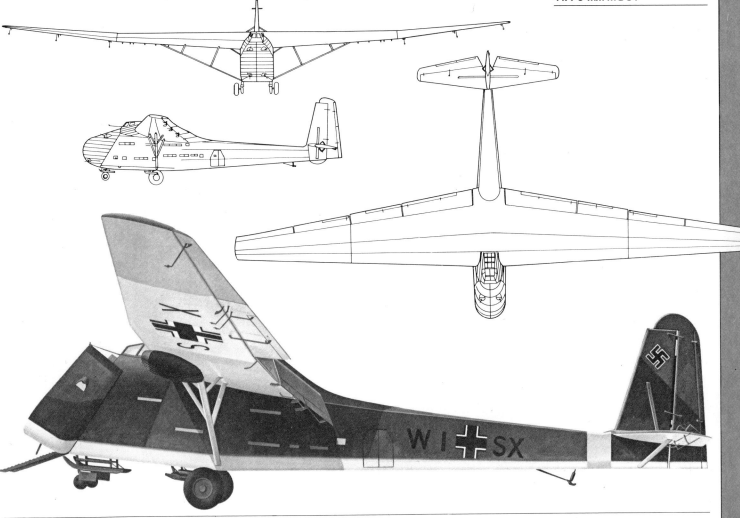

JUNKERS JU 322 *MAMMUT*

From the planning for Operation *Seelöwe* emerged the concept of the *Grossraumlastensegler,* the giant assault glider capable of lifting a Pzkpfw IV or more than 100 assault troops. The all-wood flying-wing proposed and built by Junkers was not a success. Tanks crashed through the floor and the flight characteristics were very poor and the *Mammut* programme (code-named *Warschau-Ost*) was abandoned in 1941

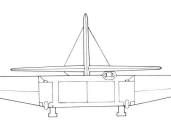

A HARD LESSON LEARNED

During the evacuation of the British Expeditionary Force and their French companions from Dunkirk, which began on 27 May 1940, Britain's Prime Minister, Winston Churchill, was already considering ways of hitting back at the Germans, who now occupied the western coastline of Europe from Narvik to the Pyrenees. On 6 June, Churchill issued a terse memorandum to General Lord Ismay for circulation to the Joint Chiefs of Staff. Churchill wrote: 'The passive resistance war in which we have acquitted ourselves so well, must come to an end. I look to the Joint Chiefs of Staff to propose me measures for a vigorous, enterprising and ceaseless offensive against the whole German occupied coastline.'

The suggestion that the British Army – digging deeply into the soil of the southern counties – was jolted by the spirit of the offensive in the Prime Minister's peremptory challenge would be a mild understatement. His memorandum concluded with demands for the means of mounting amphibious warfare, 'striking companies' and 'parachute troops on a scale equal to five thousand.' The immediate development of landing craft and the 'striking companies' or Commandos form another story but it will be seen from the date of Churchill's missive that it was only a matter of weeks after the *Luftlandekorps* landed in Holland that he was stirred into urging the formation of British airborne troops.

On 22 June, Churchill brought up the matter of parachute troops again with the Joint Chiefs of Staff. 'We ought to have a corps of at least 5000 parachute troops . . . I believe that something is already being done to form such a corps but only, I believe, on a very small scale. Advantage must be taken of the summer to train these forces, who can none the less play their part as shock troops in home defence.'

Naturally the onus for the establishment of a parachute training school lay with the Air Ministry and at first the RAF was by no means keen on the idea. Britain in mid-1940 did not possess enough aircraft to defend the homeland and it followed that few could be spared to train paratroopers let alone lift them in action. But the Prime Minister's wishes could not be ignored, and since Manchester's civil airport, Ringway, was not considered a vital strategic base for fighters for home defence, it was immediately turned over to parachute training.

The Irvin trainer parachute was then adapted so that it was worn on the back, and the ripcord operated by a static-line attached to a strongpoint inside the fuselage of the aircraft. The pupil jumped from the platform and the static-line snapped open the bag of his 'stati-chute', the canopy and rigging lines being fully released with the weight of the falling body.

All went well until on 25 July when, after 135 jumps had been made at the school, Driver Evans, of the RASC, plunged to his death. The partly developed canopy of his parachute was hopelessly intertwined with the rigging lines as the unfortunate soldier fell straight to the ground.

After a rigorous enquiry, it was deduced that the fault lay with the sequence of release of the canopy and rigging lines. 'Canopy first' worked perfectly well with the manually operated emergency ripcord types, but Driver Evans's misfortune suggested that this order of release using a static-line was likely to precipitate a foul-up of the two vital components of the parachutist's means of support.

Raymond Quilter, of the GQ Company, was asked for his

British Parachute Jump Instructor's (PJI) wings

A busy day at Tatton Park. Trainees prepare to ascend in a tethered balloon.

ARMSTRONG WHITWORTH WHITLEY MK V

Strong, graceless but business-like, the all-metal Whitley first flew in 1936 but was obsolete as a bomber by 1940. The aircraft got a new lease of life as a paratroop transport and the

Mk V carried ten men who dropped through a hole in the floor. As a training aircraft the rear turret was removed and exit rails provided. The Mk V was also equipped as a glider tug aircraft

Engines: 2 x Rolls-Royce Merlin 12	
Max speed: 230 mph	
Range: 2400 miles	
Span: 84 ft	
Length: 69 ft 3 in	
Max take-off weight: 21,660 lb	

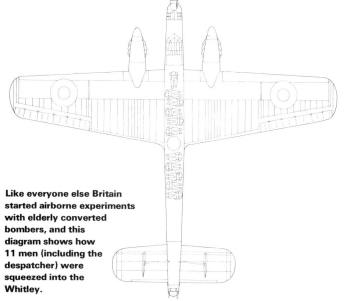

Like everyone else Britain started airborne experiments with elderly converted bombers, and this diagram shows how 11 men (including the despatcher) were squeezed into the Whitley.

Above: Whitleys enter the dropping zone. Right: Exiting from a Whitley mock-up in a hangar at the Ringway parachute school. Left: The real thing. Inside a Whitley on the way to its practice target, the despatcher (in leather helmet) communicates with the pilot

Imperial War Museum

Radio Times Hulton

opinion and within a week he produced a new bag for the Irvin-type in which the rigging lines of the parachute were withdrawn from the bag *before* the canopy. The modification was thus a combination of the Irvin parachute with a GQ packing-bag and method of operation. The parachutist now hooked his static-line, which extended from inside the bag, to a strop attached to a bar running along the inside of the roof of the fuselage. The static-line then – together with the weight of the man – broke open the bag once the length of the line was fully extended after the man's exit from the aircraft.

Pilot Officer Louis Strange, a First World War fighter ace and some time lieutenant-colonel in the Army, who was assigned to the command of the new Parachute Training School, made a start by obtaining a supply of 28-ft Irvin emergency parachutes from RAF Henlow. He also turned to the GQ Company at Woking, Surrey, for advice. G stood for Gregory and Q for Quilter – two gentlemen, who since 1934 had been in business manufacturing parachutes. As it happened GQ had already produced a 28-ft type operated by static-line with the Army in mind. Parachute jumping instructors were needed and the only NCOs in the RAF, who knew anything about how parachutes worked, were the fabric workers at Henlow; Flight Sergeant Bill Brereton, who was destined to become the ace instructor at Ringway, and eight of his colleagues promptly volunteered for special duties.

Six obsolete Whitley bombers were transferred to the 'Central Landing School' at RAF Ringway for training purposes, and the Air Ministry undertook to hold enough aircraft in reserve to drop 720 fully-armed men and 62,000 lb (28,117 kg) of equipment in action. This was just the beginning of a story of triumph and tragedy that lasted until the cease-fire was sounded in 1945.

The first Army pupils to report for parachute training at Ringway were the men of B and C Troops, No 2 Commando. After a course of ground training, the first live descents were made on 13 July from a Whitley at nearby Tatton Park. A jumping platform or open cockpit was erected in place of the rear gun turret. The pupil wearing the Irvin parachute stood facing forward gripping two side-bars, and on the instructor's command: 'Go', the jumper pulled his ripcord and was lifted from his perch as the wind developed his canopy.

The Parachute Type X Equipment – to use the official service jargon – that with minor modifications emerged from Quilter's initiative became the standard British Army parachute and was used throughout the war with a far greater degree of success than any other used by Allied or Axis airborne formations. A brief description of the X-type is as follows:–

1. *The parachute* had a canopy measuring 28 ft (8.5 m) in diameter. Canopies were made alternatively of silk, cotton (Ramex) and nylon – in that order – during the course of the war.

Twenty-eight rigging lines each 25 ft (7.6 m) long and with a minimum breaking strength of 400 lb (181 kg) converged below the periphery in four groups on 'D' rings attached to lift webs.

2. The rectangular *inner bag* when packed enclosed the folded canopy and a large flap was used to stow the rigging lines. This bag remained on the man's back after the rigging lines and canopy had been released.

BRITISH X-TYPE PARACHUTE HARNESS

A seat strap formed by the main suspension straps passed in one continuous line from one set of rigging lines and up the other set. Shoulder, back, chest and leg straps held the jumper firmly in place. The twenty-eight rigging lines converged below the periphery in four groups attached to the lift webs by D-rings

3. The *outer pack* resembled an envelope, the four flaps being lightly secured together by string in the front. The static-line was stowed in two pockets of the pack. Immediately after the parachutist's departure from the aircraft, the pack was left dangling on the end of the static-line, which in turn was hooked to the strop on the strongpoint inside the fuselage.

4. *The harness.* A seat strap formed by the main suspension straps passed in one continuous line from one set of rigging lines and up the other set of lines. Shoulder, back, chest and leg straps held the jumper in his seat strap. The man was locked in this position by a circular, metal box device. Four lift webs connected to the rigging lines formed part of the harness and some measure of flight control was achieved by reaching up and manipulating these webbing straps during the descent.

The rear platform exit of the Whitley did not allow the trainee parachutists to jump as they must in action in rapid succession. A new method had to be found of despatching a 'stick' or section of ten men and a means of doing so was discovered by simply cutting a hole in the floor of the fuselage. The Whitley aperture, which was 30 inches (762 mm) across by nearly three feet (914 mm) deep, tapered slightly like a funnel at the bottom. A stick was carried to the dropping zone sitting on the floor of the fuselage, five forward and five aft of the exit hole, the jumping sequence alternating one man at a time from each stream. An alert stick of ten men made its departure through the hole in nine or ten seconds. The principal hazard of dropping through such a restricted exit space was that there was a tendency for the lower end of

the body to be lifted in the slipstream; this often resulted in a blow to the face; 'ringing the bell' or the 'Whitley kiss' being the distinctive accolade for jumping through the hole.

Louis Strange and Sir Nigel Norman, Bt, on the RAF side, were shortly joined at Ringway by Major John Rock, Royal Engineers, and the re-named Central Landing Establishment was formed. This joint RAF/Army enterprise comprised three sub-units: the Parachute Squadron, the Glider Squadron, and the Technical Development Unit. Whilst Strange was concerned with parachuting, Norman and Rock became closely involved with planning the future of airborne forces. Both Norman and Rock were to lose their lives in the service of their country – the former in a plane crash and the latter in a glider mishap.

The problem for some time to come was the availability of air transport. Even if an aircraft could be found to carry twenty paratroopers, six would be needed to lift a single rifle company. As Student's experience in Holland had demonstrated, more aircraft still would be needed to protect them in flight. The air mobility of airborne forces was hotly debated in eminent RAF circles but the Army still had some way to go in training battalions prepared in every way to fly by air into battle.

Whilst John Rock experimented ceaselessly with suitable jumping apparel and airborne supply equipment, the volunteers at Ringway – principally No 2 Commando – were reformed on 21 November 1940 as No 11 Special Air Service Battalion. These original paratroopers were dressed in long grey-green cotton duck jackets, similar in style and length to the *Fallschirmjäger*'s smock; their headgear if only to keep the wind out of their ears was the black balaclava-style pilot's helmet. The 'Denison' camouflaged smock did not appear until 1941 by which time a sorbo (sponge rubber) head piece was the standard training helmet.

At first paratroopers, who were issued with Thompson submachine-guns, .303-in Lee Enfield rifles and Webley revolvers, carried no more on a jump than they could stow inside a small pack suspended across the chest from around the neck, or inside the front body straps of the harness of their parachutes. Experiments were conducted with containers like laundry baskets parachuted in the midst of the personnel stream leaving the aircraft and also bombcells made of sheet metal with parachutes attached and fitted to the bomb racks of the aircraft.

One solution, in the absence of a suitable transport aircraft, to the problem of lifting more substantial armaments and supplies, lay with the glider. In September 1940 an order was placed by the Ministry of Aircraft Production with General Aircraft Ltd of Feltham, Middlesex, for 400 Hotspur gliders. This was the forerunner, retained for experimental and training purposes of the operational Horsa and Hamilcar gliders. It was not until well into 1942 that the Horsa became available, and then only in slowly increasing quantities.

Although Britain's new parachute commandos were submitted daily to exhaustive airborne and ground combat training, no further significant development occurred until the Germans once again demonstrated the true potential of the airborne method. When 22,750 men of *Fliegerdivision 7* and a mountain division were landed in the Mediterranean island of Crete from over 500 Junkers transport planes, and seventy-five gliders, Winston Churchill immediately demanded news

Top: Dressed in khaki-brown copies of the German parachute smock, recruits practice training drills at Ringway in 1941. The RAF instructor explains to the men, whose dress resembles that of Crete's airborne invaders, how to make a roll which absorbed the shock of landing. Below: Like aliens in a Flash Gordon film, these men are wearing a very early model airborne helmet made of rubber. Two of them are wearing gas respirators

of progress at Ringway. Seven days after the German airborne invasion of Crete (20 May 1941), Churchill wrote another of his characteristic letters to General Lord Ismay.

The Prime Minister wrote: 'This is a sad story (about British airborne troops and gliders), and I feel myself greatly to blame for allowing myself to be overborne by the resistances which were offered. One can see how wrongly based these resistances were when we read the Air Staff paper in the light of what is happening in Crete, and may soon be happening in Cyprus and in Syria. . . . We ought to have an Airborne Division on the German model, with any improvements which might suggest themselves from experience. We ought also to have a number of carrier aircraft.'

Events now moved more swiftly in the organisation of Britain's airborne forces. But before describing just how quickly, we must turn back briefly in time to 9 February 1941 to tell the story of Operation 'Colossus', the first British parachute operation of the war. The parachute commandos of No 11 SAS Battalion were becoming restless. Constant parachute training brought their crop of injuries and the men began to wonder if they would survive long enough to see combat action. Operation 'Colossus', the airborne raid on the Tragino Aqueduct in southern Italy, was mounted partly to raise the morale of the British paratroopers and partly to lower that of the Italian Home Front. When one day in January 1941, the battalion was paraded at Ringway and asked for volunteers for the raid, every man took one pace forward.

Major T A G Pritchard, Royal Welch Fusiliers, was chosen to command 'X' troop which included a demolition team and three Italian interpreters. 'X' troop was to comprise overall a party of fifty officers and men. A mock-up of the aqueduct was erected at Tatton Park and rehearsals for the raid were organised by Sir Nigel Norman and John Rock. Eight more Whitleys were converted to the parachute role and on 7 February, Pritchard's 'X' troop emplaned at Mildenhall in Suffolk for Malta.

On arrival in Malta on the 9th, six of the Whitleys were loaded with containers packed with weapons, ammunition, explosives and rations and the other two fitted with bombloads for a diversionary attack on railway marshalling yards at Foggia. At 1700 hours on the 10th the weather forecast was encouraging and an hour later the eight Whitleys belonging to No 91 Squadron RAF and led by Wing Commander J B Tait DFC, took off and headed for the Italian coast south of Salerno.

The target lay near the small town of Calitri close to the Ofanto river in the province of Campagna, which is in the ankle of Italy. The aqueduct carried the main water supply to the south-eastern province of Apulia, the home of some two million Italians, domiciled for the most part in Taranto, Brindisi, Foggia and a few other small towns. It was hoped that if these Italians were temporarily deprived of water there would be sufficient confusion and dislocation to affect Mussolini's sally-ports for the campaigns in North Africa and in Albania. 'The Tragino Raid' was thus named after a small stream that passes under the aqueduct at the chosen point of assault. Details of the aqueduct's structure were provided by a London firm of engineers, who in the first place actually suggested it as a suitable target.

The dropping zone, which was near the snow-capped Monte Vulture, lay in an area of farmland but the high ground was wild and desolate. Air photographs exposed an hitherto unknown factor; there were two trough structures to the aqueduct, one larger than the other, running side by side. After breaching the target, 'X' troop were to make their withdrawal on foot in a westward direction to the mouth of the Sele river where a rendezvous with His Majesty's submarine *Triumph* was fixed for the night of 15/16 February.

Five of the Whitleys dropped their sticks on target on the north side of the aqueduct but the sixth deposited Capt Daly and his men in the next valley by mistake. The dropping height was 4500 feet: the time was 2145 hours; and the aqueduct was clearly visible to the parachutists as they descended in bright moonlight.

The first to land was Lt Deane-Drummond, who came to earth in a ploughed field. The containers were scattered and some of the lights fixed to them for easy location were not shining. 'X' troop retrieved most of their arms and rounded up a gang of farm hands from a nearby farm house to help porter the explosives. The Italians were in complete awe of the presence of the *paracadutisti inglese* and, far from being intimidated, they lent a hand under the staggering weight of the boxes with surprising enthusiasm!

Whilst Pritchard rallied the raiders and set up his outposts, 2/Lt Paterson, a Canadian, led his team of sappers to the aqueduct. The piers, which were made of reinforced concrete, consisted of a central column that was much taller than the two outside pairs. The more vulnerable parts of the structure were more accessible at the top of the shorter piers and it was decided to place almost the entire contents of the boxes of explosives salvaged from the drop concentrated at one point. It was hoped that the detonation of a third of a ton of gun cotton would be enough to blow a gap in the aqueduct. Meanwhile a small quantity of explosives were diverted to blow up a small bridge in the vicinity to impede an alerted *carabiniere*.

At thirty minutes after midnight, both sets of charges were fired and the small bridge went up with a bang. The damp air had caused a delay in setting off the charges at the aqueduct and the paratroopers were already sheltering behind a small hill when they heard a deafening explosion. Although the jubilant men were not immediately in a position to witness their accomplishment, the distinct sound of a waterfall was heard – 'X' troop had succeeded in their mission. Less than six hours had elapsed since the men had left their billets in Malta.

Pritchard now assembled his party for the withdrawal. Leaving one man behind with a broken leg, the raiders dispensed with all their equipment but for their submachine-guns and revolvers and moved off in separate groups for the snowline. This they skirted, keeping to the high ground. Pritchard led his own section down into a small wooded valley to lie up until the daylight hours. The Sele watershed effectively marking the best route down to the sea still lay ten miles distant. On awakening, the troops brewed up and resumed their march once again under the cover of darkness. On the second night they made twenty miles before finding another hiding place amongst trees on top of a small hill.

Traces of their bootprints were clearly visible and a farmer gave the alarm. Soon a small boy stood silently observing the paratroopers' resting place and went away again. The fugitives knew what was to come and were ready to fight but Pritchard was now more alarmed by the babble of children's voices intermingled with the barking of village dogs than the

Italian troops and *carabinieri* following on behind. Pritchard could not bring himself to order his troops to open fire on children and there was no alternative but to surrender.

Daly and his section after hearing the explosions on their belated march to the aqueduct had made off for the final rendezvous but were also soon in Italian hands. None of Pritchard's other sections made the submarine either. Conveyed in triumph by their captors to a prison in Naples, 'X' troop was subjected to interrogation and eventually escorted in handcuffs and in chains to a POW camp in Sulmona in the Abruzzese mountains. Fortunato Picchi, one of the party's interpreters and a former waiter at the Savoy Hotel in London, was, however, singled out for special treatment. He had volunteered at Ringway for 'a special mission' to his homeland. In captivity he refused to renounce his anti-Fascist beliefs and was accordingly executed by an MVSN (*Fascist militia*) firing squad.

Several officers made escape attempts at Sulmona; Deane-Drummond being at large for six weeks before recapture and transfer to Campo 27 near Pisa. In June 1942, he feigned illness and after absconding from Florence Military Hospital, this young officer walked to freedom across the Swiss frontier near Lake Como. Here his adventures did not end. In September 1944, he evaded capture after the British withdrawal at Arnhem by spending a week in the cupboard of a German HQ. A post-war champion glider pilot, SAS Colonel, Maj-Gen Anthony Deane-Drummond in 1966–1968 commanded the 3rd Infantry Division.

Four days after the German victory in Crete, Churchill's impatience had already been rewarded by the Joint Chiefs of Staff's proposal to form two parachute brigades, one in Britain and one in the Middle East, and a glider force sufficient to lift 10,000 men and essential equipment. The RAF were to provide ten medium bomber squadrons to be adapted as paratroop aircraft and glider tugs.

So far the only glider in service was the GAL Hotspur trainer. Now orders were placed for the Airspeed Horsa (the Hengist took shape only on the drawing boards) and the GAL Hamilcar. The Horsa, which was flown by two pilots operating dual control, contained twenty-five seats but normally carried only fifteen fully armed men. A wide variety of military equipment could alternatively be stowed in the main compartment. The heavy-duty GAL Hamilcar was originally designed to carry the Tetrarch reconnaissance tank or two Bren-carriers. In practice, it was generally used for heavy military loads of all description. The flight compartment was in the upper portion of the forward fuselage seating two pilots in tandem with dual controls.

In September 1941, No 11 SAS Battalion was re-formed as 1st Parachute Battalion at Hardwick Hall, near Chesterfield in Derbyshire. Hardwick Hall was the first Airborne Forces Depot and the new centre soon boasted 1st, 2nd and 3rd Parachute Battalions, forming Brigadier R N ('Windy') Gale's 1st Parachute Brigade.

A separate HQ was set up in London at St James's Palace to lay down the framework of an airborne division. On 29 October 1941, Major-General F A M Browning was appointed 'Commander Paratroops and Airborne Troops'. 'Boy' Browning, who became renowned for the perfection of his personal turn-out, envisaged a three-brigade divisional structure – two parachute infantry brigades and one glider-

Controlled descent from the parachute tower at Ringway simulating the last stages of descent

Imperial War Museum

borne – with light artillery and other support and service units. A divisional establishment of 12,148 men represented a strength of 75 per cent as compared with a conventional infantry division; 2nd Parachute Brigade did not emerge until July 1942, but plans were immediately afoot to allocate four infantry battalions to the glider rôle.

A recruiting call went out to the Army on behalf of the new airborne battalions. All the recruits to the parachute battalions were volunteers, although at only 2s extra a day for parachute pay, Browning had to rely on patriotism as opposed to the profit motive for providing an experience that has been described as 'dicing with death' and 'the second greatest thrill in a man's life'. Glider troops were not given a choice in the matter – they were 'airborne' whether they liked it or not.

A selection course was established at Hardwick Hall to sort out only the best parachute volunteers. Officers and men alike were subjected to the same physical tests. Recruits were organised into small squads each under an NCO for gymnasium, assault course and roadwork lasting a fortnight. The physical training instructor had all the grace and tenacity of a choreographer trained in the boxing ring. All candidates but the brave and resourceful were cast aside and returned with their kit bags to their parent units after only cursory examination. The system was Prussian in its application but it worked, the failure rate at the Parachute Training School being reduced to a minimum as a result of the Army's harsh selection methods.

In mid-1941, Group Captain Maurice Newnham DFC was appointed Commandant at Ringway. He was over 40 when he made his first jump, and it was he more than any one that was responsible for delivering so many thousands of British and Allied parachute troops as well as Special Operations Executive (SOE) agents expertly trained to their units. The RAF training instructors he chose were a special breed of men. Sometimes jumping a dozen times a day, and constantly engaged in parachuting experiments, these men set exemplary standards that saw many doubting pupils through their courses.

Before making a parachute descent, pupils at the PTS were introduced to carefully devised pre-jump routines. 'Synthetic' ground training using all manner of contraptions and devices was originally set up at Ringway purely for the lack of training aircraft for making actual parachute descents. The renowned circus-master of the Ringway Hangars was Wing Commander J C Kilkenny OBE and the fact that RAF ground training methods have changed little in over thirty years is a tribute to this officer's ingenuity and foresight. Not surprisingly the crux of the matter was developing a head for heights: the 'Fan' and – later in the war – the 'Tower' providing the pupil with real tests of nerve before attempting his first free parachute descent.

For the leap from the 'Fan' the pupil climbed a ladder twenty-five feet up a hangar wall and on mounting a narrow platform placed himself in a harness fastened to a steel cable wound around a drum. As he stepped off the platform and fell so two fans caused an airbrake that controlled his speed of descent. The idea for the 'Tower' actually came from the Polish Brigade that was based in Scotland. The showpiece of the preliminary course organised by the Poles before sending their potential parachutists to Ringway was a 100 foot (30 metre) tower made of steel girders. A long steel arm protruded from the top of the tower. The pupil climbed a ladder to the top and donned a parachute harness. After the command 'Go' the man found himself suspended in thin air beneath an outstretched silk canopy suspended by cable at the end of the arm until, at the press of a button, the cable ran out and he floated to the ground. This training device was adapted with great success for use in 'Kilkenny's Ringway Circus'.

The first actual descent by the pupil was made from a captive balloon hoisted aloft to 700 feet. In 1940, some of the instructors had remembered the artillery spotters of the First World War, and again purely for lack of aircraft adopted the hydrogen-filled balloon as a training aid. The balloon cage was of simple wooden and metal construction with a canvas covering. For the ascent four men crouched around the hole in the centre of the floor. As the balloon bag climbed through different air currents, the cage was apt to tilt or sway causing the incumbents to cling to metal bars for safety. After the grinding of the winch ceased, a measure of stability ensued whilst the parachutists were poised to make their exits.

Jumping through the hole whether it was from a balloon or from the various converted bombers – Albemarles, Halifaxes, Wellingtons, Stirlings – that followed the Whitleys in general paratroop service – was carried out with the body stiffly erect. The experience differed only in as much as the shape of the hole varied. The majority of parachute descents after 1942 were made through the port door of the American Dakota transport, but the mode of departure was the same.

ARMSTRONG WHITWORTH ALBEMARLE

Built of 'non-strategic' wood and metal and conceived as a fast bomber, the Albemarle served almost exclusively as a glider tug and special transport. As a paratroop transport ten men could be carried and the special transport version was fitted with underwing panniers

Engines: 2 x Bristol Hercules, 1590 hp	
Max speed: 250 mph	
Range: 1350 miles	
Span: 77 ft	
Length: 59 ft 11 in	
Max take-off weight: 22,600 lb	

Dropping sequence seen through the rear exit hole of an Armstrong Whitworth Albemarle

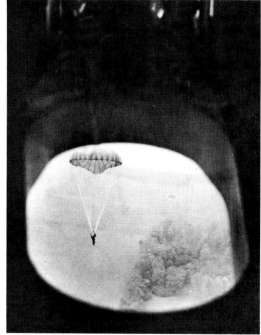

Airborne Forces Museum

An upright body on exit was more likely to ensure an un-impeded opening of the rigging lines and canopy. The effect of the aircraft's slipstream on the jumper was modified by the drag of the static-line and, if a good exit was achieved, the canopy was fully developed before much vertical height was lost. In the early days at Ringway, parachutists – like the Germans – floated to earth steered by the prevailing air currents and made a forward roll on touching down. Flight-Lieutenant Julian Gebolys, a senior Polish instructor, how-ever, pioneered the art of arresting the speed, drift and oscillation of a parachute by manipulating the shoulder lift webs. Control was exercised over drifting in any direction and so the parachutist was prepared for forward, sideways and backward landings. After hitting the ground in the line of the drift, the principle of absorbing the shock was always the same. The force of impact was distributed between the com-bined strength of both legs and on one side of the body by rolling on to the ground from the feet, through the thigh to the shoulder.

The most common impediment to a safe descent was twisted rigging lines. This meant that the front and back sets of rigging lines were interwoven above the lift webs in two strands like a thick rope. As the full development of the canopy was thus retarded so the rate of fall was increased and adequate flight control was impossible until the body was revolved through 360° and the twists eliminated. The blown periphery or 'thrown line' was much more dangerous. This abnormality was formed when part of the periphery was firstly blown inwards and then outwards through the rigging lines producing a second inverted canopy. Another kind of blown periphery was experienced when a portion of the canopy blew between the two rigging lines and the tendency followed for the canopy to roll up at the skirt. A 'streamer' was the name given to a canopy that paid out but failed to develop until the last moment. The 'roman candle', the key to the door of Heaven's gate, was the type of 'streamer' that failed to open at all.

Having paused to discuss some of the basic facts of parachuting and possible misadventures, we will now move on more optimistically with Brigadier Gale's 1st Parachute

Brigade, which arrived in March 1942 at Bulford Camp on Salisbury Plain. General Browning's 1st Airborne Division was slowly taking shape in the Bulford area; his headquarters being situated at Syrencot House, a leafy Georgian residence, in the village of Figheldean. No 38 Wing of the Royal Air Force, the new air transport arm, was also in business at the time at nearby RAF Netheravon under Group Captain Sir Nigel Norman. At the end of 1941 the Glider Pilot Regiment had been formed as part of the new Army Air Corps and the glider school was based on Devizes in Wiltshire. Moreover, Brigadier G F Hopkinson's 1st Air-Landing Brigade – 1st Borders, 2nd South Staffords, and 2nd Oxfordshire and Buckinghamshire Light Infantry – were in training in the 1st Airborne cantonment to travel in the gliders.

Potential glider pilots were drawn from trained Army units and given pilot training in powered aircraft at the Elementary Flying Training School at Derby. Glider pilot wings were awarded on completion of courses on the Hotspur followed by the Horsa. Only the most experienced pilots were chosen to fly the Hamilcars. The art of handling a military glider may seem simple on paper but the powerless aircraft was vulnerable to unkindly weather conditions and the hazards were legion.

On take-off, the glider was drawn forward along the ground by the tug until the tow rope was taut and the two aircraft were airborne. The glider pilots – two each in both Horsa and Hamilcar – knew the height and bearing of their course to the Landing Zone (LZ) from prior briefing, but since they were totally in the hands of the tug navigator for direction finding had only their maps to confirm their whereabouts. During the flight, the glider was normally positioned just above or below the slipstream of the aircraft. The glider pilot actually in control chose the moment for casting off; the release mechanism for the towrope being operated from the glider cockpit. (Communications between glider and tug was possible by means of a telephone line wound around the tow rope.) Landing conditions differed according to the terrain, windspeed and direction; the speed of approach of the glider to the ground varying at anything up to 100 mph (161 kmph).

Brigadier George Chatterton, Commander Glider Pilots, 1942–45, has described the experience of handling a Horsa on a training flight. (*The Wings of Pegasus*, Macdonald, London, 1962.)

'The tug moves slowly forward and the glider pilot holds the brakes on until the rope is fully taut, when, gradually, the glider moves forward behind the tug. It is a thrilling and strange sensation. The dust flies up from behind the tug and the speed increases – fifty, sixty, seventy-five miles an hour. The glider pilot eases back the control column, the nose wheel comes off the runway, and into the air the glider jumps. The tug-aircraft still rumbles along the runway and the glider at the end of the rope flies above it. The only sound is the rush of the slipstream – a clear roar of rushing air. The handling is rough, for there is no finesse in glider construction. Soon the tug leaves the ground, the runway drops below, and the whole combination is airborne. The ground below slowly recedes and both aircraft climb into the sky. It is a delightful sensation and one that can never be produced by other means.
'At 2000 feet the tug levels out and flies on a course. At this height the glider pilot, who is flying above the tug, drops into the low-tow position below the tug, and flies below the tug to keep the rope just above the cockpit. There are only two positions, high and low. The latter is used for bad weather flying, for by flying in the position of the 'V' of the rope, the glider can keep roughly in position. From above, it is almost impossible to keep position if in cloud or fog.
'At the end of the exercise the tug flies back to the airfield on receiving a radio signal from the ground that the glider may land. The glider pilot reaches forward and pulls the tow-rope release handle, the rope snapping away out of its sockets in the wings. There is a slight jolt, then a feeling of exaltation as the tug rushes away. The glider becomes incredibly smooth and a strange silence comes over the cockpit. On my first flight in a Horsa I felt that I never wanted to come down again, but just to drift on up there for ever. The height indicator, however, does not permit this; eyes must be kept on the air-field lest the glider gets too far away and unable to get back to the runway.
'It was borne in on me, as I flew this great bird of wood and glue and bits of tin, that the training in flying a conventional aircraft was suited also to flying gliders. We never 'rumbled in' in powered aircraft, we always throttled back and ticked over into a glider landing. I found myself using the same technique for judging and assessing height as before.
'As the pilot turns into the final run he pulls the flap lever to half flap and with a great hiss from the airbottles, and from the wings, two flaps or airbrakes come down into position. The glider checks and the nose is pushed down. At the right moment the full flap is pulled on and the glider takes on an ever steeper angle. The ground rushes up, the control column is eased back and the glider lands safely and gently and runs forward only a few yards in doing so.'

At the close of 1941, 1st Airborne Division looked confidently forward to the future. Parachute exercises were progressively increased in scale still under the watchful eye of the RAF instructors; 38 Wing's No 296 (Glider Exercise) and No 297 (Parachute Exercise) Squadrons improved daily in expertise, but British airborne troops were not yet ready to go to war on a divisional scale.

In order to discuss the dress, weapons and equipment of the British airborne soldier we must look ahead from 1941 well into 1943 to see distinctive patterns emerging. As no guide-lines existed the Airborne's philosophy in most matters was empirical: the Battle of Crete for the Germans had been a Pyrrhic victory; Britain and shortly her American ally must have time to think.

The emblem depicting Bellerophon astride the winged horse Pegasus was introduced in May 1942 and worn on both arms of all airborne soldiers. The design, which was the work of Major Edward Seago, was suggested by 'Boy' Browning, and it is said that the idea belonged to his distinguished wife, novelist Daphne du Maurier. Browning chose a blue beret but settled for a maroon colour; a happy choice that in North Africa earned 1st Parachute Brigade the title '*roten Teufeln*', the 'Red Devils'.

British airborne troops wore the maroon beret, standard khaki serge battledress, with web waist belt, web gaiters and ammunition boots. The special jump jacket copied from the Germans and worn in 1940 and 1941 was superseded by the Denison smock – the creation of a Captain Denison – but

HANDLEY-PAGE HALIFAX

The Mks II, III, V and VII of this famous bomber were used extensively as glider tugs and as paratroop transports themselves. They were also extensively used for dropping agents and weapons into occupied Europe. The specifications are for the Mk II illustrated

Engines:	4 x Rolls-Royce Merlins, 1390-hp
Max speed:	285 mph
Span:	98 ft 10 in
Length:	71 ft 7 in
Max take-off weight:	60,000 lb
Armament:	8 x .303 mg

those sartorially-minded volunteers who joined to impress their girl-friends were not rewarded with the issue of a particularly practical garment. The smock was windproof but only semi-waterproof. It was unlined and not especially warm but this was an advantage in the heat of combat. Four external patch pockets were provided as well as two internal pockets. The camouflage pattern was ragged with brown and dark green patches printed over a light green base. A tail piece was sewn to the rear hem of the smock. This flap was designed, unsuccessfully, to be fastened to press studs either on the back of the smock or, after thrusting it under the crotch, to the front hem. The Arabs in North Africa had another name for the 'red devils' – 'the men with donkey tails'.

Personal weapons were similar to those of an infantry soldier. The Thompson sub-machinegun was in general service in the British Army in 1940–41 but was progressively replaced by the 9-mm Sten carbine; the Mk I first appearing in June 1941. The Mk 2 Sten was cut down in length and fitted with a skeleton butt which folded underneath the gun. In 1943 the Mk 4 Sten was made as a prototype sub-machinegun, but it was never produced in quantity. During a jump, the Sten was carried horizontally behind the upper two front straps of the parachute body harness. Magazines could conveniently be stowed in the pockets.

The 0.303-in Lee Enfield was the airborne soldier's shoulder arm. The standard side arm of the British Army from 1936 until 1957 was the Webley (Enfield) .38-in Revolver No 2 Mk I but the Colt .45 automatic pistol was on exclusive issue to Airborne and Commando units. The Colt .45 and the 9-mm Browning replaced the Webley revolver as the official sidearm in the post-war years.

Grenades available to the British Army in the Second World War were scarcely more effective than 1914–18 types. The Airborne did, however, produce a version of their own. The Gammon grenade or 'bomb', invented by Captain R J Gammon of 1st Parachute Battalion, and officially designated the No 86 grenade, consisted of a stockinet bag with a percussion fuse in the mouth. The pitcher filled the bag with plastic explosive, took off the safety cap, and hurled the grenade. As a safety tape unwound, the detonator mechanism fired the charge and the grenade bag, which stuck to the target, went off with a bang. Widely used against tanks and other armoured vehicles, the 'Sticky Bomb' had a habit of adhering to the assailant instead. The No 86 grenade was nonetheless a successful weapon in the hands of Airborne and Commando soldiers.

The basic firepower, man-for-man, of a parachute platoon

was therefore modest. The usual infantry-scale of issue of the Bren light machinegun, the Vickers machinegun, and the 2-in and 3-in mortars were virtually the Airborne man's artillery. At Arnhem, in September 1944, another infantry (anti-tank) weapon gave 1st Airborne Division what hope they had of knocking out an élite German armoured division. The Projector Infantry Anti-tank (PIAT), similar to the American bazooka, fired a 3-lb (1.35 kg), hollow charge grenade. The PIAT weighing 32 lb (14.4 kg) was 39 in (991 mm) in length. Effective range was 100 yards (910 m).

The advance of an infantry division calls for support principally from its own artillery but also from other auxiliary troops. The conventional division is covered on its flanks by others in the line and by its own corps artillery. An airborne division, on the other hand, dropped in isolation, must bring its own menagerie to battle. Even the general must have his bodyguards!

When fully developed, the Airborne divisional artillery comprised the three batteries of the Air-Landing Light Regiment, plus two separate anti-tank gun batteries and a light anti-aircraft battery. Glider troops were equipped in the spring of 1943 at Bulford with 3.7-in howitzers but this gun was discarded in favour of the American 75-mm pack howitzer. The 75-mm gun was actually produced for mountain troops but it proved ideal for transportation in a glider. While the 75-mm acted primarily in the field rôle the 6-pounder gun was the anti-tank weapon. A typical Horsa payload included a gun, a jeep, a trailer, one or two motorcycles and six passengers. An airborne light battery totalled six guns, and each gun sub-section consisted of a gun, two jeeps and three trailers for the ammunition and stores. 'Div' artillery deployed its own observation officers but in a major battle relied on external fire support. Air defence was provided by the 20-mm Hispano Suiza (Oerlikon) and the 40-mm Bofors.

The Recce Regiment was allocated by squadron to each brigade and equipped with the seven-ton Tetrarch tank, jeeps and motor-cycles. The Tetrarch, in fact, was only sent into action on D-Day, 6 June 1944, and 6th Airborne were glad to be rid of their toy tanks when the beach-landed armour caught up with them. A Recce squadron only was sent to Arnhem but most of their armoured jeeps were lost en route.

Each parachute brigade additionally supported its own squadron of Royal Engineers, and an air-landing brigade its own company. Royal Signals ran the divisional wireless net and kept the rear links open with supporting artillery, air support and re-supply agencies and for long range communi-

GAL TWIN HOTSPUR

First of the British airborne force's operational gliders, the all-wood Hotspur was destined to serve only as a trainer, however. The Mk I was intended as a six-seat troop transport, the Mk II had reduced span wings and was used as an operational trainer, while the Mk III with dual controls was the elementary trainer. The 'Twin Hotspur' was an unsuccessful experimental attempt to double the training glider's operational capacity (Specifications Hotspur 1)

Max speed: (under tow AW Whitley) 150 mph	
Span: 45 ft 10¾ in	
Length: 39 ft 8¾ in	
Max take-off weight: 3635 lb	

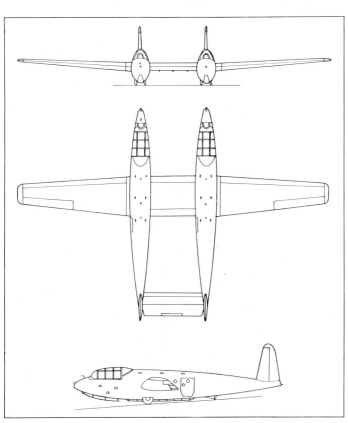

cation with home bases. Divisional units also included Ordnance, the Royal Electrical and Mechanical Engineers workshop, and Provost and Field Security sections.

Among the most remarkable features of the airborne divisions were the medical services. A parachute field ambulance staffed by nine Royal Army Medical Corps officers and just over one hundred other ranks was attached to each parachute brigade and consisted of an HQ, two surgical teams and four sections. An air-landing field ambulance was constituted on similar lines but carried a slightly larger establishment. All the medical equipment from the operating table to the surgeon's tweezers arrived by air. In Normandy supplies of blood plasma dropped in arms containers enabled airborne surgeons to perform operations on the first day of the invasion.

The Royal Army Service Corps was responsible for air cargoes dropped from aircraft. (The loading and lashing of equipment and stores into gliders was the responsibility of the troops themselves.) The divisional supply column was divided into air and ground teams; the former being responsible for loading and ejecting pre-allocated stores from the aircraft and the latter for jumping with the division and sorting out the stores on the ground.

Some mention has already been made of the means of dropping equipment into battle. The airborne kit bag and the Bren or rifle valise were developed in time for the first major airborne assignments. The kit bag was originally designed to take contents weighing up to 100 lb (45 kg) but 60 lb (27 kg) was considered a heavy enough load. It was attached by rope to the paratrooper's lower right harness strap, and secured also to the body by an ankle strap to the right leg. The 20-ft (6 m) length of rope was stowed in an exterior pocket of the kit bag and paid out when the bag was released in flight by jerking out a pin on a cord attachment from the ankle strap. A spring device absorbed the shock of the mid-air fall of the heavy bag. The Bren and rifle valises, which were made of felt, were clutched to the body on exit and secured and released in the same way as the kit bag. The prior landing of the kit bags and valises on the end of their ropes coincidentally helped to absorb the shock of the paratrooper's body on the ground.

The Central Landing Establishment experimented with many types of containers for dropping by air. In pre-war days the RAF used a small metal container about 30 inches (762 mm) long and 12 inches (305 mm) in diameter, with a lid at one end and also a beam to which small boxes or crates were tied. These contraptions were supported earthwards by a 10 ft (3 m) and 14 ft (4.2 m) parachute respectively. Neither were any use for a rifle or a machine-gun. The first invention of the Central Landing Establishment was a thick, quilted canvas mat, which when rolled up was strapped to a bar carried by the parachute. This was the 28 ft (8.4 m) diameter 'X'-type. Pockets were sewn to the surface of the mat for the inclusion of weapons.

Then came a box, 6 ft (1.8 m) long and 15 in (381 mm) in diameter and made of wood and metal. The disadvantage of this container was that as it was only fitted with lids at both ends, a midget trooper was needed to climb in to pack it properly. The next models were side opening and were finally hinged all along their length; the definitive metal arms container forming two halves. Before an aircraft door was available for troop exit and goods despatch, containers were dropped from a bomb bay or bombcell. The Central Landing Establishment (CLE) containers, which were fitted with crushable metal pans to take the shock of impact, carried up to 600 lbs (270 kg) and were parachuted as a rule without damage to the contents.

For re-supply the air despatch companies eventually handled three types of containers: the wicker pannier, the bombcell container and the SEAC pack. The pannier was loaded into and despatched from a Dakota door by means of a roller conveyor. The hinged, two-compartment metal bombcells, which usually took the rifles and Brens, could be slung on the underside of any aircraft fitted with universal bomb racks. The SEAC pack was introduced in the Far East; this was a canvas container holding up to 200 lbs (90 kg). A multiple parachute system was used for air re-supply containers with heavy loads. Two types of 18-ft (5.4 m) 'chutes with canopies made of jute hessian were specially made in India for jungle drops.

The transport of the air divisions was restricted to the jeep, motor cycles and a few scout cars. Jeeps were actually dropped by parachutes from Stirlings in 1944 during the sojourn of 2nd SAS operating with the *Maquis* in France. Motor cycles were also dropped by parachute without containerization. Two specialized Airborne transport items – the mini motorcycle and the folding pedal cycle – attracted more publicity than practical use. The Welbike 2-stroke motorcycle measured 4 ft 3 ins (1372 mm) long x 15 ins (381 mm) broad. The handle bars, steering column and saddle were arranged on a collapsible principle.

SAS wings　　　　**British Airborne wings**

The organisation of a British airborne division, 1942–45, has now been described in outline. As has been noted already the total establishment of 12,148 men was roughly three-quarters of that of an infantry division. The strength of a parachute battalion, which deployed three but sometimes four companies, was consequently scaled down to 680 men. The organisation of a parachute battalion was the same as its infantry counterpart, the 'stick' of ten men being synonymous with the infantry section. (The 'stick' or 'stick-length' was, in fact, the distance between the first and last man of the section to land on the ground and the term continued in usage when the introduction of the Dakota provided more accommodation for paratroopers.)

An air-landing battalion was stronger on the ground than a parachute battalion. Each battalion consisted of four rifle companies, each of four platoons; the additional HQ Company consisting of Signals, Pioneer, Transport and Administration platoons. A further Support company embraced Mortar, Anti-tank and machine-gun groups. The total strength of a glider battalion with first line reinforcements was 1034 officers and men.

The Special Air Service Brigade (SAS) was raised in Egypt in July 1941. This new formation, which is not to be confused with No 11 SAS Battalion – the original nucleus of 1st Parachute Battalion – was the brainchild of Lieutenant Archibald David Stirling, Scots Guards, a then twenty-six year old officer serving in No 3 Commando (Brigade of Guards). The story of how David Stirling persuaded the obdurate hierarchy of GHQ Middle East to permit him to muster what amounted to his own private army has been told elsewhere often

enough and need not be repeated here. There was no 'Brigade', incidentally, only 'L' Detachment, consisting of seven officers and about sixty men; Stirling's mission to pounce on the enemy well within the rear of their lines needed the showman's touch; for the benefit of the Germans and Italians as well as the senior officers in Cairo.

Another Commando officer, of heterogeneous connexions, J S 'Jock' Lewis, an Australian formerly serving in the Welsh Guards, in the early months of 1941, had discovered fifty 'X'-type parachutes at Alexandria, off-loaded in error from a vessel bound for India. Lewis was busy experimenting with the parachutes when Stirling enrolled him as his first recruit. Together the two Commando officers set up a makeshift camp and parachute school at Kabrit.

The ranks of the Special Air Service were filled by hand-picked volunteers and, in the absence in the early days of much help from Ringway, evolved their own system of parachute training. One feature of the ground routine at Kabrit was to make forward and backward rolls from the back of a truck moving at thirty mph (48 Kmph). This idea had in fact been abandoned at that time by the Ringway staff as backward landings from the trucks were causing too many spinal injuries. The first parachute descents at Kabrit were made from an ancient Vickers Valentia; the static-lines being hooked to the seats of the aircraft. The same method of securing the life-line was used for the next jumps from a Bristol Bombay and two men were killed on the first day of jumping. In order to restore the unit's morale, Stirling led the men straight up again to do another jump.

The basic combat training of an SAS soldier embraced

WILLYS MB JEEP

Specially modified Jeeps were
extensively used by the SAS
and the Long Range Desert
Group (LRDG) for offensive
operations in the North African
desert. Armament widely varied
but here consists of .5-in
Browning and three Vickers 'K'
machine-guns

intensive weapon handling, navigation practice and strenuous marches into the desert. Mere tents and rolling kitchens were considered a sybaritic luxury and the vagrant art of living rough for weeks on end became second nature. Emphasis was placed on personal initiative and leadership by all ranks but the SAS was always a highly disciplined and loyal force as would befit the Brigade of Guards; no badges of rank were worn in action; but with the special nature of the relationship between officers and men, the integrity and ability of the leader was seldom questioned.

The *modus operandi* of the SAS was based on the belief that the '*coup de main*' Commando method of striking in strength at one target – or in the later case of the Rommel assassination attempt 'one person' – was wasteful of man-power and equipment. Far better, in Stirling's opinion, to pounce simultaneously on several targets with small bands of resourceful men. In 1941, the chain of Axis ports, staging garrisons, airfields and supply centres stretching along the North African littoral from Tripoli to the Egyptian frontier provided many suitable objectives for SAS deep penetration.

Ironically, the first and last SAS parachute sortie into the desert was no vindication for the airborne method. The raid took place on the night of 16 November 1941, twenty-four hours in advance of General Auchinleck's offensive across the Egyptian frontier into Cyrenaica. The SAS task was to break into five different airfields in the Gazala-Timini area and blow up Axis aircraft on the ground. Fifty-five para-chutists led by David Stirling took off from Fuka airstrip in five Bristol Bombay aircraft, but atrocious winds whipped up sand storms and the RAF's task was turned into a nightmare.

The scattered drop of men and equipment was chaotic in the prevailing conditions with gusting winds blowing at three times the maximum speed acceptable in training. The raid was a complete failure and only twenty-two men survived for the pick-up in vehicles of the Long Range Desert Group. During the next eighteen months right up until the end of the fighting in North Africa, the SAS operated behind the Axis lines with conspicuous success but travelling in armoured jeeps or on foot; the LRDG playing a vital rôle in lifting the 'Parashots' to and from rendezvous points located at dis-creet distances from operational areas. SAS armoured jeeps bristled with two pairs of Vickers K aircraft guns mounted fore and aft supplemented by a heavy-calibre .50 machine-gun placed alongside the driver's seat. These armaments produced a formidable combination of fire directed at close range from an ambush position and when, after driving into an enemy airfield, the jeeps were manoeuvred in echelon amongst the dispersed ranks of aircraft on the ground the volume of fire-power was devastating.

In January 1943 1st SAS was formed with an establishment of five squadrons and about four hundred officers and men. Lieutenant-Colonel Stirling's command was equivalent to a half-battalion, but his numbers were augmented by Allied volunteers of the survivors of the French *L'Infanterie de l'Air*, the Greek Sacred Squadron and the Special Boat Section. Stirling's personal war ended one day in 1943 in the Sfax-Gabes area when he was captured by the Germans. He was taken as a prisoner to Italy but escaped four times and was recovered before being posted to Colditz. 1st SAS was subsequently commanded by Lieutenant-Colonel R B

SHORT STIRLING

First flown just before the outbreak of war and the first of the RAF's new generation of 4-engined heavy bombers, the Stirling achieved considerable success as a parachute supply aircraft. The Mk IV carried

24 paratroops exiting through a hole in the rear fuselage. The bomb-cells were retained and carried airborne supplies in universal freighter role; the Stirling Mk V was able to lift 40 fully armed troops

Engines: 4 x Bristol Hercules XVI, 1600 hp
Max speed: 280 mph
Range: 3000 miles
Span: 99 ft 1 in
Length: 87 ft 3 in
Max take-off weight: 59,400 lb

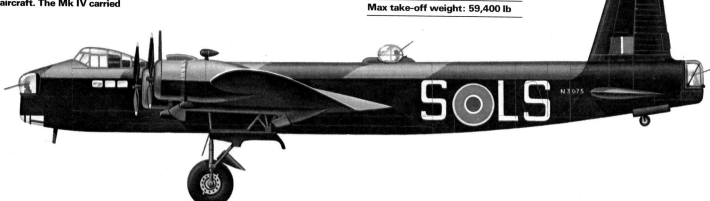

Men of the Special Boat Service (SBS) who fought their war in the Aegean, from small boats and caiques

('Paddy') Mayne. Before the conclusion of the North African campaign, 2nd SAS was formed as part of the British First Army and along with 1st SAS (temporarily renamed the Special Raiding Squadron) undertook clandestine operations in Sardinia, Crete, the Greek islands, the Dodecanese, Sicily and Italy. Stirling's brother, W S 'Bill' Stirling was the first commanding officer of 2nd SAS the Special Boat Section bifurcated from the main body of the SAS under the title of the Special Boat Service. The SBS led by Lieutenant-Colonel the Earl Jellicoe operated as raiding parties in small boats in the Aegean and Adriatic.

In mid-1941, plans existed for parachuting in India. In October an Air-Landing School was established at Willingdon Airport, New Delhi. The only aircraft and equipment available for training were a flight of Vickers Valentias, one dozen 'stati-'chutes' and a trapeze. A new Parachute Brigade emerged: the 151st (British), 152nd (Indian) and 153rd (Gurkha) Parachute Battalions. Supporting arms were raised from Indian engineer and signals units. A year later the new Delhi school, which was set up by Ringway instructors, was moved to Chaklala near Rawalpindi. Group Captain Newnham, 'on tour' from Ringway, tells an amusing story about Indian parachute volunteers; they were relieved to hear at Willingdon Airport that they would be issued with parachutes for their jumps from Hudson aircraft.

The Parachute School at Kabrit in Egypt was in 1942 transformed into an RAF unit called No 4 Middle East Parachute Training School. Lieutenant-Colonel K B I Smyth's 4th Parachute Brigade took shape as from 6 December. Smyth, who was killed in command of 10th Parachute Battalion at Arnhem in September 1944, was succeeded by Brigadier J W 'Shan' Hackett in command of 4th Parachute Brigade on 4 January 1943. Hackett, who became Vice-Chancellor of London University, had been of help to David Stirling in forming the SAS when the former was on the Staff at Cairo.

'Shan' Hackett's Brigade was to consist of the 10th, 11th and 151st Parachute Battalions. The nucleus of the 10th (Sussex) Parachute Battalion (formerly 2nd Bn the Royal Sussex Regiment) had fought with distinction at El Alamein; the 11th was recruited as was the 10th from volunteers in the Middle East. The 151st (later re-titled the 156th Parachute Battalion) was, of course, transferred from India to the Middle East. The aircraft flown at the Kabrit school included Hudsons and Wellingtons but Dakotas came into general use in 1943. No 4 Middle East Parachute Training School was later transferred to Palestine. The training centre was based on

Ramat David and the practice dropping zone was located in the Vale of Jezreel.

Lieutenant-Colonel Sir Richard de B des Voeux (also killed at Arnhem) and his 151st Parachute Battalion had been released from India as a result of a decision to turn the 50th Indian Brigade into an indigenous formation led by British officers. In June 1942, prior to the transfer of the British battalion an operational drop in Burma was made by a mixed detachment of British and Gurkha parachute troops in the Myitkyina area and Indian troops during the following month parachuted into the Sind Desert to round up a lawless band of Hur tribesmen. No 3 Parachute Training School remained at Chaklala but the 50th (Indian) Brigade moved from the Delhi cantonment to Campbellpur and indulged in intensive parachute training with the help of Hudsons and a squadron of Wellingtons. A complete wing of Dakotas later became available under the auspices of South East Asia Command. The 154th (Gurkha) Parachute Battalion brought the brigade up to full strength but was in time replaced by 1st Bn the Assam Regiment.

Back in Britain, following the formation in 1941 of 1st

British paratroop trainees at a passing-out parade before receiving their wings in March 1942. Their time of victory was soon to come

Imperial War Museum

Parachute Brigade (Gale) and 1st (Air-Landing) Brigade (Hopkinson), 2nd Parachute Brigade (Down) first saw life on 17 July 1942. Since the original Commando group had converted as No 11 SAS Battalion, the appeal for parachute volunteers had ranged far and wide throughout the British Army. Unfortunately for Browning's plans, there was no stampede to join and a new recruitment policy was implemented.

Infantry battalions were drafted to the Airborne Forces Depot and submitted to the selection course. The men were still volunteers as they could withdraw if they wished; the scheme worked well. The pride of the 'Regiment' was at stake and each man set out to do as well as his chums on the course. The first two regiments to provide battalions for conversion were the Queen's Own Cameron Highlanders and the Royal Welch Fusiliers. The 7th Battalion of the former and the 10th Battalion of the latter became the 5th (Scottish) and 6th (Royal Welch) Parachute Battalions respectively. The Camerons arriving with their pipe band, were thus the first parachute pipers! The 4th (later the Wessex) Battalion was transferred from 1st Parachute Brigade to form with the 5th and 6th, Brigadier Eric Down's 2nd Parachute Brigade.

The structure of 1st Airborne Division less support and service troops was 1st Parachute, 4th Parachute Brigade and 1st (Air-Landing) Brigade. The 2nd Brigade formed part of 1st Airborne for a time but went 'Independent' in the Italian Campaign. The 1st Brigade was commanded for most of the war by Brigadier Gerald Lathbury; the 2nd Brigade by Brigadier C H V Pritchard; and the 4th Brigade by Brigadier J W Hackett. Major-General G F 'Hoppy' Hopkinson became GOC 1st Airborne Division after Browning on 6 May 1943 but was killed in action in the Foggia area in Italy later that year. He had been succeeded in the command of 1st Air-Landing Brigade by Brigadier P H W 'Pip' Hicks. 1st Airborne was taken over in autumn 1943 by Major-General Eric Down, one of the pioneer parachutists. He was almost immediately posted to India to commence planning 44th Indian Division. The division was thereafter led by Major-General R E Urquhart.

Major-General R N Gale on 3 May 1943 formed 6th Airborne Division. Brigadier James Hill's 3rd Parachute Brigade consisted of the 7th, 8th and 9th Parachute Battalions. As was now the custom in the Parachute Regiment —now officially a Regiment of the Line — battalions were chosen on a regional basis: 7th (Light Infantry) Battalion from 10th Bn the Somerset Light Infantry; 8th (Midland) Battalion

from 13th Bn the Royal Warwickshire Regiment; 9th (Eastern and Home Counties) Battalion from 10th Bn the Essex Regiment.

5th Parachute Brigade of 6th Airborne Division was commanded by Brigadier J H N Poett. His parachute units were (after transfer from the 3rd Brigade) 7th Parachute Battalion and the 12th and 13th Parachute Battalions. The 12th was originally the 10th Bn the Green Howards and the 13th the 2nd/4th Bn the South Lancashire Regiment; these two battalions often being referred to as the 'Yorkshire' and 'Lancashire' Battalions.

Brigadier the Hon Hugh Kindersley's 6th Air-Landing Brigade's order of battle was 2nd Oxfordshire and Buckinghamshire Light Infantry, 12th Devons and 1st Royal Ulsters. 2nd Ox & Bucks and 1st RUR had originally formed part of the 1st Air-Landing Brigade, the final establishment of the latter being 1st Borders, 2nd South Staffords and 7th King's Own Scottish Borderers (KOSB).

After the departure of 7th Battalion from the 3rd Brigade, the replacement was made by the 1st Canadian Parachute Battalion. A team of Canadians had been trained at Ringway before returning to Canada to open a parachute centre at Camp Shiloh, Manitoba. Two battalions were formed. The 1st Battalion after spending four months at the American Parachute Training School at Fort Benning joined 3rd Parachute Brigade in England in August 1943.

2nd Canadian Parachute Battalion went its separate way as the 1st Canadian Special Service Battalion. The 'Devils' Brigade', as the unit was known, was a mixture of Americans and Canadians. The battalion saw action in July/August 1943 in the Aleutians and continued in a Commando rôle in the later campaigns in Italy and the South of France.

Mention has already been made of the Polish Parachute Brigade. The Poles represented the largest single foreign element of Britain's airborne forces. The Polish Brigade, however, always remained independent and General Browning did not always see eye-to-eye with the Polish commander, Major-General Stanislaw Sosabowski for this very reason. Sosabowski, who in September 1939 had led the Infantry Garrison of Warsaw, had only one ambition and that was to drop his brigade on his beloved Warsaw. The brigade colours were secretly embroidered in occupied Warsaw and smuggled out to England under the noses of the Germans. The Independent Polish Parachute Brigade was centred at Leven on the Fife coast. Sosabowski did not ask for volunteers. 'Why,' he asked, 'should only the brave die?'

The Italians: First in the Field

The Italian enthusiasm for parachuting, which had begun during the First World War with dropping agents behind the Austrian lines and – as on the Western Front jumping out of doomed kite balloons was carried on into the Second World War. Paradoxically, in spite of all the effort the Italians put into military parachuting between the wars, Italian parachutists were to fight no major airborne actions in the coming conflict.

In 1938, Air Marshal Balbo, Governor of the Italian colony of Libya, instituted the Parachute School at Castel Benito, Tripoli. The 1st Libyan Parachute Battalion, officered by Italian regulars, took part in the manoeuvres at Bir al Ghnem in the same year when a second parachute battalion was also raised. As the parachute training at Castel Benito in 1939 cost fifteen dead and seventy-two seriously injured, the 2nd Libyan Parachute Battalion was disbanded and replaced entirely by Italian volunteers. The two battalions formed a parachute regiment.

On 13 October 1939, another school for military parachuting was opened in Italy at Tarquinia. The original parachute course lasting eight months was soon reduced to two months, and initially thirty-six instructors were trained. By November 1940, one battalion of Army and another of *Carabinieri* parachutists were under training. During April/August 1941, the 1st and 2nd Parachute Regiments, each of three battalions, were raised; the 2nd Bn on 30 April dropping on the Greek island of Cephalonia. After the capture of the island, the Italian paratroopers went on to take Zante by boat.

The 1st *Carabinieri* Parachute Battalion was sent to North Africa and first saw action against the British in December 1941 at the Eluet el Asel crossroads. The battalion took part in the retreat to Agedabia, pursued by the 4th Indian Division. 1st Parachute Regiment, which also went to North Africa, was named the '*Folgore*' (Lightning) Regiment; its 1st Bn later being detached to form the 185 Parachute Infantry Bn.

The *Folgore* Parachute Division was established at the end of 1941 and earmarked for Operation 'C3', the proposed invasion of Malta. The German paratroop *Generalmajor* Hermann Ramcke was assigned to the *Folgore* as 'Chief Instructor' for the Malta plan; in effect he was the division's commanding officer. The *Folgore* Division's units were 186th Parachute Infantry Regiment (V, VI and VII Bns); 187th Parachute Infantry Regiment (II, IV and VII Bns); and the 185th Parachute Artillery Regiment, equipped with anti-tank guns. The *Folgore* Division first arrived in North Africa in July 1942 and fought in the ground rôle. In October/November the division held part of the southern sector of the line at El Alamein, but as the men had no transport the men could not escape when Montgomery's offensive broke the line. The *Folgore* gave battle to the last man and today thousands of white crosses mark their last resting places.

Another Italian Parachute Division – the *Nembo* – was in existence in Italy at this time. The *Nembo*'s units were 183rd Parachute Infantry Regiment (XV and XVI Bns); 184th

SAVOIA-MARCHETTI SM 81

A military development of the trimotor SM 73 civil transport, the SM 81 first flew in 1934 seeing extensive service in Ethiopia and Spain as both bomber and troop transport, and was the standard paratroop aircraft during Italy's period of airborne experiments until succeeded by the SM 82. When Italy surrendered five SM 81s soldiered on with the Allies, and others continued with the RSI airborne forces

Engines: 3 x Alfa-Romeo RC 35, 750 hp	
Max speed: 196 mph	
Range: 932 miles	
Span: 78 ft 8⅔ in	
Length: 60 ft 1 in	
Max take-off weight: 23,100 lb	

Left: Italy's colonial troops contributed airborne contingents before the war. Here Libyan paratroops march past in review

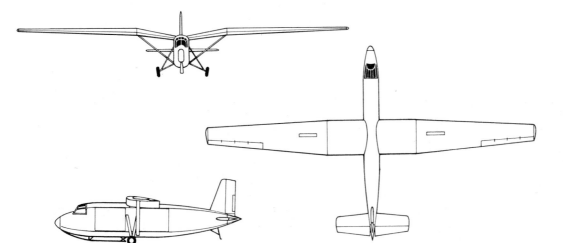

CAPRONI TM2

Italy, pioneer of airborne warfare was late to develop assault gliders. The TM2 cargo glider made its first flight in the spring of 1943 but the prototype crashed and further tests were abandoned

Span: 74 ft 9½ in	
Length: 42 ft 6 in	
Max take-off weight: 8800 lb	

Parachute Infantry Regiment (XII, XIII and XIV Bns); 185th Parachute Infantry Regiment (III, VIII and XI Bns); and the 184th Parachute Artillery Regiment. The *Nembo* saw some action in Sicily in 1943 and remained loyal to the Germans after the Italian Armistice; they ended up helping to fight Tito's partisans.

Other Italian airborne units formed before the Italian surrender in September 1943 were the San Marco Parachute Battalion, the 10th Arditi Regiment and the 1st Parachute Battalion of the Italian Air Force.

The San Marco Parachute Bn, a naval unit, was drafted from the San Marco Regiment (Marines). About 300 recruits were trained at the Parachute School of Tarquinia in 1941. These men also underwent special underwater training as well; hence the letters NP – 'Nuotatori Paracadutisti' – on their badge. The San Marco Battalion was also singled out for the Malta operation but as the invasion, which had been planned on an elaborate scale, never came off, the 'parafrogmen' found themselves in the South of France. When the battalion was later transferred to La Spezia, near Genoa, it probably numbered about 600 men.

The 10th Arditi Regiment adopted the First World War badge of Italian assault troops – two pointed blue 'flames' on the collar. The Regiment comprised three companies – *Paracadutisti*, *Nuotatori* and *Camionettisti*. (The second name, literally, means 'swimmers' and the third meant lorry and jeep troops.) The three companies amounted to a battalion, which was soon joined by another battalion of three companies to establish a full regimental scale of sub-units. During the fighting in Libya, Algeria, Tunisia and southern Italy, the Arditi carried out a number of parachute and Commando-style sabotage raids. Although most of these have not been recorded, the usual objectives were road and rail supply lines; the biggest strike by the Arditi Regiment being on 14 January 1943 at Bonira in Algeria.

The 1st Parachute Battalion of the Air Force was first mustered in April 1942 and fought in Tunisia. Another Air Force Battalion, the *Arditi Distruttori Regia Aeronautica (ADRA)*, the Air Force counterpart of the 10th Arditi of the Army, also appeared at about the same time.

In the early part of the desert war, the Italians recruited a number of Indian prisoners of war for parachute training. They wore British uniforms with yellow and green, rectangular collar patches. When later, the Indians learned that they were to be sent to North Africa, they refused their orders and were sent back to POW camps. Following the Italian unconditional surrender in 1943, some Italian parachute units fought with distinction for the British Eighth Army. The British Middle East Parachute School was, in fact, transferred from Ramat David to Gioia airfield near Bari. After the fall of Rome parachute training also took place at the Lido di Roma. The Italian parachutists were mainly used to obtain information in guerrilla areas in northern Italy in increasingly large-scale operations.

CRETE: THE ISLAND PRIZE

Hitler, in the early months of 1941, as a precautionary measure before beginning operations against Russia, decided to occupy the coast of Southern Thrace between Salonika and Alexandropolis. The Twelfth Army (List) was chosen for this operation, and included Kleist's Panzer Group. The army assembled in Rumania, crossed the Danube into Bulgaria, and from there was to pierce the Metaxas Line. When the Germans crossed the Greek frontier in April 1941, following the landing the previous month of British forces to assist the Greek Army in Salonika, the Allied forces in north-eastern Greece were out-flanked and the invaders made very rapid progress to the south.

Fliegerdivision 7's sojourn in Bulgaria had been of no special account but opportunities now arose for airborne action. As we have already learned, Student as 'Air-General' *Fliegerkorps XI*, had in 1940 singled out suitable objectives in the Mediterranean theatre, which he thought to be an area of operations well suited to Airborne strategic manoeuvre. *Fliegerdivision 7* had, in fact, been moved into Bulgaria in the winter of 1940 in preparation for the invasion of Greece. The main focus of Student's attention was, however, fixed on Cyprus and Crete.

Whilst these moves were being contemplated, the German Parachute Division, which was now commanded by *Generalmajor* Süssmann, was detailed to provide units for drops on the Cyclades islands and on Lemnos in the Aegean Sea. Both projects were cancelled as the islands were not finally considered important enough to warrant the involvement of a crack air division.

The chance for the employment of *Fliegerdivision 7* came in April when the Twelfth Army was racing southwards to Athens. The British Imperial Forces, which by now were receiving little help from the demoralized and virtually defeated Greek Army, were fast pulling back from their original positions west of the Vardar. A controlled withdrawal was in motion with the declared purpose of landing the bulk of the British and Commonwealth troops on Crete. Across their path and that of the Twelfth Army into the Southern Peloponnese lay a strip of land cut by the Corinth Canal.

The road route along this slender land-line spanned the Corinth Canal by means of a single bridge, the capture of which was assigned to *Oberst* Albert Sturm's *FJR 2*. The airborne landing was to be made ahead of the Twelfth Army to facilitate its advance to the southern ports of the Peloponnese. By the end of the third week in April, the vast majority of the retreating forces had reached their evacuation areas but some stragglers still remained on the Greek mainland. The seizure of the Corinth Canal Bridge had thus already lost much of its tactical importance when the Germans struck on 25 April.

Oberst Sturm's plan was to drop his two parachute battalions (1st and 2nd) on either side of the bridge. Whilst this battle group adopted defensive positions, a party of engineers was scheduled to land in gliders to capture the bridge. During the 24th, *FJR 2* assembled at the Greek airfield of Larissa and at 0500 hours the following morning a Junkers fleet of 270 aircraft took to the air. The 'bridge party', lifted in three DFS 230 gliders, numbered fifty-two parachute engineers *(Fallschirmpioniere)*; their officer in charge being *Leutnant* Häffner.

The gliders sailed in at 0700 hours: the bridge was defended by British troops, but, after exchanging fire with sentries, the German engineers were quickly in control of their objective. *Hauptmann* Kroh's 1st Battalion had made a successful drop and thrown out a protective cordon on the north side of the bridge but the landings by *Hauptmann* Pietzonka's 2nd Battalion were scattered and were of little help to the engineers. A fierce battle developed at the southern end of the bridge. Although the German engineers had removed the British demolition charges, it was now a question of whether they could save the bridge from destruction by increasingly accurate artillery and mortar bombardment.

The story that the bridge was exploded by a Bofors shell hitting a pile of dismantled charges may be apocryphal; but it was destroyed, perhaps by a round from a heavier weapon. Nobody is sure! A temporary structure was erected and three days after the attack, advance guards of the Twelfth Army crossed the Corinth Canal.

The evacuation of Greece by the Royal Navy was completed by 29 April. Although the Germans had been successful in encircling some of the retreating units at Nauplia and Kalimata, 43,000 troops were rescued from Greek ports, 27,000 of whom were landed in Crete. The Allies had every intention of turning the island of Crete into a fortress stronghold but Hitler decided that it was one of the keys to his Mediterranean strategy and *Fliegerkorps XI* was alerted for an immediate landing.

In the words of Basil Liddell Hart, the eminent military historian: 'The capture of Crete by an invasion delivered purely by air was one of the most astonishing and audacious feats of the war. It was also the most striking airborne operation of the war. It was performed at Britain's expense – and should remain a warning not to discount the risk of similar surprise strokes "out of the blue" in the future.' (*History of the Second World War*, Cassell, 1970).

Generalleutnant Student's first step in mounting the Cretan operation was to present his case to Keitel, Head of *OKW*, *Flieger-General* Löhr in turn outlining the *Luftwaffe* plan to Göring. Both Keitel and Göring were impressed and Hitler gave his approval on 21 April, the day of the Greek Army's surrender. Hitler had some reservations as to the practicability of an airborne invasion of Crete but spared nothing in words of encouragement to make the operation a success. Crete was to be the supreme test of the viability of airborne warfare.

Winston Churchill suspected the possibility of an airborne attack on the island. He ordered more tanks to be despatched there from the Middle East but only a few could be spared. A warning was sent to General Freyberg, whose command in Crete totalled 28,000 British, Australian and New Zealand troops, who was sceptical of airborne intervention. The General, a New Zealander, argued that there was no cause for nervousness.

The mounting of Operation *Merkur* ('Mercury') called for the total commitment of *Fliegerkorps XI* but as was always to be the case in a major airborne battle conducted by any Army, the overall responsibility lay with the Air Force. For Crete, bomber and fighter support was assigned to *Generalleutnant* Freiherr von Richthofen's *Fliegerkorps VIII*. The spearhead of the bomber group was formed by 150 Ju 87

Left: Generaloberst *Löhr*, commander of Luftflotte IV. He proposed an airborne attack on Crete to Göring in April 1941. *Below:* Kurt Student the guiding intelligence behind the successes of the German airborne forces. His paratroops were a decisive element in the

success of Hitler's 1940 victories but Crete was to be the greatest prize. He died in July 1978 at the age of 88

dive-bombers. Further support for the *Blitz* on Crete was provided by Do 217 bombers and Ju 88's; six groups of fighters – Bf 109s and Bf 110s – providing cover for the transport and bombers.

At the Hotel Grande-Bretagne in Athens, General Student issued his operational orders for the battle. Ten air transport groups of Löhr's *Luftflotte IV*, attached to *Fliegerkorps XI*, boasted approximately 500 Ju 52s, and three glider-towing groups of *Luftlandegruppe I*. The skytrain was commanded by *Generalmajor* Conrad. Seven emplaning points were chosen within easy flying distance of Crete: Corinth, Dadion, Elevsis, Mégara, Phaleron, Tanágra and Topolis. The problem of the limited range of the Stuka dive-bombers was solved by basing the bulk of them on the island of Scarpanto (now Karpathos), which lay only a few minutes' flying time across the Kasos Strait from Crete.

It will be remembered that in Holland, *Fliegerdivision I* had been partnered by *Luftlandedivision 22* as air-transported troops. This air division, which in spring 1941 had been sent to Rumania on oilfield protection duty, was committed to the Eleventh Army for the invasion of Russia, and so was not available for Operation 'Mercury'. Its place in *Fliegerkorps XI* was taken by *Generalleutnant* Julius Ringel's *Gebirgsdivision V* (5th Mountain Division). Ringel, an Austrian, who had served as Chief of Operations of *Gebirgsdivision III* in Norway, was re-assigned to train the 5th Division for the

invasion of Greece. After breaking through the Metaxas Line with great success, Ringel's men were route-marched to Athens and given three weeks in which to prepare for their new rôle.

The *Fallschirmjäger* were as ready for large-scale action in May 1941 as they would ever be again during the Second World War. The German paratrooper was well trained and equipped and his morale in the triumphant tide of Nazi victory was of the supreme order. Although the impending onslaught on Russia was making heavy demands on the *Luftwaffe*, the matter of air transport techniques had been thoroughly studied and rehearsed. Student's proposal to capture Crete from the air, which was strategic in concept, demanded the all-embracing master plan should be bridled with daring experiment if disaster was to be averted.

The German paratrooper's combat dress, which has already in part been described, featured a long, loose-fitting, weatherproof gabardine overall. Originally olive-green, the 'bone sack' was made in a number of different colours and versions; several camouflage patterns being associated with the *Fallschirmjäger*'s smock from late 1940. Light khaki was adopted for tropical wear. All pockets and openings were closed with zip fasteners or press studs. Side-lacing jump boots were made of heavy leather with thick rubber soles; baggy trousers were tucked into the boots. Side-lacing boots were later abandoned for a front-lacing version. The smock

FALLSCHIRMJÄGER, 1941

When it first appeared the German parachutist's uniform and special equipment were far in advance of combat clothing worn by any other army. The *Fallschirmjäger* of 1940/41 wore a combat dress quite distinct from the rest of the *Wehrmacht*. A thigh length smock was worn over the *Luftwaffe*-grey tunic and field-grey trousers. The smock was loose fitting and provided with four capacious pockets. Padded leather gauntlets and knee and elbow pads protected the soldier from the shock of landing. The close-fitting padded helmet with forked chin strap had almost no neck shield. Special equipment shown here include an ammunition bandolier in blue-grey cloth and a Mauser 98K with sniper-sight

John Fraser

was worn over the webbing equipment for the jump. Long gauntlet gloves protected the hands and rubber knee protectors were worn. One familiar aspect of the *Fallschirmjäger*'s fighting attire was a special ammunition bandolier carried in combat around the neck and secured by two ties to the belt.

The best-known parachutists' rifle was the specially produced *Fallschirmjäger Gewehr* (FG) 42. This weapon was a combination of rifle and light machine-gun but was not available in time for the Crete operation. The FG 42 automatic rifle fired standard infantry ammunition (7.92-mm). In the early part of the war use was made of the standard infantry Mauser 98K bolt-action rifle. The paratrooper dropped with the pistol P 08 and two full magazines on the person. The standard Wehrmacht-issue MP 38 and later the MP 40 were characteristic Airborne weapons. Both machine-carbine models were fed by thirty-two round detachable box magazines using 9-mm ammunition. When jumping the MP 38 and MP 40 were either slung around the paratroopers' necks or broken up and stowed in their overalls. Spare magazines were carried in leather or canvas pouches, usually worn on the belt, three to each side. Each pouch contained two magazines. The platoon support weapon was the MG 34 machine-gun and again this weapon was standard infantry issue.

Arms containers were not dissimilar in size and shape to the British CLE patterns. Two or three different types were employed in Crete. One container holding up to 260 lbs (135 kg) of arms and equipment was shared between twelve jumpers and handles and a pair of bogie wheels were fitted for ease of handling on the ground. The containers or *Waffenbehälter* were brightly painted for swift recognition and clearly inscribed with unit markings. These canisters were dropped from specially adapted racks in the Ju 52 'bomb' bays at the same time as the personnel.

Fliegerdivision 7 was equipped with a modest scale of light and medium artillery guns, broken down into basic components for air transportation. The Airborne field weapon was the mountain gun of 75-mm calibre and experiments were made for the landing in Holland with dogs and ponies for towing the guns. The animals proved less amenable, however, to flight discipline than human porters and the scheme was abandoned. Experiment with the *leichte Geschutz* (*lG*) 75-mm in Crete was not entirely successful but the design was modified and the gun was produced in quantity in 1942. The lG 40 75-mm had a small carriage of motorcycle wheels and could be stripped down to four loads for parachuting in containers. Other late-war developments in Airborne artillery were the lG 42 and lG 43, although both of these were preceded by the RFK 43. The lG series were light recoilless artillery and not to be confused with the standard Army 75-mm mountain gun. The PzB 41 anti-tank gun, infantry version, was easily handled by paratroopers; a refined model appearing for airborne forces in 1942.

DFS 230 gliders were used in Crete but as they were so small they made no significant contribution to the battle. Principally troop carriers, these aircraft were more suited to the raiding rôle, as demonstrated at Eban-Emael and Corinth. There was no question of the DFS 250 lifting light artillery or heavy freight; the Ju 52 transport carrying five times the payload of the glider.

NSU KETTENRAD

A typically ingenious yet over-complex example of German engineering, the Kettenrad tracked motorcycle gave great tractive power for light weight and was ideal for airborne use. Few however were used operationally by the airborne forces

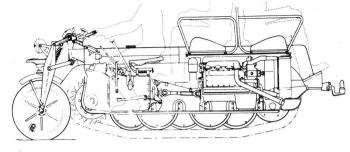

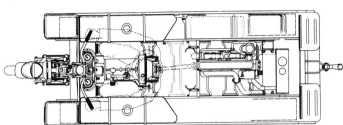

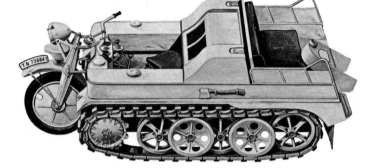

Kettenrad and IG 40 combination with paratroop crew

7.5-cm IG 40

Krupp had been developing recoilless weapons for airborne use in parallel with Rheinmetall and produced a 7.5-cm model with the firing mechanism mounted on top of the breech. Rheinmetall also produced a 10.5-cm weapon known as the IG 42 and both weapons were used in Crete.
While light guns had a very useful performance and surprise value they were greedy for propellant, the jet efflux at the rear made concealment difficult and they were impossible to dig in

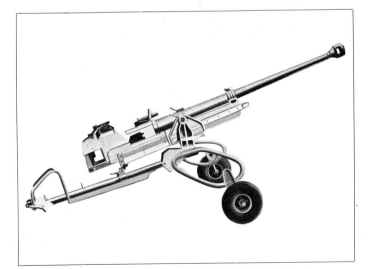

2.8-cm PzB 41 Ausführung für Fallschirmjäger

Called a *schwere Panzerbüchse* (heavy anti-tank rifle), this gun based on the Gerlich taper-bore principle was a formidable anti-tank weapon when it first appeared in 1941. The airborne model featured a simplified trail, small aircraft-type wheels, had no shield and weighed some 260 lb (118 kg) in action

Operation *Merkur*
The assault on Crete

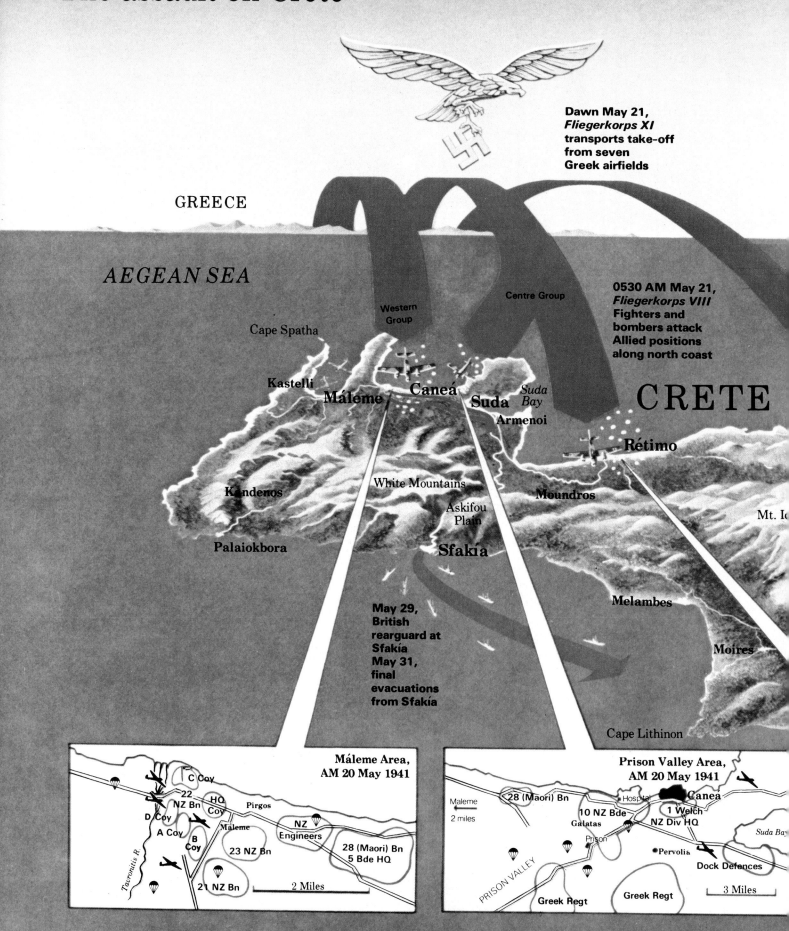

Dawn May 21, *Fliegerkorps XI* **transports take-off from seven Greek airfields**

GREECE

AEGEAN SEA

0530 AM May 21, *Fliegerkorps VIII* **Fighters and bombers attack Allied positions along north coast**

Centre Group

Western Group

Cape Spatha

Kastelli

Máleme   **Caneá**   **Suda**   *Suda Bay*

CRETE

Kandenos

Armenoi

White Mountains

Rétimo

Askifou Plain

Moundros

Mt. Io

Palaiokbora

Sfakía

May 29, British rearguard at Sfakía May 31, final evacuations from Sfakía

Melambes

Moires

Cape Lithinon

Máleme Area, AM 20 May 1941

C Coy

22 NZ Bn   HQ Coy   Pirgos

D Coy   Máleme   NZ Engineers

A Coy   B Coy

23 NZ Bn   28 (Maori) Bn 5 Bde HQ

Tavronitis R.

21 NZ Bn   2 Miles

Prison Valley Area, AM 20 May 1941

Maleme
2 miles

28 (Maori) Bn   Hospital   Canea

10 NZ Bde   1 Welch

Galatas   NZ Div HQ

Prison   *Suda Bay*

Pervolia

PRISON VALLEY   Dock Defences

Greek Regt   Greek Regt   3 Miles

1941

APRIL 25: Führer Directive 28 orders 'Operation Merkur' – the attack on Crete. Units of XI Fliegerkorps alerted in Germany.

APRIL 29: End of the main evacuations from southern Greece.

APRIL 30: Wavell visits Crete – General Freyberg is appointed commander of the defending forces.

MAY 16: The last British reinforcements arrive in Crete.

MAY 19: Freyberg orders the last airworthy aircraft to be flown out.

MAY 20: 'Operation Merkur' begins. German glider and parachute forces are pinned down at Heráklion, Caneá, and Rétimo, but gain a footing at Máleme. British retire from Point 107.

MAY 21: Germans gain control of Máleme airfield; failure of British counterattack.

MAY 22: Freyberg cancels the proposed second British counterattack at Máleme and orders withdrawal to a shorter line.

MAY 24: General Ringel organises his forces for the main German attack. Withdrawal of the British 5th Brigade completes the formation of the Staliana/Khania Line.

MAY 25: Germans fail to break through at Galatas.

MAY 26: Germans enter Perivólia and Galaria. Freyberg orders withdrawal to Sfakía.

MAY 27: Freyberg receives Wavell's authorisation for evacuation. Germans enter Caneá, gaining control of Suda Bay.

MAY 28: British rearguard fights the last action north of the White Mountains. British evacuate Heráklion.

MAY 29/30: British rearguard maintains the Sfakía beach-head. The Rétimo garrison is forced to surrender to the Germans.

MAY 31: Final British evacuations from Sfakía.

Roy Castle

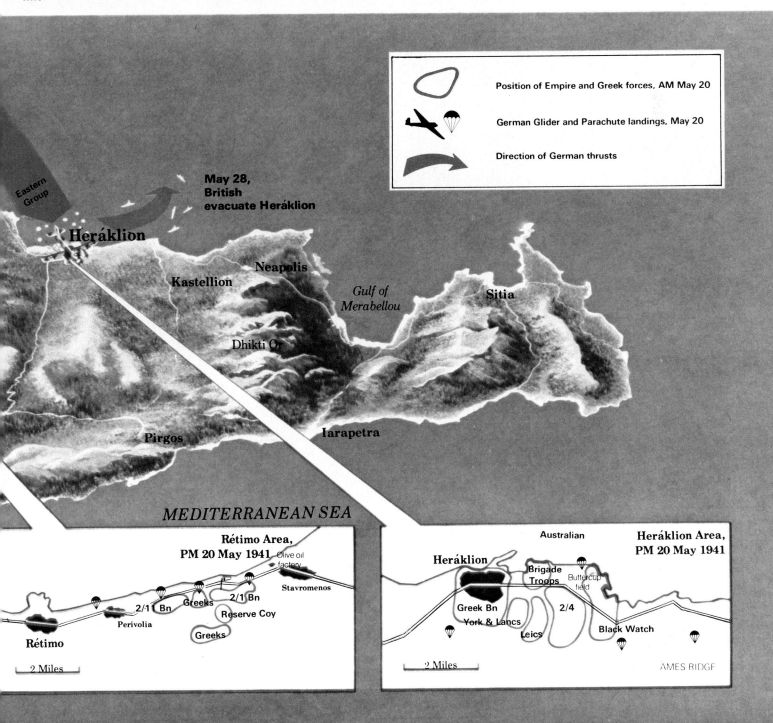

Position of Empire and Greek forces, AM May 20

German Glider and Parachute landings, May 20

Direction of German thrusts

May 28, British evacuate Heráklion

Eastern Group

Heráklion

Neapolis

Kastellion

Gulf of Merabellou

Sitia

Dhikti Or

Pirgos

Iarapetra

MEDITERRANEAN SEA

Rétimo Area, PM 20 May 1941

Olive oil factory

Stavromenos

2/1 Bn

Greeks

2/1 Bn

Perivolia

Reserve Coy

Greeks

Rétimo

2 Miles

Heráklion Area, PM 20 May 1941

Australian

Heráklion

Brigade Troops

Buttercup field

Greek Bn

York & Lancs

2/4

Leics

Black Watch

AMES RIDGE

2 Miles

A German glider-borne soldier goes into action on Crete from beneath the wing of a DFS 230

The Luftwaffe freight gliders mainly saw service on the Eastern front. The Me 321 *Gigant*, built for 'Operation Sealion', was operational before the end of summer 1941. The main problem was finding tug aircraft capable of towing the giant glider. The most usual method was provided by the Heinkel IIIZ *Zwilling* an ingenious but dangerous alternative being the *Troikaschlepp*. In the latter system, three Messerschmitts were arranged in a triangular system as tug aircraft. The ground manoeuvres before take-off were the most complicated; four highly skilled pilots in effect being needed to get the *Gigant* airborne.

The Gotha Go-242 glider was also a feature of air transport supply in Russia. It carried twice the payload of the DFS 230. The Go-244 was a powered version with two engines, and two Ju 52 squadrons were converted to Go-244s in the summer of 1943. The Go-345 was introduced in 1944 as a freight glider; it was subsequently projected as a ten-seat battle glider. This aircraft was fitted with two auxiliary engines suspended from the wings.

As regards tug aircraft – in summary – the Ju 52 was the workhorse of the DFS 230. The Heinkel III 'twins' and the Me 321 – *Gigant* formed a bizarre combination in the sky. The *Troikaschlepp*, three Bf 110 fighters, with the Gigant on tow may also be said to have been a brave gesture in aviation antics. The Go-242 was usually towed by the Heinkel III but Dornier Do 17s and Italian Savoia Marchettis were also pressed into service.

The original German airborne division, which was formed in July 1938, was still incomplete at the outbreak of war with only two parachute regiments. Under Student's leadership, *Fliegerdivision 7* had reached its full establishment in 1941. The total strength of the parachute division numbered approximately 16,000 men. Three Parachute Regiments of 3206 men each were broken down into nine battalions, three per Regiment, which each also supported Regimental HQ, Mortar or Light, and Anti-Tank Companies. A battalion consisted of three rifle companies and light support sections; the company being sub-divided into three rifle platoons; the sections making ten men each. The scale of weapons allocated to a parachute rifle battalion less support weapons was: rifles or carbines 410; pistols 257; sub-machine-guns 214. The division was staffed by the usual Headquarter support units.

The strategic reasoning for the German invasion of Crete was to provide a base for the air war against Britain in the eastern Mediterranean. Crete, a mountainous island some 100 miles (161 km) long by 40 miles (64 km) wide, also provided suitable harbour facilities for naval vessels. Although Löhr's Air Fleet (*Luftflotte IV*) seemed formidable, it would not be possible to land *Fliegerkorps XI's* assault waves in one lift. Two lifts were necessary involving the aircraft in two runs to distribute the airborne troops along a broad portion of the northern coastline of the island.

The objectives of the first wave on the morning of 20 May 1941 were Máleme and Caneá. The former lay at the western end of the island and the latter, the capital, not far to the east of the first objective. The second wave in the afternoon was assigned to Rétimo and Heráklion, being further east still in the centre of the coastal area. The second wave spearheaded by paratroops was scheduled to include one regiment of Ringel's *Gebirgsdivision V* and supporting light armour

German Gliders and Tugs: Winning Combinations

HEINKEL HE IIIZ ZWILLING

In mid-1940 development work on the enormous Ju 322 *Mammut* and Me 321 *Gigant* cargo gliders was well under way but there was no tug aircraft available with sufficient power to haul these giants into action.

The *Troikaschlepp*, triple-tow by three Bf 110s, proved clumsy and dangerous but a simple solution was proposed by twinning two He IIIs with a fifth engine in a new constant-chord centre wing section and the first prototype flew in autumn 1941. Full defensive armament was maintained and the test aircraft proved remarkably successful although operationally it was a disappointment, but through no fault of its own.

Seelöwe was cancelled, *Herkules* (a projected attack on Malta) was cancelled, and projected assaults with He IIIZ and Me 321 combinations on Astrakhan and Baku were similarly cancelled, and most of these remarkable aircraft were expended ignominiously in resupply operations in Russia

Engines: 5 x Junkers Jumo 211F-2, 1350 hp
Max speed: 272 mph
Span: 116 ft 1⅔ in
Length: 53 ft 9½ in
Max take-off weight: 62,556 lb
Armament: 1 x 20-mm MG FF, 5 x 7·9-mm MG 15, 2 x 13-mm MG 131

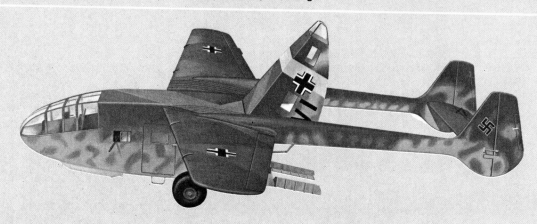

GOTHA GO 242

The success of the DFS 230 prompted the RLM (German Air Ministry) to investigate the development of larger transport gliders and Dipl Ing Kalkert at the Gothaer Waggonfabrik was quick to make proposals based on a large uninterrupted cargo hold with near ground-level loading. The Go 242 was built largely of wood with a skid landing gear and hingeing tail providing easy access to the hold under the shoulder-mounted wings and twin-boom tail

GERMAN GLIDER TOW TECHNIQUES

1: Mistelschlepp (Parasite-tow)
DFS began to investigate in 1942 the merits of a *Huckepack* (pick-a-back) configuration. Tests under tow led to the definitive DFS 230B and Bf 109 E-1 combination but the *Mistelschlepp* scheme was not adopted operationally

2: Starrschlepp (Rigid-tow)
For night or bad weather missions a rigid-tow arrangement could be used – the glider anchoring to an articulated joint at the rear of the tug aircraft

3: Troikaschlepp (Triple-tow)
Before the operational appearance of the giant He IIIZ tug aircraft, the Me 321 *Gigant* was hauled into the air by three Bf 110s in the hair-raising technique known as *Troikaschlepp.* The technique needed a very high degree of proficiency by the tug pilots. Straining at the end of 10-mm steel cables, the central cable being 328 ft long and port and starboard 262 ft long, the combination needed a concrete runway 4000 ft long and the preliminaries were so complicated that only one glider could be sent up at a time, even with the assistance of hydrogen-peroxide ATO underwing rockets

4: Seilschlepp (Cable-tow)
The most common towing technique used by the *Schleppgruppen.* In a typical combination the DFS 230, for example, was joined to a Ju 52/3 m by a 131-ft cable

configuration.
The *Luftwaffe* accepted its first 12 Go 242s in August 1941 and production continued with several modified versions. The Go 242 A-1 was intended primarily for freight carrying and the A-2 for assault with additional doors and a braking 'chute. Go 232 B variants featured full fixed undercarriages. The Gotha glider saw most service on the Eastern Front in air resupply operations

Max speed: (under tow Ju 52/3m) 130 mph
Span: 80 ft 4½ in
Length: 51 ft 10 in
Max take-off weight: 16,094 lb

Bundesarchiv

The perimeter of Máleme airfield marked by crashed Ju 52s. Already the Germans were bringing in heavier equipment including AA-guns and motor-cycle combinations

and guns to be landed in the vicinity of Heráklion. The two waves were actually split into three main battle groups: Group West (Meindl); Group Centre (Süssmann) and Group East (Ringel).

Meindl's Group, which included a glider element, was centred for the attack on Máleme around the Assault Regiment. Two *Fallschirmjäger* companies were to land first at 0715 hours in DFS 230 gliders. Meindl's Assault Regiment (three battalions) was to capture Máleme aerodrome. The right wing of the assault was further reinforced by three parachute battalions and a machine-gun company. The main weight of the blow was in the hands of Süssmann's Group Centre. Süssmann, the parachute division's commander, was responsible for two battle zones. His right arm, which also included glider assault troops, was pointed at Canea and the nearby naval base at Suda. This element comprised *FJR 3*, part of 100th Mountain Infantry Regiment, the glider troops numbering two companies and artillery and other support troops. His left arm – chiefly *FJR 2* – was directed at Rétimo.

Ringel's Group East – *FJR 1*, 2nd Bn *FJR 2*, the remainder of 100th Mountain Infantry Regiment – was to be strengthened further by a Panzer Battalion, a Light AA Battalion and an enlarged Machine-gun Battalion. Ten Air Transport Groups of *Fliegerkorps XI* (Conrad) were split into three *Geschwader*. Group West and the right echelon of Group Centre were allotted to the first wave (morning) and the left echelon and Group East to the second wave (afternoon). The rear squadrons of the second wave were to reinforce all four landing zones. Two Light and two Heavy Ship Flotillas were allocated for the sea transport of reinforcements and heavy weapons.

Clouds of dust climbed high in the sky as the German transports took off from their Greek airfields. Löhr had favoured landing the entire *Fliegerkorps* in one place but Student's insistence on dispersed landing zones would have

been sounder if the plan had been based on more accurate intelligence. On Crete, Freyberg knew that invasion was imminent but he expected amphibious landings. His dispositions were consequently arranged along a broad stretch of the northern coastline and served equally well to counter scattered landings from the air. Student had also underestimated the strength of the British and Commonwealth garrison of 28,000 men. In addition, Freyberg could count on but not necessarily enumerate the large numbers of Greek and Cretan troops on the island.

Preceded by *Luftwaffe* raids on the assigned objectives, the Western and Centre Group elements commenced landing in the early morning of the 20th in the Máleme and Caneá areas. Many of Group West landed some distance both to west and east of the airfield but re-grouped quickly to put in their attack. The commanding feature of the locality was Hill 107, which was held by the 22nd Battalion of the 5th New Zealand Brigade. The New Zealanders brought heavy fire to bear on the Germans as they scrambled into action, inflicting severe casualties. The *Fallschirmjäger* overran the airfield but were obliged to secure their defences against fierce counter-attacks. Hill 107 overlooked the airfield across a coastal road: a parachute battalion had dropped to the left of the hill feature; and gliders had sailed in accurately south of the road to the right. After deploying, the paratroopers encircled the hill but with their inadequate equipment were in no position to dislodge the New Zealanders. One German company well to the south seized a bridge, thus cutting a road leading north to Máleme, but their success had no tactical use.

Group Centre (right) landing simultaneously with Group West dropped on top of the 4th New Zealand Brigade. Hundreds of *Fallschirmjäger* were dead on arrival on the ground; well-aimed rifle fire greeting the crouching bodies suspended from their parachute lines. The 4th Brigade, which had been facing seawards, turned inland to engage the parachute and glider troops, who straddled a road leading northeastwards to Caneá. The 2nd and 3rd Bns of *FJR 3* dropped to the west of the road whilst the 3rd Bn was to be located near Perivolia to the east in territory manned by the 19th Australian Brigade. The commander in this sector was *Oberst* Heidrich and the pivot of his battle zone developed west of the road to Caneá around Galatas. A prison formed a prominent landmark in this area, which became known as 'Prison Valley'. Some gliders had landed almost due south of Caneá and more further east along the coast; an area defended by 1st Rangers, 1st Welch Regiment and the Northumberland Hussars.

For the Germans, both the Máleme and Galatas landings by comparison with expectations had been disastrous. The airfield, by the end of the first day, was not under control and the situation in 'Prison Valley' critical. Heidrich's force, reduced by one-third on the dropping zone, was extended over an area, three miles in diameter. Counter-attacks by the Australians and New Zealanders made the possibility of the Germans holding their positions without annihilation unlikely.

As morning turned to afternoon and the Cretan sun intensified, *Oberst* Sturm's *FJR 2* east of Rétimo and *Oberst* Bräuer's *FJR 1*, at Heráklion, fared even worse. Airfields were the principal attractions in both areas although Kroh's 1st Bn area at Rétimo boasted an olive oil factory of doubtful military value. Both at Rétimo and Heráklion, the *Fallschirmjäger* jumped on to Australian outposts and were decimated by the advance of offensive patrols of a Black Watch battalion.

At *Luftwaffe* Battle Headquarters in Athens, Kurt Student in the early evening of the first day of the Battle of Crete was short on Signals reports. A rear-link message from Máleme suggested that the battle was not going well. The *Fliegergeneral* held two trump cards: Freyberg was possibly overconfident; and the 5th Mountain Division was so far virtually intact and uncommitted to battle. Student was now more inclined to Löhr's preference for concentration in strength. Student's instructions accordingly were to send all available air-landing battalions plus supporting arms to Máleme and for the enlarged Group West to roll-up the Allied defences from west to east.

At Máleme on the second day, Meindl was replaced by *Oberst* Ramcke, a First World War veteran who after Crete was to be attached to the Italian *Folgore* Division and formed his own Brigade at El Alamein. Ramcke vigorously proceeded to batter down the 'gateway' to the east along the coast.

Ringel's mountain troops now commenced arriving in Junkers transport planes at Máleme airfield and on the beaches and in the surrounding countryside. The descending aircraft were greeted with a barrage of anti-aircraft and machine-gun fire. Piles of wrecked Junkers lay everywhere but casualties were not as great as they might have been if the pilots had put down on the airfield regardless of the consequences.

The first indication that the tide of fortune was turning in the Germans' favour was when patrols probing forward at Hill 107 found the position abandoned. This meant that the airfield was no longer under fire and further reinforcements were safe to land. Student could scarcely believe his luck when he received the news that the New Zealanders had left

Hill 107 and he immediately ordered more troops in transport planes to Máleme.

The 5th New Zealand Brigade was now fast pulling back to Caneá and Suda. At this stage, Ringel (Süssmann being dead) took over command of all forces on the ground. His first manoeuvre after Caneá fell was to outflank the Suda defences. Suda Bay formed the best anchorage on Crete and its swift capture would ensure the delivery of seaborne supplies and heavy equipment. Contact was made with Heidrich and the remnants of Group Centre and then a major attack was mounted to clear the Canea-Suda area. After freeing German prisoners taken in the Rétimo area, Ringel now steam-rollered eastwards. By 24 May, General Freyberg had virtually conceded victory to the Germans and the decision to evacuate the island was made on 27 May. The Royal Navy immediately commenced a mammoth rescue operation, concentrating the bulk of the mercy fleet at the southern port of Sfakía. Stuka dive-bombers unmercifully strafed the Allied troops as they retreated southwards across the mountainous interior of Crete. A ring of British Commandos was thrown around Sfakía but they could provide no protection from the systematic dive-bomber attacks.

In the Rétimo area, an armoured battalion landing from the sea enforced large-scale surrender; German troops on motorcycles rounding up isolated detachments. Many of the Greek and Cretan soldiers as well as British, New Zealand and Australian stragglers took to the mountains where they remained to fight on as guerrillas. The last evacuation was made from a beach at Sfakía on 31 May.

Of the estimated Allied garrison of some 42,500 men, approximately half were safely carried by the Royal Navy to Egypt. The casualties amounted to about 17,500 killed, wounded and prisoners, but it was never possible to accurately assess the losses of the Greek and Cretan soldiers and inhabitants. In addition, nine British warships had been sunk and seventeen damaged in the sea battle that had taken place around the island's shores.

Student himself arrived on Crete on the second day of the battle. In Churchill's words the 'spearhead of the German lance' was shattered. It was now his task to compare the fruits of victory with the expenditure in human lives. More important from his point of view, the airborne method had been put on trial and *Fliegerkorps XI*'s future development depended on Student's superiors' evaluation of the Battle of Crete. Of the force of 22,000 men committed to the battle, 6000 were dead and many more wounded. The dead included several senior officers who had helped build the *Fallschirmjäger* Division. No less than half of the 500 Junkers transport planes had been destroyed.

When Student visited Hitler's headquarters at the *Wolfschanze* in an East Prussian forest two months later, the heavy losses in Crete had not shaken the General's belief in the Airborne concept. The Führer acknowledged that *Fliegerkorps XI*'s success signalled a pyrrhic victory but argued that the cost of winning the battle was too great. Airborne forces were much too vulnerable to warrant deployment en masse. *Fliegerdivision 7* was sent to Russia for operations in the ground rôle with only limited airborne tasks. Under Göring's guidance, German airborne forces after 1941 nevertheless grew steadily in numbers but the day· of the parachute division in its true rôle was over.

THE US AIRBORNE

Between the two World Wars, the Americans, like the British, had given some study to the air-transport concept but little or none to parachute and glider training. In the 1920s, the United States Marine Corps experimented with aviation for evacuating the sick and wounded on minor expeditionary duties. Three soldiers and a machine-gun were dropped by parachute at San Antonio, Texas, in 1928 but the experiment was not repeated. More jumps made in the 1930s by soldiers over Army Corps bases formed no part of a co-ordinated plan to develop military parachuting. Similarly, the air-landing of an infantry section on manoeuvres in Delaware in 1932 stimulated interest but no immediate action in implementing airborne training for suitable units.

On 29 June 1940 (three weeks before the first parachute descents were made by British Commandos at the Royal Air Force Parachute Training School at Ringway in England), the American Parachute Test Platoon jumped for the first time at Fort Benning. This Test Platoon, which was led by Lieutenant William T. Ryder, numbered 48 volunteers drawn from the 29th Infantry Regiment. The unit had been raised by Major William Lee, who was charged with conceiving a plan for the training and organization of airborne units. 'Bill' Lee had few guidelines to follow apart from news of the German *Fallschirmjäger*'s sensational participation in the invasion of Holland, class-room conjecture on the airborne method by Staff College men at Leavenworth, and the advocacy, originating in 1918, by his now deceased countryman, 'Billy' Mitchell, of 'vertical envelopment' by parachute troops.

No ground training apparatus existed at Fort Benning, so Lee's unit moved temporarily to New Jersey, where two 250-ft (76.2 m) towers had been erected. These simulated training structures, copied from the 'parachute tower' built for the 1939 New York World's Fair, were unfortunately of no help in learning flight techniques. The 'fun'-jumper's exit and descent controlled by vertical wires around the periphery of the canopy afforded no more than a mild thrill compared with the shock of slipstream drag from an aircraft, mid-air oscillation and drift, and the 'tooth-rattling' impact with the ground. The first aircraft jump was made on 16 August 1940 at Fort Benning and this was followed 13 days later at the same location by a 'mass' demonstration jump. Douglas B-18 bombers were employed for both drops, which were watched by Service observers with great interest.

The first parachute used by these pioneer American airborne troops was the standard T-3 Air Corps escape issue, which was worn with an experimental reserve. The manually operated T-3 was adapted as the T-4 for opening by means of a short static-line. The Irvin-designed T-4 consisted of a flat, circular canopy measuring 28 ft (8.5 m) in diameter; its large square pack was fastened by three hooks to the harness. The T-4 sequence on opening was canopy before rigging lines; the idea worked well for the Americans although the reverse principle was preferred by the R.A.F. when perfecting their 'X-'-type model. The American paratrooper has always carried a rip-cord-operated reserve 'chute worn clipped to the front of the harness in the chest position.

The standard American war-time paratroop 'chute was the T-7. This version was actually designed for release by static-line. The pack, which contained the same canopy as the T-3, was again attached to the harness by three hooks and firmly secured to the man's back by a wide body band, which also helped to support the reserve. The static-line was stowed '*Fallschirmjäger*-fashion' outside the oblong-shaped main pack. This pack or bag, which was not as bulky as the 'X'-type, opened to release the canopy within seconds of the paratrooper's aircraft exit, when the static-line broke a line laced through the flaps of the pack's cover panel. Another breakable tie released the apex of the canopy from the cover, which remained attached to the static-line, by now left suspended through the door from the strongpoint in the aircraft. Excessive oscillation and drift were controlled, so far as was possible, by manipulating the 'risers' or 'lift-webs' as these webbing straps are known in British jargon.

Those who were able to make a practical comparison between the American 'canopy-first "T-type"' and the British 'rigging-lines-first "X-type"' aver that the U.S. parachute battalions in the Second World War would have suffered fewer jump casualties had the British parachute been adopted. The pioneer parachute designer – American Leslie Irvin – introduced the same canopy for both models but it was Englishman Raymond Quilter of the GQ Parachute Company, who, in 1940, reversed the release order, after the pre-war Irvin parachute modified for use by static-line had caused a fatality at Ringway and was deemed unworkable. The 'T'-type nevertheless saved lives on very low altitude drops when, if the rigging lines had been 'first out', the canopy might well have had insufficient time in which to develop before the crucial impact with the ground.

On 16 September 1940, the Parachute Test Platoon provided a nucleus of the officers and NCOs for 1st Parachute Battalion, which six months later was renumbered the 501st Battalion. Now risen to Lieutenant-Colonel, 'Bill' Lee formed the Parachute Group at Fort Benning; this was an experimental unit assigned to training parachute volunteers. One of the parachute towers was brought back to Benning from New Jersey and other simulated training devices were devised for instruction on jump procedures. Aircraft were scarce until some DC-3s were posted to the new Benning Parachute School. At this time the DC-3 was a commercial air-liner in regular service although official plans were already on file to turn it into a military transport. Few alterations were made to the original DC-3 for the early parachute training courses; the door was removed and a strong-point cable was run along the ceiling of the fuselage cabin.

In July 1941, the 501st Parachute Infantry Battalion was transferred to the Panama Canal Zone and replaced at Fort Benning by the new 502nd Parachute Infantry Battalion. The 503rd and 504th followed on shortly afterwards. Thus far the U.S.A. was still a neutral country but the Japanese assault on Pearl Harbor on 7 December 1941 saw the nation at war. On 30 January 1942, it was decided to expand the existing parachute battalions into Regiments, each of three battalions. At the same time the Parachute Group was turned into the Airborne Command; Lee was still the Commanding Officer. Thought was already being given to the training of glider troops and the 88th Infantry Battalion accordingly joined the Command for this purpose. In Panama, the 550th Infantry Regiment in liaison with the 501st carried out air transport and air-landing manoeuvres.

In Britain, in mid-1942, the build-up of British airborne forces was moving on. Major-General 'Boy' Browning's 1st

*American paratroopers training
on the tower at Fort Benning*

Imperial War Museum

Teamwork: The C-47 Dakota and the WACO Glider

Of all the Allied wartime planes in use with the airborne forces, the C-47 Dakota was probably the best-known and the most widely used. It served both for parachute drops and as a glider tug in the Mediterranean sphere and in the Allied invasion of Europe in 1944. As a tug, one of its most common responsibilities was the Waco glider seen on these pages, which, with the Horsa and Hamilcar gliders, was the staple gliding transport of the Allied airborne forces. Together, the C-47 Dakota and the Waco glider proved a reliable and successful team which, despite occasional disasters through unforeseen conditions, greatly contributed to Allied victory

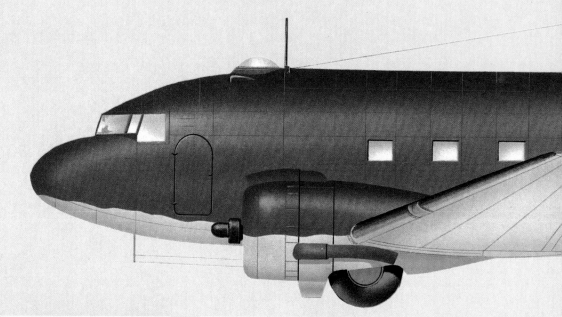

US Airforce

Above: C-47 Dakota transports of the Troop Carrier Air Division of the 12th Air Force in formation over the Mediterranean en route to drop paratroops during the invasion of the South of France, 15 August 1944. Left: Here a C-47 Dakota pulls a Waco glider full of US troops of the First Allied Airborne Army into the air and en route to the landing areas around Eindhoven, in Holland, 17 September 1944

Imperial War Museum

DOUGLAS C-47 'SKYTRAIN'

Known as the Dakota I by the British, the C-47 was manufactured by the Douglas Aircraft Company Inc. of Santa Monica, California and was a military adaptation of the DC-3 airliner. The C-47 was essentially a freight carrier and displayed a reinforced metal floor, a large door (for loading) and reinforced landing gear. The twin-engine Dakota was a low-wing cantilever monoplane. In the supply role, it carried up to 6000 lb (2700 kg) of equipment. As a paratroop aircraft, it was equipped with folding benches for 28 fully-armed troops.

Engines: 2 x Pratt & Whitney 'Twin Wasp' R-1830	
Max speed: 270 mph	
Range: 3000 miles	
Span: 95 ft	
Length: 64 ft 5½ ins	
Height: 16 ft 11½ ins	
Max weight with load: 65,000 lb	

WACO CG-4A

Known as the Hadrian by the RAF, this glider was designed by the Waco Aircraft Co. The CG-4A was a rigidly-braced, high-wing monoplane of fabric-covered wood and steel construction. It could carry freight or 15 fully-armed troops including pilot and co-pilot. The nose was hinged for direct loading of equipment. The normal troop entrance was port side forward. The CG-4A could also be fitted with two 'power eggs'; i.e. cells each containing a 6-cylinder engine, fuel tank and engine instruments. Originally delivered to North Africa in packing cases for the invasion of Sicily, this was the only glider used in any number by the USAAF. It was also used by the RAF in the Sicily invasion and in Burma by Colonel Phil Cochrane's Air Commando in support of the Chindits.

Max touring speed: 125 mph	
Max gliding speed: 38 mph	
Span: 83 ft 8 in	
Length: 48 ft 3¾ in	
Height (tail up): 16 ft 10 in	
Weights: 4700–9150 lb	

Airborne Division based on Salisbury Plain had then been in existence for over six months as had the Glider Pilot Regiment forming part of the new Army Air Corps. In June 1942, Generals Arnold, Eisenhower and Somervell took Lee, who had been promoted to one-star General, to England to discover how American airborne troops might play their part in the Second Front. Browning stressed the need for properly integrated parachute and glider units organized at the divisional level and the Americans bought the idea with enthusiasm. 'Hap' Arnold, the U.S.A.'s foremost airman, in the tradition of Benjamin Franklin and 'Billy' Mitchell, especially favoured filling the skies with airborne warriors and was prepared to give maximum Air Force support. On the return of the American mission to the United States, Lee immediately recommended the formation of airborne divisions with supporting artillery, engineers, signals and service units. Two airborne divisions were authorized on 30 July 1942: each was to number approximately 16,000 officers and men. After several changes of mind, the mainstay infantry element was to comprise two Parachute Regiments and one Glider Infantry Regiment, each of three fighting battalions.

The 82nd 'All American' Airborne Division was enrolled in August 1942 in the Order of Battle of the United States Army. Only that February it had been the 82nd Infantry Division; subsequently it had been turned into a motorised division but had barely received its motor vehicles before it was given its new airborne rôle and a new commander. General Matthew B. Ridgway was a resourceful and rather religious officer, who combined aggressive soldierly qualities with a keen intellect. When he commenced training the 82nd, which was moved from Fort Benning, Georgia, to Fort Bragg, N.C., he was determined that it would become the finest division in any army.

As the first experiment in Anglo-American Airborne co-operation, 2nd Battalion, 503rd Regiment, was attached to the British 1st Airborne Division in England but the remainder of the 503rd was despatched to Australia where it was brought up to full strength by replacements from the 501st in Panama. The battalion in England was shortly redesignated 509th Parachute Battalion, scheduled for the North African landings, while the 503rd in Australia was destined for the Pacific.

The 101st Airborne Division – the 'Screaming Eagles' – was built around a cadre from the 82nd and Ridgway negotiated a compromise with Lee, who was to command the 101st, over an equitable split of the best men. Both divisions were based on Fort Bragg and trained hard to perfect their parachute and glider techniques. The men indulged in physical training and long marches and a fighting spirit, second to none, developed in all airborne units. In April 1943, the 82nd embarked for North Africa to prepare for the invasion of Sicily and four months later the 101st sailed in two British ships for Liverpool.

The aircraft used for parachuting and air-landing exercises during 1940 and 1941 were B-18 bombers, C-39 transports and DC-3 air-liners but, from January 1942, the C-47 Skytrain was the standard troop carrier in U.S.A.A.F. service. The C-47, or Dakota as the R.A.F. called it, was in fact the military

USA wings, left to right: Basic plus combat jump, Basic, Senior, Senior, Master, Special Force, Para-glider. Senior and Master were introduced after 1945

adaptation of the DC-3 and from mid-1942 was the work-horse of American airborne troops. Designed some years before the war by the Douglas Aircraft Company, the twin-engined C-47 was essentially a freight carrier, and displayed a reinforced metal floor, a large loading door and reinforced landing gear. In the supply rôle, it carried up to 6,000 lb (2,722 kg) of equipment; for example, two jeeps or three crated aero engines with sufficient fuel for a range of 1,500 miles (2413.5 km). As a transport aircraft, it was fitted with folding benches for 28 fully-armed troops but the maximum stick-load of paratroopers was 20 men. Exits were performed from the door, which was located port side aft.

The C-47, which was superior to the Ju-52, its German counterpart, was produced in quantity. By 1945, over 2,000 had been delivered to the R.A.F. alone. A robust aircraft, the C-47 was ideal for dropping paratroopers: it was able to take off from improvised grass airstrips; it could achieve a satis-factory range; and its cruising speed of about 200 mph (322 km/h) could be effectively controlled over the dropping zones. The pilot approached the DZ with both engines throttled back, gradually losing height at between 85 and 100 mph (138/161 km/h). The strong-point cable was fixed to the starboard side of the fuselage and, because of the slow speed of the aircraft, the jumpers usually experienced no trouble in the slip stream after orderly exits. (The tendency to somersault and for rigging lines to become twisted were problems the British paratrooper experienced in the faster-flying converted bombers in RAF service.) Dropping heights on training runs varied from 800 to 1,200 ft (244/366 m) but combat jumps were made according to operational necessity at lower altitudes.

Several experimental, prototype gliders were produced before the introduction of the Waco CG-4A enabled the training of glider troops to begin in earnest. Known almost invariably by the Americans as the CG-4A, this glider in RAF service was called the Hadrian. The CG-4A was a rigidly-braced high-wing monoplane of fabric-covered wood and steel-tube construction. It could carry freight up to 3,800 lb (1,724 kg) or 15 troops, two of whom were the pilots, who sat side by side with dual controls in the nose of the glider. The nose was hinged for direct loading of equipment. The normal troop entrance was port side forward. The freight capacity was equal to one jeep or anti-tank gun, the equipment being unloaded through the nose door by means of two small ramps. The CG-4A, which was designed by the Waco Aircraft Co., could also be fitted with two 'power eggs'; that is, two cells each containing a 6-cylinder engine, fuel tank and engine instruments. A larger Waco glider, the CG-13, which lifted 42 men or a 105-mm gun or 8,500 lb (3,856 kg) of supplies, was in operation in the Philippines towards the end of the war. The Waco CG-4A was the mainstay of American airborne troops during the Second World War but the British Horsa was also used on operations in Europe.

The USAAF set up Air Transport Command, later named 1st Troop Carrier Command, in Indianapolis in April 1942 but troop carriers rated low priority in essential aircraft production. The USA's mounting capacity to wage war in the air was reflected in the thousands of bombers and fighters scheduled for swift manufacture and there was indeed disagreement at top levels on the correct ratio of the allocation of transport aircraft for airborne forces and everyday supply flights. Even the aircrew drafted to 1st Troop Carrier Com-mand were classified as less promising than their colleagues assigned to the bombers.

The airmen made the grade through imaginative training and sheer dedication. Troop carrier units were assigned to Lawson Field, Fort Benning, and Pope Field, Fort Bragg, and others worked closely with trained paratroopers in mounting airborne exercises on an ever-increasing scale. In March 1943, the 82nd and 101st made a mass drop at Fort Bragg for the benefit of General George Marshall, Field Marshal Sir John Dill and Mr Anthony Eden, the British Foreign Secretary. But a demonstration in December 1943 by the newly-formed 11th Airborne Division, which involved over 10,000 men in a parachute glider and air-landing exercise, did more than anything else in the United States to convince all but the complete sceptics of the viability of the airborne forces.

Potential glider pilots drawn from the Air Corps progressed from their basic training schools to advanced centres for tactical experience. The tug aircraft was the C-47 and the transport pilots co-operated with the glider pilots at airfields in Texas and Arkansas in perfecting take-off and release techniques. By mid-1943, the pilots had learned the art of flying two gliders on 'double-tow' from a single aircraft. The practice of retrieving a glider from the ground by an aircraft in flight was also introduced at this time.

The American paratrooper was a tough and surprisingly nimble-footed store cupboard of personal weapons and equip-ment. The standard uniform was similar to the olive-drab sateen M.1943 combat dress: the jacket displayed a fly front and large diagonal patch breast and side pockets and the trousers were fitted with a large patch pocket on the outside of the thigh. Steel helmets with forked chin strap and rubber cup were usually camouflaged in action. High lace-up brown ankle boots with rubber soles worn both for business and pleasure were the paratrooper's special status symbol until they became standard Army issue.

On a jump, the American paratrooper was not encumbered by the personal kit-bag carried tethered to the leg of the British parachute soldier. Much reliance was placed on the safe and well-aimed arrival on the DZ of parachute containers copied from the British and German models or bundles, but nonetheless an extraordinary amount of equipment was loaded on to the man's body. The baggy pockets of the shower-proof combat jacket and trousers concealed ammuni-tion, maps, compass, torch, pocket knife, spoon, socks and cleaning gear, including razor. The pockets also contained the three-meal 'K' rations and emergency 'Parachute' chocolates. The shoulder braces and webbing belt supported ammunition pouches, shovel, water bottle, first aid kit, binoculars and bayonet. In lieu of the British small pack, spare clothing, blanket and more ammunition were stuffed in a bag slung around the waist. Further body accoutrements included a length of rope, gas mask and a jump-knife attached to the leg. (Americans, unlike the Germans and British, did not wear a smock over their equipment. It was thought to be a hindrance if combat took place immediately on landing.)

The M1 semi-automatic carbine, which was conveniently fitted inside the parachute harness on a descent, was the favourite weapon of the American paratrooper; a folding butt introduced for the M1A1 reduced the risk of injury on land-

US paratroop NCO in a uniform similar to the M.1943 combat dress but with different pocket arrangements. He is equipped with an entrenching tool and armed with a .30 MI carbine with folding stock, specifically intended for airborne use

John Fraser

ing. (The M1 carbine was described as 'useless' by a distinguished American airborne general because it was inclined to jam.) The later M2 carbine fired bursts from a 30-round magazine. The M3 sub-machine gun, or 'grease-gun', was a widely used automatic weapon. The heavier semi-automatic Garand M1 rifle could be strapped down one side of the body without undue risk of DZ injury. Many preferred to jump with a Thompson M1 sub-machine gun clutched to the body above the reserve pack. It was as a result of General Ridgway's orders that the Colt .45 pistol, with its holster fastened to the webbing belt, became an essential additional weapon for all American airborne troops. Squad fire-power was further augmented by the limited-scale issue of the Browning Automatic but this rifle was stowed in the containers. The body armoury finally embraced fragmentation and smoke grenades; the Hawkins anti-tank mine and Gammon bomb (both borrowed from the British) proved their worth in fighting tanks.

On an operational jump, the Garand M1 rifle was carried loaded and ready for use; 156 rounds of ammunition were carried in the pouches. The U.S. Army originally developed what was familiarily called a 'violin case', in which the rifle could be enclosed broken down into two parts. But after their first combat experience, the Americans decided that the rifle should be placed underneath the reserve parachute against the soldier's body and then moved into a vertical position for the exit from the aircraft. Once the parachute opened and the vertical descent began, he manoeuvred the rifle into a horizontal position so that it did not interfere with the landing.

The 82nd's artillery battalion, which was raised shortly before the division's departure for North Africa, was armed with the 75-mm Pack Howitzer, a light mountain gun destined to be the regular issue US and British airborne field gun. A very small scale of 105-mm Howitzers was also included in the divisional artillery allocation. The anti-tank guns were the 57-mm M1 (6-pounder) and 3-in (76.2-mm) M5. A Waco glider could only support one of these guns but the 75-mm could be stripped down for parachuting without difficulty.

Mortars, heavy and light machine-guns, ammunition, radio sets and medical equipment were packed in suitable containers and dropped either singly or in bundles from the C-47's six bomb racks or pushed out of the door. The machine-guns on which the rifleman so much relied were the 7.62-mm GPMG, .30 Browning and its heavier calibre .50 version. Last but not least of the US infantry weapons adopted by airborne troops was the 2.36-in M9A1 Rocket Launcher. Better-known as the Bazooka, this two-man anti-tank weapon fired a hollow-charge projectile at short ranges. The Bazooka was standard infantry issue but the 505th Parachute Infantry Regiment was the first ever unit to be equipped with it in North Africa.

The American-conceived jeep was lifted by the Waco glider and was on limited allocation to US airborne forces. It was the only tow-vehicle available for the guns and provided the sole means of ground transportation for zealous commanders who were impervious to enemy fire. The first jeeps to arrive in England in 1941 were at once directed by the US military attaché to RAF Ringway, where experiments were successfully made to fit the vehicle into a Horsa glider. It was also possible to drop a jeep with a cluster of parachutes from a C-47 and the RAF made effective use of Stirlings for the same

M3 .45-in

Above: A robust design, the
M3 was a mass-produced
submachine gun which
supplemented the Thompson.
It came into service in 1942 and
had a low rate of fire which
helped accuracy. It was a
practical weapon but suffered
from feed troubles. The M3
weighed 8 lb 15 oz and had a
rate of fire of 450 rpm

REISING 55

Below: This was basically the
same as the Model 50 but had a
wooden pistol grip and a folding
wire stock, which made it ideal
for airborne use. The weapon
was designed by Eugene Reising,
patented in 1940 and continued
in manufacture until 1945. The
Model 50 had a 0.45-in calibre
and fired 550 rpm with a 12 or
20 round box magazine

*Above right: American paratroops
inside their Waco glider,
equipped with MIAI Thompson
SMGs*

purpose on re-supply missions to the SAS operating behind
the enemy lines post 'D'-Day in France in 1944.

The American M22 (Locust) light tank was designed for
US airborne forces and finalized in prototype form in mid-
1941; the first operational models to be completed entered
service in the spring of 1943. More than 800 were manufactured but the Locust never saw action with the US Army.
The reason for this was that the USAAF did not possess either
a glider or an aeroplane to carry it. The Locust would,
however, fit into the mammoth British Hamilcar glider and
some were used for the Rhine-crossing in March 1945.

The Hamilcar was in fact designed principally with the
British Tetrarch tank in mind as its cargo load. The Tetrarch
weighed only 16,800 lb (7,620 kg) fully loaded and equipped.

This light tank carried a crew of two men and its main
armament was a 2-pounder gun. A 7.92-mm Besa machine-
gun was also provided. Although its armour, ranging from
0.15 in (4 mm) to .54 in (14 mm) in thickness, afforded little
protection, the Tetrarch was fast: 40 mph (64 km/h) could
be achieved on roads and 28 mph (45 km/h) cross-country.
The Tetrarch was landed in Normandy in June 1944 and was
deployed as a reconnaissance vehicle but 6th Airborne were
in more ways than one relieved when the main battle tanks
caught up with them and the Tetrarchs were withdrawn from
the line. The Locust was virtually the same as the Tetrarch in
size but its armour was thicker (.35 in [9 mm]/.78 in [25 mm])
and it was manned by a crew of three. The gun, which was a
37-mm M6, was also very similar to a 2-pounder.

AIRBORNE IN NORTH AFRICA

The Allied seaborne landing in French North Africa on 8 November 1942 came a fortnight after the British offensive on General Rommel's positions at El Alamein and four days after General Montgomery's advance westward from Egypt commenced. General Eisenhower, as supreme commander of Operation 'Torch', deployed three main task forces in the assault on the North African coastline. The Western Task Force despatched from the United States was to capture Casablanca. The Central Task Force, also all-American, was embarked in the United Kingdom in predominantly British ships destined for Oran. The Anglo-American Eastern Task Force, also sailing from the United Kingdom, was to capture Algiers. Within three days of the landings at Safi, Casablanca, Port Lyautey, Oran and Algiers, Admiral Darlan had surrendered the French garrison in Algeria and the Allies were driving eastwards into Tunisia.

The Airborne involvement in North Africa did not extend beyond the early days of the campaign but British and American parachute troops were to fight many bloody battles as infantry of the line. It will be remembered that the US 2nd/503rd Parachute Infantry Battalion had been attached during the year to the British 1st Airborne Division in England. This battalion, which was to be expanded into the 509th Parachute Battalion, took off from England on the night of 7/8 November in 39 C-47s for a 1,500-mile (2,414 km) journey to capture the French airfields at La Senia and Tafaroui south of Oran. The airborne expedition (commanded by Lt-Col. Edson Raff) miscarried because of bad weather; the leading aircraft lost its way over the North African coast and the pilot was forced to land to ask a French-speaking Arab the way to Oran! The battalion, running short of fuel, made an unopposed landing at Sebkra. The men re-emplaned and dropped on another target, Lourmel airfield, Morocco.

Meanwhile, on the Axis side of the battle and in spite of Hitler's reluctance after Crete to engage in large-scale airborne operations, General Student considered such plans for projected attacks on Malta, Gibraltar, the Cape Verde islands and Toulon harbour. The highest operational priority was given to Operation 'Hercules', the plan to seize the island fortress of Malta. Assigned to the Italian *Folgore* Parachute Division trained by the *Fallschirmjäger Generalmajor* Ramcke, the invasion of Malta never took place. None of Student's other proposed assaults transpired and, at Hitler's instigation, he lost his air support to the Afrika Korps.

With the cancellation of Operation 'Hercules', the *Folgore* Division, along with Ramcke's Battle Group, consisting of four parachute battalions with artillery, anti-tank and engineer support, were despatched to Egypt. The *Folgore* was decimated at El Alamein but the German paratroopers made good their escape from the battle in vehicles captured from a British supply column. Ramcke was later assigned to raising a second *Fallschirmjäger* Division in the south of France.

Wrecked Junkers Ju-52 transport aircraft in a scrap heap at El Aouina airfield, North Africa

Left to right: Libyan Btn (Italian Colonial), Italian army (1st type), Libyan Btn

1st Parachute Brigade in North Africa. After the early airborne drops, the 'Red Devils' saw hard action as infantry of the line until the Axis surrendered on 13 May 1943

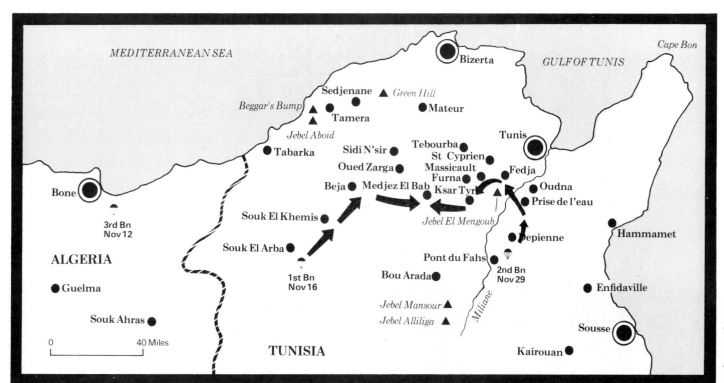

MEDITERRANEAN SEA

GULF OF TUNIS

Cape Bon

● Bizerta

Sedjenane ● ▲ *Green Hill*

Beggar's Bump ▲
▲ Tamera

● Mateur

Jebel Aboid

● Tabarka

Sidi N'sir ●

Tebourba ●

● Tunis

St Cyprien ●

Oued Zarga ●

Massicault ●

Furna ●

Fedja ●

Beja ● Medjez El Bab ● Ksar Tyr ● ● Oudna

● Prise de l'eau

Souk El Khemis ● *Jebel El Mengoub* ▲

● Bone

3rd Bn Nov 12

● Depienne

● Hammamet

Souk El Arba ●

ALGERIA

1st Bn Nov 16

Pont du Fahs ●

2nd Bn Nov 29

● Guelma

Bou Arada ●

Jebel Mansour ▲

● Enfidaville

Souk Ahras ●

Jebel Alliliga ▲

Miliane

● Sousse

0   40 Miles

TUNISIA

Kairouan ●

Peter Sarson and Tony Bryan

Italian paratrooper armed with stick grenade and Beretta machine-gun. This was an Air Force paratrooper, from the Special Force Unit, who did not wear the characteristic Army smock

Italian airborne insignia, left to right: Folgore Division (2nd series), X Flotilla para-frogman, X Flotilla, San Marco Regt, Folgore Division, Army parachutist (2nd series)

John Fraser

After the early promises of the Vichy government to resist the Allied invasion of North Africa, a plan to drop *FJR* 5 in Algeria was cancelled. Instead, the regiment, led by *Oberstleutnant* Koch, the veteran of Eban-Emael, was air-landed in Me 323 supertransports in Tunisia to secure key defensive positions. A rapid build-up of Axis strength in Tunisia followed the French surrender; *Hauptmann* Saur's enlarged paratroop battle group seized Tunis and its port facilities.

On 9 November, a strong element of Lt-Col R J Pine-Coffins's British 3rd Parachute Battalion took off from Cornwall in USAAF C-47s and flew via Gibraltar to Maison Blanche, an airfield 12 miles (19 km) from Algiers. The remainder of Brigadier Flavell's 1st Parachute Brigade (the 1st, 2nd and balance of the 3rd Battalion), which was then at sea, arrived in Algiers harbour 11 days later. Pine-Coffin was immediately alerted for a drop on Bône airfield along the coast on the Algerian side of the frontier with Tunisia.

The paratroopers knew that they were engaged in a race against time; a German parachute battalion was known to be in Tunis and might already be airborne, bound for the same objective. The drop at Bône was intended as a night operation but the American Dakota pilots had no experience of handling parachute troops, so the 3rd Battalion's descent was put forward to the early morning of 12 November. After the drop, the parachutists were scattered over a wide area of stony ground. The exit height was only 400 feet (122 m) but the atmospheric conditions played havoc with parachute performance. Twelve men were seriously injured on landing (one officer was unconscious for four days) and one man 'roman candled' and was killed instantly on impact with the ground. The airfield was taken with little difficulty, much to the pleasure of the Arabs who were overjoyed at the prospect of profitably converting the silk parachutes into underwear. The Arabs' haul might have been greater if the *Fallschirmjäger* had joined the battle but the FJR 5 battalion witnessed the British drop and the Ju 52s turned back.

After capturing Bône airfield, and defending it with the help of No. 6 Commando landed from the sea, the 3rd Battalion rejoined its Brigade now on standby with the American 509th Parachute Battalion at the Maison Blanche airfield in Algeria. When the British First Army attacked across the Tunisian Border on 15 November, 1st Parachute Battalion (Hill) was ordered to drop on the Souk el Arba plain and capture the road junction at Beja, and the airfield, and to persuade the French garrison to join up with the Allies. At the same time, the 509th was to drop on airfields nearer at hand at Tebessa and Youks les Bains. The Americans jumped on the 15th as planned but when Hill's Battalion arrived in their Dakotas over Beja the town was obscured by cloud and the drop was cancelled. The British Battalion took off again from Maison Blanche on the 16th.

James Hill, mounted the following morning in the leading Dakota, in clear visibility, made a wide survey of the terrain and ordered the descent near the village of Souk el Arba. Hill borrowed a fleet of old buses and the battalion moved off, spending the night in a bivouac outside Beja. The next morning, the CO marched his battalion twice through the town, the men on the first occasion wearing their steel helmets and on the second their red berets. The French garrison commander was so impressed by the bearing of the British parachute battalion that the French troops rallied to their

ME 323 E2-WT

The Me 323 was an invaluable supply transport on the Eastern Front, where it first appeared but in North Africa and elsewhere its slow speed made it an easy prey for Allied fighters. It was used by German airborne troops to provide reinforcements in Tunisia. After heavy losses during the evacuation of Tunisia, little more was heard of this huge aeroplane. The version illustrated is the Me 323 E2-WT, identifiable by the power-operated turrets, mounting a 20-mm MG 151 cannon installed above the central engine nacelle in each wing – the answer, it was hoped, to the enormous casualty rate. Early models were provided with eight wheels, later increased to ten. The plane was capable of lifting 130 troops or 60 wounded or 21,500 lb freight (9765 kg) – three times the capacity of the Ju 52. This enabled it to carry, for example, one 88-mm gun and its tow vehicle. There was a crew of five

Engines:	6 x 990 hp Gnome-Rhône 14N 48/49 radials
Max speed:	137 mph
Range:	696 miles
Span:	181 ft 1¼ in
Length:	93 ft 4½ in
Height:	27 ft 6 in
Take-off weight:	95,901 lb
Max payload:	24,251 lb

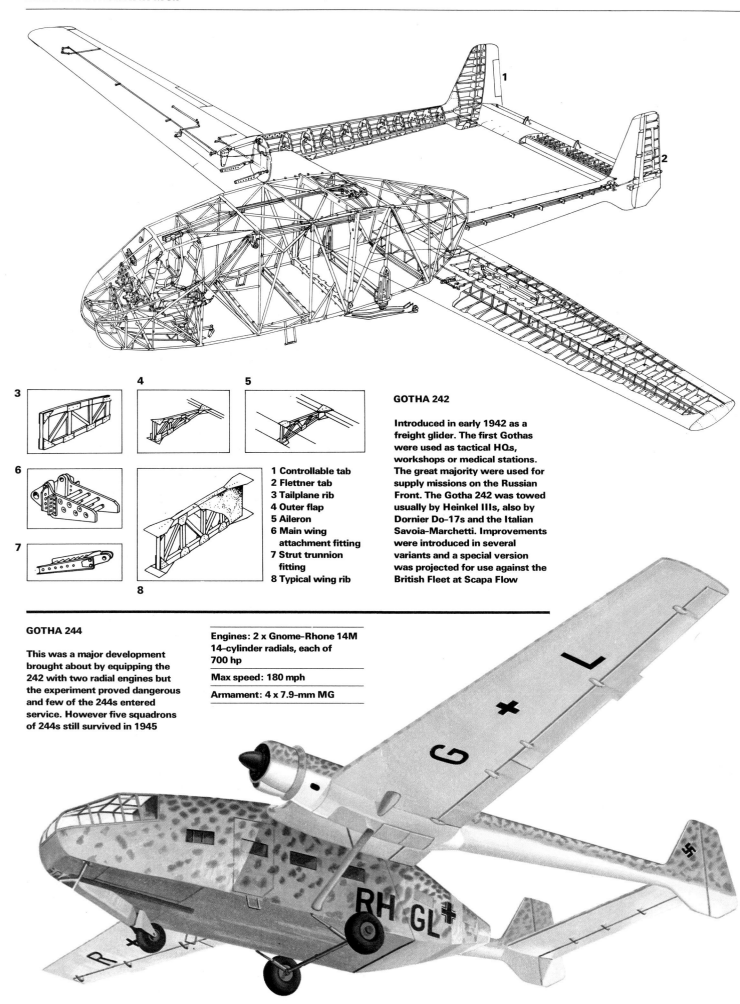

GOTHA 242

Introduced in early 1942 as a freight glider. The first Gothas were used as tactical HQs, workshops or medical stations. The great majority were used for supply missions on the Russian Front. The Gotha 242 was towed usually by Heinkel IIIs, also by Dornier Do-17s and the Italian Savoia-Marchetti. Improvements were introduced in several variants and a special version was projected for use against the British Fleet at Scapa Flow

1 Controllable tab
2 Flettner tab
3 Tailplane rib
4 Outer flap
5 Aileron
6 Main wing attachment fitting
7 Strut trunnion fitting
8 Typical wing rib

GOTHA 244

This was a major development brought about by equipping the 242 with two radial engines but the experiment proved dangerous and few of the 244s entered service. However five squadrons of 244s still survived in 1945

Engines: 2 x Gnome-Rhone 14M 14–cylinder radials, each of 700 hp

Max speed: 180 mph

Armament: 4 x 7.9-mm MG

British officer, 1st Airborne Division, armed with Sten Mk V with bayonet. He wears the characteristic jumping helmet and Denison smock. The smock was windproof but only semi-waterproof. It was designed by Captain Denison

John Fraser

side and the combined force fought several hard engagements against German tanks before 1st Parachute Brigade was assigned to V Corps as infantry of the line.

The 2nd Battalion held in the reserve at Maison Blanche had been earmarked to jump further forward of the First Army at Pont du Fahs and Depienne airfields, south of Tunis, but as these objectives were reported to be abandoned by the Germans another target some 20 miles (32 km) south of the capital was chosen at Oudna. The battalion was now commanded by Lieutenant-Colonel J D Frost, who had won the Military Cross for his exploits at Bruneval. Frost's Battalion was airborne on the morning of 29 November in USAAF Dakotas of Nos 60 and 64 Group, under the protection of long-range Hurricanes, Lightnings and Spitfires.

The battalion dropped near Pont du Fahs, 12 miles (19 km) from the target. As the troops formed columns in the late afternoon for the night approach march they were totally unaware that General Eisenhower's concerted bid to capture Tunis and thus hasten the link-up with the British Eighth Army advancing from the east had been abandoned. Even then, the Germans were attacking strongly and driving the Allies back to Medjez el Bab, which held the key to the road and rail communications in the contested battlefield of northern Tunisia.

The signal informing Frost of the postponement of the Allied advance was received at dawn on the 1st but, since he found no aircraft on the airfield objective to be destroyed, he had already decided to withdraw the battalion. The story of 2nd Parachute Battalion's fighting retreat, lasting three days, to the Allied lines at Medjez el Bab deserves more space than the scope of this narrative permits. The battalion was in fact already almost surrounded at Oudna and suffering casualties when Frost rejected a German emissary's demand to surrender and made his decision to pull out. In the process, 2nd Parachute Battalion suffered 75 per cent casualties; sixteen officers and 250 other ranks died and the wounded were left.

There were no more Allied airborne operations in North Africa, partly because of the weather but more so because the British and American paratroopers were wanted in the line. The Parachute Regiment won nine Battle Honours in North Africa: Soudia, Oudna, Djebel Azzag, Djebel Alliliga, El Hadjeba, Tamera, Djebel Dahra, Kef El Debna and (in summary) North Africa 1942–43, by which time the 'Regiment' had suffered casualties amounting to 1,700 men killed, wounded and missing. In March 1943, German radio signals intercepted in the field referred to 'den Roten Teufeln' – 'the Red Devils'. British airborne troops accepted their sobriquet as a soldierly compliment. The nickname derived from their maroon beret and the title has remained with them ever since.

It would be invidious to omit mention of the Italian parachute troops of X Arditi Regiment that made several sabotage drops in Algeria during the North African Campaign. Their aim was to destroy the rail route to the front line but there is no evidence that these raids caused any serious dislocation of the Allied supply line. 1st Parachute Brigade met the *Fallschirmjäger* face-to-face many times in combat in North Africa until organized resistance of the Axis forces ended on 13 May 1943; the toughest battle between the paratroopers was in the Tamera Valley, where, today, hundreds of white crosses lie peacefully in harmony marking the last resting places of both friend and foe.

The Bruneval Raid

In late 1941, the Royal Air Force reported an improvement in German Flak (AA) and fighter interception which was being controlled by a new radar system located along the coast of occupied France and Holland. The system known as Würzburg acted as a rangefinder for the guns and vectored fighters onto incoming bombers. The Würzburg, which was produced by D/T Telefunken, had a large saucer aerial capable of following a fast moving target over a range of 20 miles (32 km). As Britain at that time possessed no comparable position finder or gun layer, scientists were anxious to study sample components of this superior radio-location equipment.

Aerial photography in January 1942 clearly pinpointed one such station situated on a cliff-edge in the Seine Maritime, 12 miles north of Le Havre, near the village of Bruneval. Commodore the Lord Louis Mountbatten, of Combined Operations, immediately submitted a plan to the three Chiefs of Staff proposing a Commando-style raid on the Würzburg site. Britain's fortunes at this time, and those of her new American ally, were at a low ebb and Mountbatten's initiative, although approved, was not greeted with reassuring enthusiasm. Mountbatten then went to Major-General Browning, as GOC 1st Airborne Division, and the plan for the Bruneval raid was swiftly evolved.

At the Parachute Training School at RAF Ringway, Captain John Frost completed the jump course and, exchanging his three pips for a crown, was transferred with the 120-strong 'C' Company, composed almost entirely of Scotsmen, to the Glider Pilot Regiment's depot at Tilshead on Salisbury Plain. The company commander was at first under the impression that his assignment was to organize an airborne demonstration for the Service chiefs but when Flight-Sergeant C W H Cox, a radio mechanic, arrived to join the company, Frost surmised that there was more to the job than met the eye. General Browning informed Major Frost that his company was to carry out a real raid on the coast of France; Cox had the key job of removing the Würzburg radar components and bringing them back to England, where they could be analyzed at leisure.

The Bruneval raid, planned for late February, was to be a truly combined operation, involving 'C' Company, 2nd Parachute Battalion, dropping from twelve Whitleys; a naval evacuation force; and an infantry party landed from the sea to cover the beach evacuation. A final evacuation exercise was mounted on the night of Sunday, 23 February, from a beach on Southampton Water. Favourable tide conditions at Bruneval at the projected hour of withdrawal and a full moon dictated that the raid must take place within the next four nights. The outlook for the weather over the next few days, however, was daunting; on 27 February the French countryside was covered with snow but the wind had dropped and the operation was 'on'. In the afternoon the naval flotilla put to sea and 'Jock' Company arrived in trucks at Thruxton.

The Würzburg equipment was sited about 1,200 yards (1,097 m) from Bruneval in front of a large, lonely villa housing the technicians; the village itself was built on either side of a ravine leading to the sea. About 400 yards (366 m) along a track to the north of the villa, a wood enclosed a farmhouse called La Presbytère. French Intelligence reported that the farmhouse was the garrison HQ for about 100 troops who manned 15 defence posts along the cliffs. A

German infantry regiment and a Panzer battalion were also stationed within easy striking distance of the area.

'C' Company was divided into three assault groups: 'Nelson', 'Drake' and 'Rodney'. Lieutenant 'Junior' Charteris's 'Nelson' party numbered 40 men and was scheduled to drop first to silence the machine-gun defences on the cliffs and seal off the village. 'Drake' comprised 50 men: Lieutenant P.A. Young's party was to seize the radar installation, which was built into a hole in the ground about 200 yards (183 m) from the villa; and Major Frost's party was detailed to break into the villa and take prisoners. 'Rodney' formed the reserve group ordered to protect the rear area. Lieutenant Young's task was essentially to provide cover while Flight-Sergeant Cox and Captain D. Vernon, a sapper, got to work; then the party was to carry the dismantled equipment to the boats.

The men were armed with Sten guns, .45 pistols and grenades; demolition and radio equipment was packed in the containers. The flight of the 12 Whitleys to the French coast near Le Havre in bright moonlight took two hours. But the moonlight that helped the navigators to identify their landmarks was also a help to the Flak gunners and two of the pilots were obliged to alter course for the target.

The order to 'Prepare for action' was given half an hour before the drop and, as Major Frost swung his legs into the hole of his aircraft and surveyed the night scene with its carpet of snow, he regretted that there had been no time to obtain white smocks. By now the Flak batteries were very active, causing the pilots to take frequent evasive action. All but the two Whitley stragglers made the drop approaching midnight with complete accuracy. 'Drake' and 'Rodney' groups advanced from their assembly area, at the double, in the direction of the radar installation, the villa and the wood surrounding La Presbytère. Frost, to his surprise, found the front door of the villa open; blowing a loud blast on his whistle, he leaped in, his men at his heels. The ground floor rooms were empty so the company commander rushed upstairs shouting 'Surrender' and 'Hände hoch' followed by four men. A German, the only one present, was promptly killed in one of the upstairs rooms.

Meanwhile, Lieutenant Young had found the Würzburg radar positioned in a shallow pit. It was well-defended by machine-gunners in a trench and there was a sharp engagement in which five out of the six German soldiers manning the post were killed. The survivor ran for it but toppled over the cliff, landing on a ledge 10 feet (3 m) down. By now, Major Frost had reinforced the radar site, which was under heavy machine-gun fire from La Presbytère. Flight-Sergeant Cox and Captain Vernon swiftly completed their exercise in radio-dislocation, with bullets striking the main apparatus, and Major Frost ordered the withdrawal.

Lieutenant 'Junior' Charteris and half of the 'Nelson' group flying in the two Whitleys that had changed course after crossing the French coast had landed about 3,500 yards (3,200 m) south of the villa and had been unable to tackle the machine-gun posts along the cliffs leading to the escape beach. The distance from the villa to the Bruneval ravine was about 800 yards (732 m); the 'going' was difficult in the snow drifts and several men, including Sergeant-Major Strachan, were hit. While Cox and his porters hugged their fragile loads close to their bodies, Frost ordered Lieutenant Timothy's

An artist's impression of the Bruneval raid, which compresses two stages of the raid into one picture. The paratroopers float down on the radar station while an MTB and landing craft wait to take the raiders off

reinforced 'Rodney' Group to eliminate a German strongpoint on the shoulder of the cliff where the ground sloped down steeply to the beach. The missing sections under Charteris now arrived on the scene and a combined assault was made on the pillbox; the attack was completely successful and, after capturing a solitary telephone orderly in a small house, the raiders assembled on the beach. It was 02.15 hours but there was no sign in the mist of the evacuation craft.

The Naval flotilla, after avoiding two enemy destroyers and several smaller vessels, had been lying off-shore for two hours when look-outs spotted signals from Very pistols exploding in the air above the beach and three ALCs and three MTBs were rapidly despatched for the pick-up. At approximately 02.35 hours, Major Frost heard the cry, 'Sir, the boats are coming in'. It was not a moment too soon; the beach was under heavy plunging fire from the cliff tops. Then German troops arriving in trucks from Bruneval ran into a heavy barrage from the flotilla guns. Two of Frost's men were confirmed as dead and six were missing but there was no time

left to wait for them. The radar prize and six wounded men – Strachan had three bullets in his stomach – were put on board the ALCs. As 'C' Company embarked, the infantry leapt ashore from the MTBs and contributed to the deafening noise with well-aimed fire at the cliff-tops. They were the last to leave the beach.

The capture of the Würzburg radar equipment told the British scientists what they wanted to know and one result of the experiments that followed was the operational use of metal-strip reflectors dropped from the air to create false echoes in the enemy radar. From a purely military point of view, the success of Operation 'Biting' was greeted with jubilation by Winston Churchill, who insisted on hearing the full story from John Frost. The Germans were astounded by the audacity of the British parachute troops and many years later General Student, who himself was impressed by the raid, reported that the Führer received the news of the Bruneval affair on the night of 27/28 February 1942 with 'a profound sense of shock'.

THE INVASION OF SICILY

The end of the North African Campaign in May 1943 saw the Mediterranean open to Allied shipping and the stage was set for the next phase of operations, the invasion of Sicily and then Italy. In April, General Matthew B. Ridgway's US 82nd Division had embarked for North Africa. The 82nd comprised two parachute regiments, the 504th and the 505th, each of three parachute battalions, and the 325th Glider Infantry Regiment of only two battalions. After six weeks in French Morocco, Ridgway's Division moved to Kairouan in central Tunisia, the jump-off point for Sicily.

In June, the battle-tested British 1st Parachute Brigade, now commanded by Brigadier Gerald Lathbury, assembled near Mascara south of Oran and was joined in the same month by 2nd Parachute Brigade (Down) and 1st (Air-Landing) Brigade (Hicks); 4th Parachute Brigade (Hackett), which was raised at Kabrit, in Egypt, in December 1942, arrived from Palestine. 1st Airborne Division was thus at full operational strength for the invasion of Sicily. General Browning, who was now serving on General Eisenhower's staff as 'Airborne Adviser', had passed over the command of 1st Airborne to Major-General G F 'Hoppy' Hopkinson, an able and popular commander who was to meet his death in action in Italy.

The Allied forces in the Mediterranean theatre were ready for the invasion of Sicily by early July. General Eisenhower's forces consisted of the Fifteenth Army Group, under the direction of General Alexander, comprising the United States Seventh Army (Patton) and the British Eighth Army (Montgomery). The assault from the sea was to be preceded by American parachute landings near Gela and by British glider landings near Syracuse. Allied strategy for the Sicily invasion was based on a pincer movement, with the Seventh Army disembarking on the south-eastern portion of the coastline between Licata and Scoglitti and the Eighth Army on the east coast, south of Syracuse. Jim Gavin's reinforced 505th Regiment was to seize the high ground (Piano Lupo) in the Gela area to prevent the enemy from reaching the bridgehead. 'Pip' Hicks 1st (Air-Landing) Brigade was to capture the Ponte Grande canal bridge on the approach to Syracuse.

On the evening of 9 July the Air-Landing Brigade took off as planned from Tunisian airfields to launch Operation 'Husky', the Allied invasion of Sicily. The 2,000 British troops of the glider battalions were followed into the air shortly afterwards by Gavin's 4,400 American paratroopers. The glider force, bearing men of the 2nd South Staffordshire Regiment, 1st Border Regiment and support units, consisted of 137 Wacos and eight Horsas to carry stores, 2-pounders, machine-guns and mortars.

The wind began to rise in the night sky from the southeast before the glider formation passed Malta but soon it increased to gale proportions. Wind speeds at their worst reached 45 mph (72 km/h) and, when the aircraft reached the Sicily coast, the off-shore wind whipped up a wall of dust from the arid soil, blotting out the landmarks completely. The fly-in to Syracuse was a disaster: many of the tug pilots turned away too soon; the glider pilots blindly slipped their tow ropes in the darkness before crash-landing in the sea. The waters beneath were soon bristling with floating wooden wreckages. Troops clung to fuselages or dismembered wings and many of them were rescued by the passing assault boats; others, including the Brigade commander, swam for the shore. Altogether 252 men were drowned. Only 52 of the gliders

made landfall and only 12 of these landed near the target.

The American Dakota pilots on their approach flight to Gela were having similar navigational problems. As the Sicilian sun rose in the morning sky, the sight of the 82nd's deflated canopies and many unopened containers spread out over hundreds of square miles of terrain at least had the desirable effect of causing pandemonium amongst the German and Italian commanders, who believed they had been invaded by a whole army of paratroopers. But the Americans, during that first night in Sicily, were equally bewildered in their scattered positions.

As two thirds of Ridgway's command was still in Tunisia, the General landed on D-Day (10 July) by boat to assess the battle situation before ordering Reuben Tucker's 504th Regiment into the air the following night. One of the 504th's battalions had already dropped with Gavin's Regiment but it was still a formidable force and urgently needed to help consolidate the American beach-head. The C-47s came in over the invasion fleet just as a heavy German air attack was ending. The gunners on board the Allied ships mistook the low-flying American aircraft in the dark for German bombers and opened fire. Twenty-three C-47s were shot down, a tragic error costing 97 lives. No order had been given to the ships to withhold their fire as the troop-carrier aircraft ran in.

The 82nd's parachute landings contributed significantly to safeguarding the US Seventh Army's footholds in Sicily and Patton's left pincer arm rapidly fanned out, with the airborne division thrusting westwards. Ridgway's two parachute regiments, with their 75-mm pack howitzer battalion and some reinforcing artillery, met isolated but often determined resistance before arriving in the port of Trapani on the western tip of the island. In its drive west, the division moved 150 miles (241 km), mainly on foot, in six days, and captured 15,000 prisoners.

Meanwhile, on 10 July, a party of South Staffords landing from their gliders were led in an assault on the Ponte Grande bridge by Lieutenant Withers; the objective was taken before midnight after a bloody encounter with the German defenders. The South Staffords formed a small garrison with men of the 1st Borders under continued shellfire but their posts were overrun during the afternoon. Within half-an-hour, 17th Infantry Brigade, advancing from their beach-head, launched a counter-attack in the area and the bridge was re-taken before it could be blown up by German engineers. Syracuse swiftly fell to the Eighth Army and, on 13 July, Montgomery was poised to drive northwards to Catania. After re-assembling its scattered units on land and the survivors from the sea, 1st (Air-Landing) Brigade was withdrawn from the battle.

After his victory offensive from the Western Desert into Tunisia, General Montgomery was now presented with the opportunity of deploying parachute troops as tactical support for the first time. He did not hesitate to alert Lathbury's 1st Parachute Brigade in Tunisia and, on the evening of the 13th, the 1st, 2nd and 3rd Battalions emplaned for the Catania plain in 105 Dakotas and 11 Albemarles. In addition, Halifaxes and Stirlings towed eight Waco and 11 Horsa gliders carrying anti-tank guns, gunners, engineers and field ambulancemen.

Brigadier Lathbury's orders were to land the 1st Brigade west of the main road from Syracuse to Catania. The 1st Battalion (Pearson) was to capture the Primosole Bridge spanning the River Simeto at a point a few miles south of

Left to right: US 11th Airborne Division, US 13th Airborne Division, US Airborne Command, US 17th Airborne Division, US 82nd Airborne Division, US 101st Airborne Division

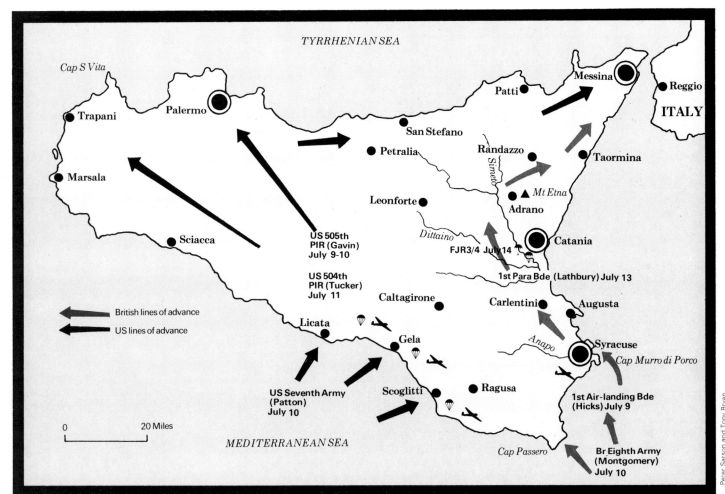

Peter Sarson and Tony Bryan

The British and American airborne landings in Sicily. The American dispositions represent the actual as opposed to the proposed landings in the Gela area

75-MM PACK HOWITZER

The basic artillery weapon of the US and British airborne forces, designed in the USA as a mountain weapon suitable for mule transport. Carried in Horsas, Waco CG–4As and Hamilcars. Length of barrel 52 in (130 cm), all-up weight approximately half a ton (508 kg), initial rate of fire 6 rpm, muzzle velocity with HE shell 1250 fps (380 metres ps), effective range 9475 yd (8660 m)

US Airforce

Far left, top: US airborne forces loading a Jeep into a Waco glider in North Africa prior to the landings in Sicily, July 1943. Far left, bottom: British paratroopers on exercise, preparing a 3-inch mortar for packing in a container. Left: Loading a 105-mm gun into a

Waco glider in North Africa in readiness for the invasion of Sicily

Catania. Montgomery's line of advance along the main road over the bridge was to be further protected by the 2nd Battalion (Frost) and the 3rd Battalion (now Yeldham) capturing the high ground on the approach to Syracuse.

The 1st Brigade took off from airfields near Kairouan and followed the same route over Malta previously taken by the glider Brigade. The aircraft adopted a tight 'V' formation and the pilots, barely rested from the invasion lifts, anticipated a smooth flight along the Sicily coast in the now more favourable weather conditions. These hopes were dashed off Syracuse, when the Allied invasion fleet repeated the same grievous error inflicted on the 504th Regiment and turned their anti-aircraft guns on the in-coming aircraft. In the mêlée that followed, two Dakotas were shot down and many aircraft sustained damage and turned back for North Africa.

The fire from friendly vessels and presently from German and Italian anti-aircraft guns caused the pilots to take evasive action even over the dropping zones. Many pilots of aircraft that had been hit crash-landed in the sea and on the beaches; tug captains advised their glider colleagues to cast off where and when it seemed safe to do so. Of the 1,900 men of 1st Parachute Brigade who had taken off at Kairouan, only one officer and 50 men of the 1st Battalion were available on the ground in the vicinity of the Primosole bridge to launch the attack in the early hours of the morning.

The bridge was quickly captured against little opposition and Pearson promptly assembled more men, including some from the 3rd Battalion, who had dropped further north, ordering them to entrench and form a defensive position. The artillery battery mounted in the Horsas had fared quite well and at first light was sited at the bridge and on high ground overlooking the location.

The Axis defence of Sicily, under General Alfredo Guzzoni, was based on 12 Italian divisions with some light tanks supported by the German 15th Panzer Grenadier and Hermann Göring (Armoured) Parachute Divisions. The Allied pincer movement was developing strongly when *General-major* Richard Heidrich's *Fallschirm-Division 1* was placed

on standby in the Rome area and *FJR 3* and *4* were emplaned with artillery, machine-gun and engineer elements for the Catania Plain. The German paratroopers, who dropped from their Junkers aircraft in three phases, were quickly locked in battle with the British 1st Parachute Brigade on the Syracuse road. The clash was fiercest at the Primosole Bridge where the opposing airborne troops actually dropped at the same time; a German enquired politely of a British paratrooper in the night if he had found his 'Schmeisser' in one of the weapons containers.

Pearson's force clung to the bridge but, when tanks, infantry and a self-propelled gun were brought up to reinforce the German paratroopers, the British were obliged to evacuate the position under heavy fire. British armour now joined in the battle and, after a two-day engagement, men of the Durham Light Infantry, probing forward on the dawn of 16 July found the enemy had gone. The cost of the operation to 1st Parachute Brigade, in killed and wounded on the Catania Plain, was 12 officers and 283 other ranks.

British Special Air Service troops were also involved in the Sicily adventure. After David Stirling, the Regiment's founder, was captured by the Germans in early 1943 in the Western Desert, 1st SAS continued their harassing raids behind the enemy lines. The SAS soon split up into two units forming R B 'Paddy' Mayne's Special Raiding Squadron and Lord Jellico's Special Boat Squadron. In May 1943, 2nd SAS came into being in North Africa: its commanding officer was Lieutenant-Colonel W S 'Bill' Stirling – 'Colonel David's' brother. The new SAS Regiment, as part of No. 62 Commando, participated in a number of raids on the Dodecanese and Greek islands, Sardinia and Crete. SRS and 2nd SAS at this time came under the command of Hopkinson's 1st Airborne Division. North Africa was also the base of Force 133 Mission that in April 1943 inaugurated parachute drops under the auspices of the Special Operations Executive (SOE) in Yugoslavia to forge friendly contacts with Tito's partisans.

2nd SAS Regiment, after flying with the RAF on DZ reconnaissance flights over Sicily, made two parachute drops in support of the campaign. A diversionary sortie was conducted by six men at Lake Omodeo in Sardinia; and at Randazzo, on the approaches to Messina, two SAS parties made a sabotage raid.

Post-war historians have alleged that the Allied airborne participation in the invasion of Sicily was a fiasco. Many British and American lives were lost on the fly-in: the inexperience of the air-crew, the weather conditions and the incompetence of HQ Fifteenth Army Group that caused the troop carrier aircraft to be fired on by Allied guns, all contributed to the disastrous opening of the campaign. It has been said that General Patton had an easy landing on the southern coast of the island; the heaviest Axis resistance was certainly experienced on the American sector where General Guzzoni made every effort to throw the US 1st and 45th Divisions into the sea. General Student, however, has given the 82nd Airborne Division the credit for stopping the Hermann Göring Division from assaulting Patton's beachheads. The way was thus open for the spectacular advance by the US Seventh Army, whose function was principally to protect the flank of the British Eighth Army; Patton accordingly seized Messina, which was Montgomery's objective, ahead of the British troops.

THE ITALIAN CAMPAIGN

In late August 1943, the US 82nd Airborne Division, after returning briefly to North Africa, was back in Sicily but the British 1st Parachute Brigade, having also returned there, remained with 1st Airborne Division. Prior to the Italian unconditional surrender, which was signed at Cassibile in Sicily on 3 September, an Allied scheme was afoot to woo the Italians away from Mussolini and the Germans. A plan seriously considered in Anglo-American Command circles involved dropping the 82nd into the Rome area to negotiate the disaffection of the Italians from their German ally and facilitate a rapid advance by the Allies, chasing the Germans in headlong flight up the Italian peninsula.

General Ridgway considered the operation ('Giant II') suicidal: Rome was out of range of supporting fighters for the skytrain and six German divisions were known to be based in or near the capital itself. On expressing his doubts to General Alexander, his British superior replied: 'Don't give this another thought, Ridgway. Contact will be made with your division in three days, five at the most.' The measure of Ridgway's wisdom may be adjudged from the fact that, after the Allies landed in Italy on 3 September, nine months elapsed before the fall of Rome. Ridgway said, 'When the time comes that I must meet my maker, the source of most humble pride to me will not be accomplishments in battle, but the fact that I was guided to make the decision to oppose the thing, at the risk of my career, right up to the top.'

The Americans were, nevertheless, sitting in their C-47s and ready to take-off from Sicilian airfields when the flight was cancelled. A secret meeting had been arranged in Rome between General Maxwell D. Taylor, the 82nd's artillery commander and a future Commanding General of the 101st Airborne, accompanied by Colonel Gardner, an Air Corps Officer, and General Carboni and Marshal Badoglio, the former Chief of Staff, who was to lead the new Italian Republic, dissolve the Fascist Party and declare war on Germany. Taylor's radio signal, using the code word 'innocuous', meant that the airborne operation was impractical. In spite of the imminent likelihood of the Badoglio surrender, the Germans fully intended to contest every inch of Italian soil.

On 3 September, the Canadian 1st and the British 5th Divisions landed in the 'toe' of Italy around Reggio. On 9 September, General Mark Clark's Fifth Army, comprising the US VI Corps and the British X Corps, went ashore at two points in the Gulf of Salerno; on the same day Hopkinson's 1st Airborne Division, sailing from Bizerta, arrived in Taranto harbour. The disembarkation of the division was marred by the disaster that befell the 6th (Royal Welch) Parachute Battalion. HMS *Abdiel*, bearing 400 men of the battalion and some support troops, hit a mine in the harbour and sank within two minutes. Fifty-eight men were killed and 154 injured. Hackett's 4th Parachute Brigade led the advance from Taranto and was soon in action in the Moltala area. It was when the 10th Battalion was in action against the German defences at Castellaneta that Major-General Hopkinson fell mortally wounded. The command of the division, until his transfer to India, was held by Major-General Eric Down.

Mark Clark's Fifth Army was clinging to a ridge overlooking the Salerno beach-head by nightfall on the 3rd. No progress was possible in the coming days against fierce German opposition and on the 12th the invaders at Salerno were in danger of losing their foot-hold in Italy. Clark despatched a P-38 pilot to Ridgway in Licata, in Sicily, with a letter asking for an airborne drop that night. Eight hours after Ridgway received Clark's letter, Reuben Tucker's 504th Regiment, plus Company B of the 307th Airborne Engineers, took off for the night drop at Salerno. The troops were to drop near Paestum on a flaming 'T'-shaped beacon produced by oil cans filled with sand soaked in petrol. Ridgway was assured by Clark that the beach-head guns would be silent for the run-in.

In the event, no beacon at first showed but the DZ was clearly discernible in the moonlight to the leading pilots of No. 52 Troop Carrier Command. As the first stick dropped, the 'T' exploded into flame and the 504th made a successful landing. Back in Licata, Gavin's 505th Regiment was under orders to parachute on to the same DZ the following night. The descent from the same C-47s was made in perfect order. The two parachute regiments were then linked in the van of the beach-head defenders. The airborne intervention tipped the scales in favour of the Fifth Army: the 82nd, backed up by heavy artillery cover, broke up a major German assault and General Clark ordered the advance towards Naples.

On the same night (the 13th) that the 504th flew into Salerno, the 2nd Battalion of the 509th Parachute Infantry Regiment was dropped on the small town of Avellino, which lay in the mountains 20 miles (32 km) inland from Clark's beach-head. Many of the planes of the 64th Troop Carrier Command missed their dropping zones, and 640 paratroopers were scattered over a hundred square miles. All but 130 of them eventually found their way back to the Allied lines, individually and in small groups, after mining roads, blowing up bridges and ambushing German search patrols. The battalion commander was one of those to go into captivity, after parachuting into the middle of a German tank park.

The 82nd advanced into Naples, where they remained as occupation troops, less the 504th Regiment, which was seconded by Mark Clark for the Volturno river crossing. Reuben Tucker's 504th remained in Italy after the 82nd was officially withdrawn to Britain, where they arrived in December. The 504th saw some hard fighting and were severely mauled in the long-drawn-out battle commencing in late January 1944 in the Anzio beach-head. This regiment did not rejoin Ridgway's command until May 1944 but its rehabilitation was incomplete when the 82nd dropped in Normandy the following month and the 504th was left behind in England.

1st Airborne Division, less 2nd Parachute Brigade, was also back in England in December 1943. The 2nd Parachute Battalion had mounted a minor drop on 2 October at Pescara to guide escaping Allied prisoners through the lines and the 3rd Battalion had conducted a similar mission in the Ascoli area on the same day. On 10 December, the command of 1st Airborne Division was assigned by 'Boy' Browning to Major-General R E Urquhart, an officer who was new to airborne forces and whose recent experience had been as GSO 1 51st Highland Division in North Africa and Commander of the Malta Brigade in Sicily.

Brigadier C H V Pritchard's 2nd Parachute Brigade remained in Italy and saw no airborne action until June 1944, when three officers and 57 men were dropped from three Dakotas near Torricella in the rear of the Germans then withdrawing from Rome towards the Pisa-Rimini (Gothic)

US Airforce

Above: C-47 Dakotas with their Waco CG-4A gliders prepare to take off from Comiso airfield during 52nd Troop Carrier Wing manoeuvres in Sicily prior to the invasion of the Italian mainland

Imperial War Museum

Left: This picture was taken on 15 March 1944 as 2500 tons of bombs rained down on Cassino in Italy. When the barrage lifted, the fight for the ruins began. Below: Indian troops storming Monte Cassino

line. The parachutists acted in three guerrilla groups and successfully blocked a supply road for more than a week. In the meantime, 2nd Independent Parachute Brigade had seen continuous action as part of Freyberg's 2nd New Zealand Division on the left flank of the Eighth Army. In March 1944, Pritchard's Brigade was sent with the New Zealanders to the Cassino area. Five months later, in mid-August, the 2nd Brigade at last took part in a major airborne operation, Operation 'Anvil', the 'Champagne' invasion of the southern coast of France.

There were three parachute divisions in existence on the German side in Italy, in autumn 1943. *Fallschirm-Division 2* (Ramcke) was in action in the summer against Marshal Badoglio's government forces. On 9 September, the 2nd Battalion (800 men) of *FJR 2* were dropped to capture the Italian Army HQ at Monte Rotondo and Ramcke's Division ruthlessly gained control of Rome after the Italian capitulation. Shortly afterwards, the Allies captured the Dodecanese islands of Kos, Leros and Samos: the assault on Kos was

Imperial War Museum

J. G. Moore

spearheaded on 14 September by a parachute drop by 'A' Company of the British 11th Parachute Battalion. But 17 days later the British were evicted by the Germans after a seaborne attack led by a battalion of the Brandenburg Regiment parachuting on to Antimachia airfield. On the next day, another Brandenburger company descended from the air, seizing the Aegean island of Stampagia.

On 17 September, the 3rd Battalion of *FJR 7* was parachuted into the neighbourhood of Portoferraio, the principal harbour on the north coast of Elba. The Italians on Elba had accepted the terms of the Armistice but, after a sharp engagement, a force of 10,000 of them were forced to surrender to the Germans. On 12/13 November, 1st Battalion *FJR 2* (700 men) and a company of the Brandenburg Regiment made another island parachute assault expelling the British defenders of Leros.

Generalmajor Heidrich's *Fallschirm-Division 1* was evacuated from Sicily and saw the war through to the bitter end in Italy. On 29 February 1944, Heidrich's *Fallschirmjäger* were assigned to the defence of Monte Cassino. The

town and heights had already been under heavy attack by Allied troops since January and the German paratroopers were to be subjected for ten weeks to one of the most violent series of air, artillery and infantry attacks of the war. After the US II Corps, New Zealand II Corps, Indian 4th and British 78th Divisions had failed to break the human locking pin of the Gustav line at Monte Cassino, the United States Strategic Air Force flew in 500 heavy and medium bombers on 15 March and dropped more than 1,000 tons of high explosive and fragmentation bombs on the town. Some 800 guns directed their fire simultaneously for six hours on Heidrich's positions. The New Zealand II Corps and the Indian 4th Division stormed into the town and engaged in hand-to-hand fighting, principally with *Oberst* Heilmann's *FJR 3*, but they were repulsed. Cassino finally fell on 11 May to the Polish Corps after the fourth major assault of the battle for the mountain fortifications. Heilmann's paratroopers were the last to go on 17 March.

Fallschirm-Division 4 (Trettner) was formed in Italy, at Perugia, during the late autumn of 1943, from cadres pro-

*Far left: Skorzeny's 'Commando'
prepare for the raid on the Hotel
Albergo-Rifugio, on the Gran
Sasso peak, to rescue Mussolini.
Below: Mussolini, in civilian
clothes, ready to leave on the
hazardous escape flight from
Gran Sasso*

J G Moore

vided by *Fallschirm-Division 2* and pro-German elements of the Italian *Folgore* and *Nembo* Parachute Divisions. Trettner's Division was ready for action in January 1944 and was thrown with the Hermann Göring Panzer Division against the Allied beach-head at Anzio. *Fallschirm-Division 4* fought throughout the Anzio battle, withdrawing north after the fall of Rome. At the time of the landings at Anzio, the German 1st Parachute Corps (Schlemm) was established; it comprised this parachute division and the 3rd Panzer Grenadier Division. As the Corps fell back northwards in June, the command passed to *Generalleutnant* Heidrich; the 1st and 4th Parachute Divisions alternated as part of his Corps structure.

One spectacular feat must be recorded from the period of the Italian surrender and downfall of the Fascist regime in autumn 1943. It was accomplished on 12 September by *Obersturmbannführer* Otto Skorzeny, Hitler's favourite Commando and Germany's most successful Irregular soldier of the war. Mussolini had been taken as a prisoner to the Hotel Albergo-Rifugio near the top of the Gran Sasso, the loftiest peak in the Apennines range of mountains, a hundred miles from Rome. Skorzeny, a Viennese, who bore scars on his face from 14 duels fought in his student days and carried himself with the air of a fourteenth-century Condottiere, was selected by Hitler to find Mussolini and rescue him from captivity. Mussolini's secret location on the Gran Sasso plateau was soon discovered. Skorzeny at once decided that since the funicular and mountain approaches to the hotel were guarded, the situation called for airborne intervention.

He rejected the idea of a parachute mission, as the swirling thermal wind currents in the mountain atmosphere might cause the collapse of the canopies during a descent but he was certain that a gliderborne swoop on the Hotel Albergo-Rifugio would succeed. His operational plan was submitted to General Student, who accepted its feasibility and himself set up a control centre at the Practica di Mare airfield near Rome. At 1 pm on Sunday 12 September, Skorzeny and a mixed force of 107 paratroopers and *Waffen SS* Special Forces boarded 12 DFS 230 gliders.

Eight of Skorzeny's gliders landed without difficulty in the Hotel carpark. Il Duce, who had been threatening to commit suicide, was sitting at an open window when one glider

suddenly loomed into view with a parachute, acting as a rear brake, blossoming out before the glider crashed with a shattering noise a few hundred yards away. At 3 pm, looking sick and unkempt in ill-fitting civilian clothes, Mussolini was crammed with the tall Skorzeny and the pilot into a small Fieseler Storch which had managed to land in the meadow near the Hotel. As the plane gathered speed it lurched dangerously over rocky terrain into a yawning gully but the pilot miraculously pulled the Storch out of its death dive and flew safely into the valley. Within an hour, the Storch, General Student's own personal aircraft, landed at the Practica di Mare airfield and Mussolini and Skorzeny were put aboard a trimotor Heinkel on the next leg of their journey toward an audience with Hitler.

The persistent tempo of the Partisan onslaught against the Germans in Russia and Yugoslavia became the keynote of increasing Communist guerrilla activity in northern Italy in the winter months following the fall of Rome. In Yugoslavia, the airborne supply of weapons, equipment, ammunition and clothing by the Allies was a constant, if sorely inadequate, adjunct of Marshal Tito's war against the Nazi invader. The Germans adopted ruthless measures in their attempts to liquidate patriotic resistance in Yugoslavia and both German and Italian parachute troops were employed on numerous counter-guerrilla operations. In May 1944, a plan was evolved to capture Marshal Tito by landing parachute and gliderborne troops near his mountain hideout in the Drvar district of Bosnia but the execution of the plan was unsuccessful.

The SAS (SRS and 2nd SAS) moved with the British forces after the Sicily Campaign to operate on the eastern sector of the Italian Front. After capturing Bagnara on first landing in Italy, the SAS fought Commando-style actions, participating on 3 October 1943 with No. 40 Royal Marine Commando in the capture of the port and town of Termoli. Operating always ahead of the main forces, small SAS parties exploited the sabotage techniques perfected in the Western Desert, successfully ambushing road convoys and derailing trains.

Six men of 2nd SAS on 7 September parachuted into the Borgo Val di Taro area and destroyed a railway tunnel but there were no more airborne assaults until the turn of the year. Two deep-penetration parachute drops by 20 men (Operation 'Maple') were mounted on 7 January 1944 by 2nd SAS at Aquilla and Ancona. They resulted in the destruction of 14 troop trains. In February, Mayne's freebooters raided an airfield at Perugia. During March, the SAS, although not lost to the Italian theatre, was recalled to Britain to train for the invasion of France, ostensibly as part of Urquhart's 1st Airborne Division.

Now the fictitious Special Air Service 'Brigade', thus-named by David Stirling at Kabrit, in July 1941, really existed! The Brigade cantonment in Ayrshire, on the east coast of Scotland, included 1st, 2nd, 3rd, 4th and 5th SAS. Lieutenant-Colonel Blair Mayne still commanded the 1st Regiment but the 2nd received a new CO when Lieutenant-Colonel Brian Franks succeeded 'Bill' Stirling. The 3rd (Conan) and 4th (Bourgoin) were converted French parachute battalions originating in North Africa and the 5th (Blondeel) was a Belgian parachute company. 'F' Squadron Phantom Signals (GHQ Reconnaissance Regiment) was attached to the Brigade and parachute-trained at Ringway for the forthcoming SAS undercover rôle in N W Europe.

Parachutists of 2nd Special Air Service in action with a 3-inch mortar, in support of the Partisans in the Alba area

OML 2-INCH MORTAR

Muzzle-loaded, the 2-inch mortar was an invaluable weapon in the support role. It fired $2\frac{1}{4}$-lb HE or 2-lb smoke bombs with great accuracy over a range of 500 yards. Maximum rate of fire was 8 rounds per minute. Length 21 inches. Weight 19 lb with base or $10\frac{1}{2}$ lb with spade. Also fired illuminating and signal ammunition. Mks VII and VIII were assigned as the airborne models. These could be stripped down for packing

Returning to the Italian campaign, in December 1944, 3rd Squadron of 2nd SAS was despatched to the mountainous area north of the Arno River near Florence to fight with the partisans. 'Galia', which was the first of these operations, involved 33 men of No. 1 Troop led by Major Bob Walker-Brown and covered the hinterland of the coastal town of Spezia, south of the road from Parma, through Reggia and Modena to Bologna. No. 1 Troop's venture commenced on 27 December with a drop at Rossano and lasted for 50 days. Mules were used to porter mortars and machine-guns but heavy snow inhibited movement. The SAS nevertheless succeeded in inflicting about 100 casualties on the Germans and destroyed a quantity of their transport.

Major Farran, the squadron commander, himself commanded Operation 'Tombola', commencing on 4 March 1945. His base in a valley south of the River Secchia, between Spezia and Bologna, was ideal for attacking German interior lines of communication south of the Po valley. Thirty-six men were on this occasion dropped from Dakotas to aid the partisans.

The most memorable raid associated with 'Tombola' was the attack on the German Corps headquarters at Albinea, a village in the Po valley. It was an audacious plan with the object of killing as many German officers as possible before setting fire to the HQ, which was housed in the Villas Calvi and Rossi. After a long approach march, a small party of 10 SAS men, 20 Italians and some Russians reached Albinea without being seen and, during a 20-minute engagement, killed 60 Germans, including the Chief of Staff; they also burnt maps and vital documents. This raid, which is usually known as the attack on the Villa Calvi, was probably one of the most successful of its kind in the war.

The guerrilla campaign in northern Italy continued until the last day of the war on the Peninsula. Operation 'Tombola' ended in mid-April when Major Farran was ordered by Fifteenth Army Group to harass the main German escape route in the Bologna area. The clandestine raiders succeeded well and four German divisions were thrown into confusion.

On 20 April, Italian parachutists jumped at Ravarino with an assignment to disrupt communications in the rear areas. This force was known as 'F' Company and the men wore British uniform; they were attached to the Eighth Army and recruited originally from the *Folgore* Parachute Division.

THE RUSSIAN FRONT

In April 1941, prior to the outbreak of hostilities in Russia, the Soviets had formed five airborne corps (Nos 1 to 5) consisting of three brigades with a total strength of approximately 10,000 men. Stalin's airborne forces were only partially organized within this framework, however, when, on 22 June, Hitler launched Operation 'Barbarossa', the invasion of Russia. The swiftness of the German advance, spearheaded by the Panzers, in the North towards Leningrad and on the (Russian) Western and Southern Fronts converging on Moscow, gave little opportunity for airborne manoeuvre by the defenders. Trained parachutists were immediately thrown into the battle as conventional ground troops. But in October an effective air-lift was organized on the Bryansk Front, on the southern sector, when 5,500 infantrymen were air-landed with some 13 tons of ammunition northeast of Orel, at Mtsenk. The air operation was mounted by the Moscow Special Air Group (the Civil Air Fleet) and the Russian resistance at Mtsenk by two Tank brigades and the airborne infantry came as a complete surprise to the 2nd Panzer Group.

The Soviet High Command saw the main use of the airborne arm as a means of supporting the partisans. Small groups of varying strengths were dropped behind the lines throughout the war to conduct sabotage raids and to encourage the patriotic offensive by the people of the occupied territories against German troop concentrations, staging posts and lines of communication. The Partisan War, which made a major contribution to the German defeat in Russia, raged over a vast area, embracing the Karelo-Finnish, Estonian, Latvian and Lithuanian Soviet Republics and many regions of the Russian Federation, Byelorussia, the Ukraine and Moldavia.

In December 1941, the Germans were halted at the gates of Moscow and the Russians began to hit back. Between January and April 1942, Russian airborne troops, having already sustained serious losses in the first six months following the German invasion, were deployed en masse as sky battalions on the Western Front, hinging on the Smolensk area. Parachute troops were dropped at Medyn in January. During the third week of the month, the largest of these operations was launched when two battalions of the 201st Airborne Brigade, and the 250th Infantry Regiment of 4th Airborne Corps, totalling more than 1,640 men, were dropped 25 miles (40 km) south of Vyasma, near Zhelanye. By the end of the month, the 8th Brigade of 4th Airborne Corps, numbering 2,000 men, was air-lifted to Ozerechuya. The airborne troops played their part in sending the Germans back 155 miles (250 km) in the Vitebsk direction. Elsewhere, a battalion dropped in February, near Azhev, to reinforce encircled troops and to help them break out from the trap. In October, Naval parachutists were involved in a drop on a German airfield in the Caucasus.

The battles of Stalingrad and Kursk, which ended victoriously for the Russians in February and August 1943 respectively, saw the beginning of the end for the German Army in Russia. In autumn 1943, the German High Command ordered their armies to dig in along the entire front but the Russians were poised for the kill. By mid-September, the Red Army offensive, which had started while the great tank battle at Kursk was still raging, had cleared the east bank of the Dnieper river. Once bridgeheads had been established, the engineers were faced with the mammoth task of erecting pontoon bridges and repairing the road and rail bridges destroyed by the Germans.

The only large-scale parachute operation that was in fact attempted on the Dnieper crossings was a failure. This event took place on 24 September when the 3rd and 5th Airborne Brigades were dropped under cover of darkness near Kremenchug on the 2nd Ukrainian Front, about 25 miles (40 km) south-east of Kiev. The plan was to create a corridor for the tanks and infantry debouching from the bridgehead in the area but the timing of the airborne drop was poorly co-ordinated with the ground offensive. The two Russian parachute brigades were indeed beleaguered 25 miles (40 km) behind the German lines. The Russians dug in, forming their defences, but the odds were against them and there were no survivors from a battle lasting several days.

Although the Russians, both in defensive and offensive operations, made use of air-landed troops on all fronts in times of crisis, there is little mention of parachute troops again, after the Kremenchug fiasco, in the story of their war against Germany. In 1944, some 'SAS-type' operations were conducted by Russian paratroopers in Czechoslovakia and Bulgaria. The first of these was mounted during July/August together with Czech troops jumping in small groups into the mountains to aid the partisans; the second was a raid on an airfield at Burgas in Bulgaria. The end of the war saw Russia fighting Japan and, in August 1945, airborne troops were air-landed to capture key cities in northern China, Manchuria, Korea and the Kurile islands.

The Red Army paratroopers, who in 1941 were placed under Air Force control, jumped with a parachute with a square canopy. As this was slow to open, the Russians were dropped in action at a height of about 1,000 feet (305 m). The canopies were made of silk or rayon, as nylon was not available in Russia at this time. They appear to have carried little during a descent apart from the PPSh 41 sub-machine-gun with a spare 71-round drum magazine on the belt. A wide range of both large and small containers were used to parachute weapons and equipment. These were slung below the ANT-6, beneath the fuselage, but the Russians in support of partisan operations often flew in very low, jettisoning their containers and bundles by free-fall.

The ANT-6 four-engined bomber, which dated from the late 1920s, carried a maximum load of about five tons; it was obsolete before the war started and was phased out of service in the middle period of the war in Russia. This venerable aircraft, which had played an important part in pre-war airborne training and manoeuvres, had a range of 250 miles (402 km) and carried up to 30 parachutists. The American DC-3 (Dakota) was already being built in Russia under licence in 1939 and, as the Lisunov Li-2, came into widespread wartime use as a Red Air Force transport aircraft.

Gliders were principally deployed to reinforce and supply ammunition and equipment to the partisans. The Antonov A-7, which was similar in appearance to the German DFS 230, was made entirely of wood with a fabric covering. The A-7 supported a single pilot and nine fully-equipped troops or the equivalent in loads. The Polikarpov BDP S-1 glider was planned as a 20-seater with the alternative capacity for a jeep or a light gun. In late 1944, two 140 hp engines were fitted to the Polikarpov but this glider was barely satisfactory in powerless flight and a total failure as a powered aircraft.

Right: Hungarian airborne insignia.
Far right: German cuff titles

Fallschirm-Division

Fallschirm-Jäger Rgt. 1

*German artillery being loaded
into an Me323 D-1. The D-1 was
the most commonly used of the
Me323s for freight transport*

JUNKERS JU 352

Three-engined transport for
freight and heavy loads, with a
rear-loading door through which
vehicles could be driven straight
in; the tail was first lifted onto a
trestle. Not a commonly used
aircraft for airborne assaults

Engines: 3 x Jumo 211F 12-cylinder radials	Span: 111 ft 10½ in
Max speed: 272 mph	Length: 82 ft 4½ in
Range: 2473 miles	Armament: 1 x 13 mm in turret 2 x 7.92 MG in beam positions

The Germans, like the Russians, employed trained parachute troops in the Eastern European theatre as infantry of
the line. Both the original *Fliegerdivision 7* and *Infanterie
(Luftlande) – Division 22* were transferred to Russia in the
early months of 'Barbarossa' in 1941. *Generalleutnant* Peter-
sen's parachute division, which was reformed with a nucleus
of the survivors of the capture of Crete, served on the Leningrad, Rzhev and Mius sectors. Renamed *Fallschirm-Division 1*
in autumn 1942, the formation was withdrawn from Russia
the following March and posted to the South of France for
rehabilitation.

The only German combat jumps in Russia were performed
by the Brandenburg Regiment *zbv – zur besonderen Verwen-
dung*, for Special Purposes. This regiment was raised in 1939
and trained as a parachute/glider unit for raiding and intelligence tasks. The Brandenburg Regiment, which contained,
for linguistic reasons, a large proportion of foreigners, was
controlled by *Abwehr II*, the infamous Army counter-intelligence organization.

Two Brandenburg raids in Estonia and Lithuania marked
the initial phase of 'Barbarossa' in July 1941 and another
followed in August 1942, when the objective was one of
Hitler's oil refinery goals in the Caucasus. In 1943, the
Brandenburgers were employed in the Mediterranean theatre,
where they jumped on to and seized the Dodecanese islands
of Kos, Stampagia and Leros. In 1944, the Brandenburg
Regiment was expanded into a *Panzergrenadier* Division
during the retreat from Russia but the revised formation
retained a parachute battalion.

In September 1942, *FJR1* and *FJR3* of *Fliegerdivision 7*,
the 2nd Battalion of the Assault Regiment and support troops,
guns and equipment were flown in to help the Sixteenth Army
hold the Red Army's counter-offensive at Leningrad. These
airborne reinforcements were committed to the Russian Neva
bridgeheads at Petruschino and Wyborgskaya. But apart from
this and some supply tasks by the giant Me 321-Gigant glider,
the participation of the *Fallschirmjäger* on the Eastern Front
was almost exclusively an infantry affair.

The Me323 D-2, with Heine fixed pitch wooden propellers, was rarer than the D-1. Here army personnel are handing over to the Luftwaffe responsibility for loading horses on the Russian front

'D'-DAY: OPERATION NEPTUNE

The arrival of the United States 101st Airborne Division in Britain in August 1943 marked the beginning of the build-up of the Allied airborne arm for the invasion of France. Led by General 'Bill' Lee, the 'Father of American airborne forces', the 101st disembarked at Merseyside and moved to their billets in rural Wiltshire and Berkshire. The units of the 101st were the 502nd and 506th Parachute Infantry Regiments, the 327th Glider Infantry Regiment, the 907th Glider Field Artillery and the 326th Airborne Engineers. With the arrival of the 501st PIR in January 1944, the 101st had over 12,000 men available.

The British 6th Airborne Division, which was stationed on Salisbury Plain, had been in existence since 3 May 1943; its divisional commander, Major-General R N Gale, assumed his duties on 7 May. The division was to comprise the 3rd and 5th Parachute Brigades and the 6th (Air-Landing) Brigade. New parachute battalions were formed from County regiments on a regional basis as follows – *3rd Brigade*: 7th (Light Infantry) Battalion from 10th Btn the Somerset Light Infantry; 8th (Midland) Battalion from 13th Btn the Royal Warwickshire Regiment; 9th (Eastern and Home Counties) Battalion from 10th Btn the Essex Regiment. *5th Brigade*: 12th (Yorkshire) Battalion from 10th Btn the Green Howards and 13th (Lancashire) Battalion from 2nd/4th Btn the South Lancashire Regiment. The glider troops of the *6th Brigade* were the 2nd Btn the Oxfordshire and Buckinghamshire Light Infantry, the 1st Btn the Royal Ulster Rifles and 12th Btn the Devonshire Regiment. 6th Airborne Division possessed its full complement of support and service units, which included the 53rd A/L Light Regiment RA (75-mms), two anti-tank batteries (6-pounders) and a Light Anti-Aircraft Battery (20-mm Oerlikons and 40-mm Bofors). In July 1943, the 1st Canadian Parachute Battalion arrived from Camp Shilo, Manitoba, and was assigned to 3rd Parachute Brigade; 7th Parachute Battalion was transferred out to bring 5th Parachute Brigade up to full strength.

General Ridgway's battle-tested 82nd Division, less the 504th PIR (left behind in Italy in the Anzio beach-head), went into training in December 1943 in Northern Ireland for the 'D'-Day invasion. The 505th PIR and 325th Glider Infantry were reinforced in January 1944 by the 507th and 508th PIRs arriving from the USA. In February, the 82nd

AIRSPEED HORSA

The Horsa Mk I, a troop and freight carrying glider, was manufactured by Airspeed Ltd of Portsmouth, Hampshire. The Airspeed Horsa was a high-wing cantilever monoplane. Both wings and fuselage were all-wooden constructions, with plywood coverings; the wooden tail was covered in fabric. Two large fuselage doors were situated front side forward for freight and starboard side aft for troops. As a trooper, the Horsa contained 25 seats but normally carried only 15 fully armed troops. A wide variety of military equipment could alternatively be stowed in the main compartment. The Mk II introduced in 1944 was of the same length and wing span as the Mk I but displayed a hinged nose to permit direct loading of light ordnance and vehicles

Max towing speed:	180 mph
Stalling speed:	60 mph
Span:	88 ft
Length:	67 ft
Height:	19 ft 6 in
Weight, loaded (Mk I):	15,500 lb

British Horsa and US Waco gliders after disgorging airborne troops in the Allied landings in Normandy, 10 June 1944

moved to the Midlands of England into camps in the general area of Leicester, Nottingham and Market Harborough.

On 24 April, General Browning mounted a British 1st Airborne Corps exercise that ranged for three days over the green fields of Oxfordshire, Wiltshire and Gloucestershire. Exercise 'Mush', in which 6th Airborne was lifted by air and 1st Airborne acted as the enemy, was the former's 'D'-Day dress rehearsal. Browning's Command, which now included Sosabowski's so-far-uncommitted Polish Independent Parachute Brigade and the SAS, had thus achieved Corps status prior to the invasion of N W Europe. The American divisions also reached the peak of their training efforts and set up their own parachute school to train replacements and exercise by night and day. Finally, on 9 May, the entire 101st dropped on the Berkshire Downs around Hungerford and Newbury: the exercise was marred by navigational errors and jump injuries but there was now little time to spare for renewed experiment.

On 8 May 1944, the Supreme Commander Allied Forces Europe, General Dwight D Eisenhower, designated D-Day as 5 June but, because of the bad weather, he decided to postpone the assault on the Normandy coast-line until the following day. 2,876,000 men were ready to cross the English Channel for the greatest seaborne military operation in history; more than 200,000 invasion troops were scheduled to go ashore from ships and assault craft on D-Day, plus 1 and 2. Commencing at 06.30 hours on 6 June, the United States First Army was due to land on the right of the line on the Cotentin Peninsula, southeast of Cherbourg, on Utah and, further east, on Omaha beaches; the British Second Army, including the Canadian 3rd Division, were scheduled to go ashore 50 minutes later on the left, east of Arromanches, on Gold, Juno and Sword beaches. Some 5,000 vessels made up the cross-Channel fleet and RAF bombers were poised to strike along the entire invasion coastline.

The American attack was to be spearheaded by the US 82nd and 101st Airborne Divisions landing from the air shortly after midnight astride the Merderet river in the

Ministry of Defence

Above: General Montgomery carries out an inspection in March 1944 of British Airborne troops who were to take part in airborne operations in Europe some months later

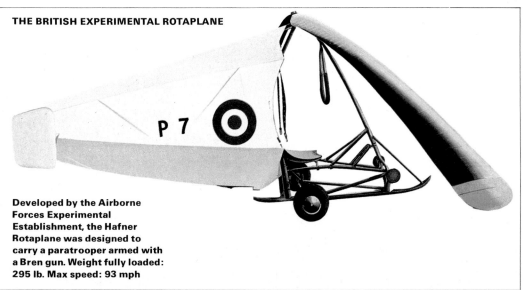

THE BRITISH EXPERIMENTAL ROTAPLANE

P 7

Developed by the Airborne Forces Experimental Establishment, the Hafner Rotaplane was designed to carry a paratrooper armed with a Bren gun. Weight fully loaded: 295 lb. Max speed: 93 mph

Right: Part of the RAF air armada before it set off from Britain for the French coast on the evening of 6 June 1944

WESTLAND LYSANDER

Evolved as a two-seat Army co-operation aeroplane, the Westland Lysander was destined to play an unusual but useful role in the Second World War. The Mark IIIA (447 built) was used for air-sea-rescue and landing agents in occupied territory. Here the low flying speeds and remarkable STOL characteristics of the Lysander provided a unique performance, especially for landing in and taking off from small fields or roads in Occupied Europe. Four passengers could be crammed in

Engine: One 870 hp Bristol Mercury 30 radial

Max speed: 212 mph

Range: 500 miles

Span: 50 ft

Length: 30 ft 6 in

Height: 14 ft 6 in

Max take-off weight: 6318 lb

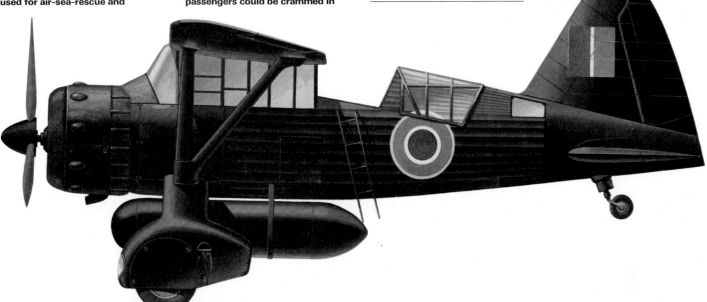

vicinity of St Mère Eglise to facilitate the advance of the US VII Corps. At the same time, the British 6th Airborne Division, landing 40 miles to the east, was to secure the Allied left flank between the Orne and Dives rivers. The Special Air Service Brigade, which had moved from Scotland to its airfield base at Fairford in Gloucestershire, was also ready to play its part in the 'D'-Day Operations. The French SAS were committed to four drops on 6 June to solemnize their return to their native soil and, on the same day, 1st SAS were committed to three; the largest of the British sorties involved 'A' Squadron, (Operation 'Houndsworth'), at Rouvray. The purpose of the SAS on 6 June was to create diversions and – as was the forthcoming SAS-style – to establish firm, clandestine bases in liaison with the resistance fighters.

At 21.30 hours on 5 June, the American Pathfinder Group of 9th Troop Carrier Command took off from an airfield in Lincolnshire and headed for the Dorset coast at Portland Bill.

The Pathfinders' task was to plant the REBECCA and EUREKA radar navigational aids and mark the dropping zones in the 82nd and 101st operational zones on the Cherbourg Peninsula. One hour later 822 C-47s, bearing 13,000 American paratroopers, gathered speed after taking off from numerous airfields scattered throughout the English Midland, Eastern and Southern counties.

The US Airborne Divisions formed part of Major-General Lawton Collin's US VII Corps, landing on the eastern shore of the peninsula, a few miles north of the Vire estuary; the assault on the Utah beaches was led by the US 4th Infantry Division. The 82nd Division was to drop on both banks of the Merderet River, seize the river and neighbouring marsh crossings and capture the road junction in the village of St Mère Eglise. Further south, the 101st Division's assignment near Carentan was to capture four causeways across the marshland and guard VII Corps' southern flank.

Far left: Supreme Allied Commander-in-Chief Dwight D Eisenhower visiting US Airborne forces during training in England prior to the D-Day invasion of Europe, May 1944
Left: Major General R N Gale, GOC 6th Airborne Division, talking to paratroops before they emplane

General Ridgway's 505th PIR was to land to the east of the Merderet and the 507th and 508th to the west. General Maxwell D. Taylor, who had assumed command of the 101st after 'Bill' Lee was invalided home, was also allocated three DZs; the 501st, 502nd and 506th PIRs with the 377th Artillery Battalion were to land in a mixed regimental pattern. The initial glider commitment was drastically cut when pre-'D'-Day reports indicated that obstacles had been placed on all the likely air-landing zones. (These obstacles, known as 'Rommel's asparagus', were formed by sharpened poles supporting webs of barbed wire.) One hundred gliders shared equally between the two divisions were, however, to accompany the airborne assault and 200 more were due to fly in during the course of 'D'-Day.

The skytrain flew safely to the French coast but German heavy and light anti-aircraft batteries caused the aerial column to be broken up as the pilots were forced to take evasive action. General Ridgway's first encounter on French soil was a solitary cow, which registered no emotion or response on being challenged at pistol point for the password by the Commanding General of the elite US 82nd Airborne Division. The time was about two o'clock in the morning and none of the stick from which he had only just parted company were anywhere to be found. Both divisions had, in fact, been widely scattered by the wind over a vast area and the chances of assembling by unit before daylight were remote. The gliders fared particularly badly; few of them landed in unison on the designated landing zones. What was worse, the heavily-laden paratroopers who dropped into the flooded marshland areas had little or no chance of survival. Hundreds of men died in this way; their bodies were never recovered from their watery graves.

On the northern approaches to St Mère Eglise, Lieutenant-Colonel Krause of the 3/505th assembled about 100 of his men in the darkness and advanced cautiously towards the village. German Flak guns had already been in action against the incoming aircraft and a Grenadier Regiment in the area was on full alert. Six Americans, dropping into the village square, were greeted by a hail of rifle fire and killed instantly. A seventh, Private Steel, was more fortunate; he feigned death for two hours as he hung suspended by his parachute from the top of a church tower, watching helplessly as his comrades died in the street below. He was rescued by one of Krause's parties fighting its way into the village. By dawn, St Mère Eglise had been cleared of Germans and the Americans were in possession of the road junction.

Elsewhere in the 82nd Division's zone, troops who had missed meeting at their rendezvous commenced converging in daylight to seize their bridge objectives and to form road-

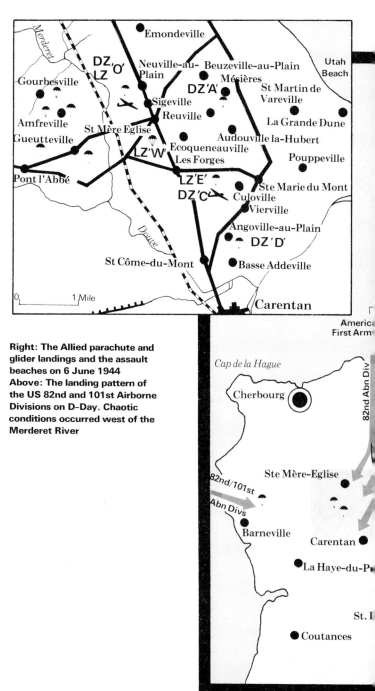

Right: The Allied parachute and glider landings and the assault beaches on 6 June 1944
Above: The landing pattern of the US 82nd and 101st Airborne Divisions on D-Day. Chaotic conditions occurred west of the Merderet River

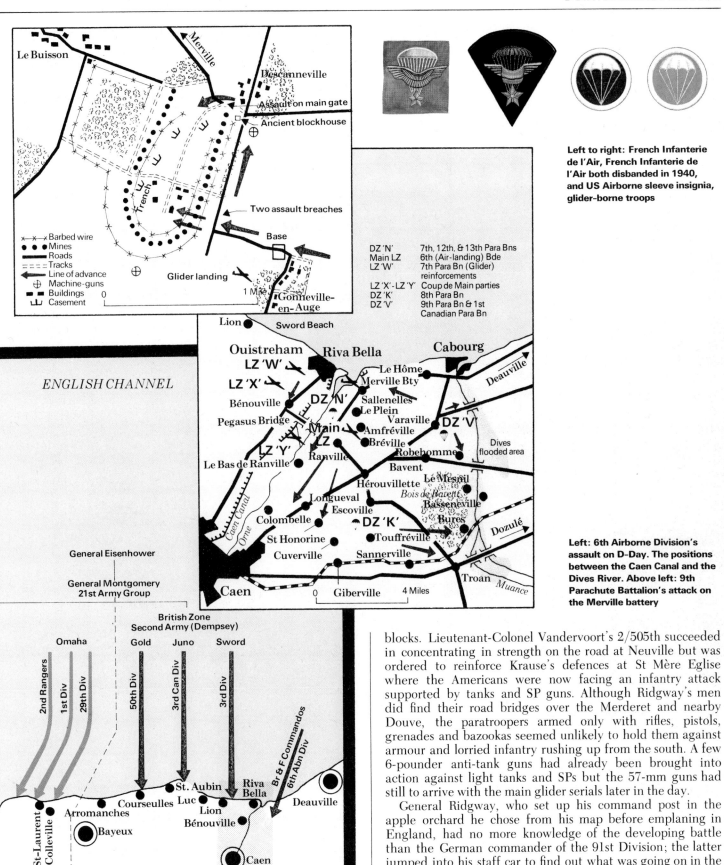

Left to right: French Infanterie de l'Air, French Infanterie de l'Air both disbanded in 1940, and US Airborne sleeve insignia, glider-borne troops

DZ 'N'	7th, 12th, & 13th Para Bns
Main LZ	6th (Air-landing) Bde
LZ 'W'	7th Para Bn (Glider) reinforcements
LZ 'X'-LZ 'Y'	Coup de Main parties
DZ 'K'	8th Para Bn
DZ 'V'	9th Para Bn & 1st Canadian Para Bn

Left: 6th Airborne Division's assault on D-Day. The positions between the Caen Canal and the Dives River. Above left: 9th Parachute Battalion's attack on the Merville battery

blocks. Lieutenant-Colonel Vandervoort's 2/505th succeeded in concentrating in strength on the road at Neuville but was ordered to reinforce Krause's defences at St Mère Eglise where the Americans were now facing an infantry attack supported by tanks and SP guns. Although Ridgway's men did find their road bridges over the Merderet and nearby Douve, the paratroopers armed only with rifles, pistols, grenades and bazookas seemed unlikely to hold them against armour and lorried infantry rushing up from the south. A few 6-pounder anti-tank guns had already been brought into action against light tanks and SPs but the 57-mm guns had still to arrive with the main glider serials later in the day.

General Ridgway, who set up his command post in the apple orchard he chose from his map before emplaning in England, had no more knowledge of the developing battle than the German commander of the 91st Division; the latter jumped into his staff car to find out what was going on in the wild night of confused shooting and met his death from the bullets of an 82nd patrol. 'I am glad', said Ridgway to the jubilant Lieutenant, 'that the dead Divisional commander was a German!'

By daylight, D + 1, 7 June, the 82nd had secured a *logement* some six miles in depth east of the Merderet River. The captured territory was roughly triangular in shape; St Mère Eglise in the south-eastern corner was firmly in American hands and Krause's 3/505th repelled all German attempts to

103

Waco and Horsa gliders lie scattered among the fields of the Cherbourg peninsula hours after the drop on the night of 5/6 June 1944 in support of the 'D'-Day landings

take the town. Vandervoort had sent a reinforced platoon under Lieutenant Turnbull north to Neuville to accomplish the mission originally assigned to his battalion but the Neuville area was not in the 505th's hands until Vandervoort moved the main body of his battalion up from St Mère Eglise.

In spite of the earlier confusion, Colonel 'Jumping Jim' Gavin had made an excellent job of organizing the 505th's units. At the western tip of the triangle, at La Fière, he was faced with a tough job in capturing and holding the Merderet bridge. Kellam's 1/505th first encountered the Germans at the bridge and a fierce battle ensued; small arms and mortars were no match for tanks and SP guns. The 507th and 508th Regiments were, on the face of it, cut off west of the Merderet and well-coordinated attempts to cross the bridge to link with the main force proved disastrous. It was only on the second attempt, with artillery support, that the 325th Glider Infantry succeeded in digging in on the west bank.

Three days had now elapsed since the first landings and the 82nd was completely exhausted but help was on its way from the beaches. The US 90th Division, disembarking from the boats, moved up via St Mère Eglise to La Fière and threw everything they had into the battle for the crossing. The 90th, which started apprehensively, having been alarmed by the signs of death and destruction as they approached the firing line, swept all before them and within a matter of days reached the west coast of the Cherbourg peninsula.

Meanwhile, General Maxwell D Taylor's 101st Airborne Division was no less heavily engaged in the south where their task was to establish the US 4th Division's lines of advance from the Utah beaches. The 101st, which landed on four DZs and one LZ, was in fact disposed north of Carentan, both east and south of the 82nd's positions. In addition to capturing the four causeways across the marshland, General Taylor had the additional assignment of securing the northern flank of his divisional zone by seizing St Germain de Varreville and the bridges over the Douve near Carentan. On the first night, the 101st troopers, like those of the 82nd, were either drowning in the inundated areas or wandering in small parties all over the Cherbourg peninsula.

The 502nd's initial objectives were situated in the north of the sector, involving the crossings at Adouville and St Martin-de-Varreville. A small party of the 2/502nd found the St Martin gun battery abandoned and by dawn the battalion was assembled in sufficient strength to establish defensive positions on the northern flank where the 1/502nd was already in action. Lieutenant-Colonel Cole of the 3/502nd was obliged shortly after landing to knock on the door of a house in a small town to find out where he was. He was surprised to find he was in the 82nd's zone in St Mère Eglise; as his battalion's objectives were some four miles to the east, at Beach Exits 3 and 4, Cole made haste in the night to find his men. Collecting groups of them as he went along, Cole took both his objectives unopposed by 7.30 in the morning.

Lieutenant-Colonel Cassidy's 1/502nd had the job of clearing a German artillery barracks at Mézières. Staff Sergeant Summers, who was given 15 men to complete the assignment, reached the objective unobserved and, on entering the mess hall, the NCO personally shot 15 Germans sitting down to breakfast. The Americans then came under intense fire in open ground from upstairs vantage points but well-aimed bazooka shells at the ammunition store and roofs set the barracks ablaze. Germans escaping from the burning buildings were cut down by the dozen and the remainder of the garrison surrendered. Summers afterwards confessed that he had been sickened by the experience and hoped that he would never have to do it again. Command of the 502nd passed to Colonel John H Michaelis after Colonel George Mosley broke his leg on the DZ. The 502nd's experience of the battle was one of fierce but isolated encounters; with the crossings secured at Adouville and St Martin-de-Varreville, units of the 4th Division were free to advance.

The 506th Regiment had been much heartened before take-off at Welford, in Berkshire, by a visit from General Eisenhower. The men's morale had been visibly increased as the General walked amongst their ranks on the airfield wishing the blackened faces well in battle. The 2/506th's mission was to capture Beach Exits 1 and 2 at Pouppeville and Houdienville. The former was taken by 50 men and the latter with a rather larger force but not without strong resistance.

Although Colonel Robert Sink had rallied the 506th without great difficulty, inter-regimental contact in the 101st Airborne Division was non-existent. General Taylor's arrival in France had been similar to that of General Ridgway: Taylor's first encounter was with a cow and, so far as he could tell in the solitude, he was the only man available to fight the Germans. It was some time before the Commanding General was able to piece together news of his division.

The 3rd Battalion's DZ was near the River Douve. Unfortunately, the Germans had anticipated a parachute landing in the very area of the drop zone. As the C-47s flew in, the Germans lit fires to direct their machine-gunners and mortarmen to the area. Luckily, this time, navigational errors produced bonus points for the 3/506th but those who dropped on target did so to murderous enemy fire. Lieutenant-Colonel Robert Wolverton – a religious man who had led his battalion in prayer before emplaning in England – was killed instantly as was his Executive officer, George Grant. None of the Company commanders were available to lead their groups. The first men to reach the two bridge objectives were Privates Zahn and Montilio: the former was rewarded by being commissioned in the field and the latter by being promoted to sergeant. Both men received the Distinguished Service Cross. The object was to destroy the bridges to prevent German reinforcements from moving up to the beach-heads; this was promptly achieved by the Airborne sappers.

The Regimental assignment of Colonel Johnson's 501st was to hold the 101st's southern flank. More bridges were to be blown on the road and railway routes running north from Carentan to Cherbourg. Naval gunfire was brought to bear on targets selected by 501st officers and indicated by Navy OPs. At this stage German paratroopers were thrown into the battle: Freiherr von de Heydte's *FJR* 6 advanced north from Carentan to meet the 501st.

The Glider operations in support of the US 82nd and 101st Airborne Divisions on 'D'-Day were more successful in terms of landing personnel than the recovery of jeeps and anti-tank guns. The 505th PIR had already landed at St Mère Eglise when the first contingent, numbering 30 gliders, crashed shortly afterwards into the swampland and obstruction poles surrounding the town. A much larger force of Wacos and Horsas (also destined for the 82nd's zone of operations) arrived over Utah beach the following evening but as their

D-Day Weapons for the British Airborne Forces

A great variety of weaponry was either created for or especially adapted for the use of airborne forces, much of it with the eventual aim of the D-Day invasion in mind. Some of the armament was more successful than other pieces. The Tetrarch tank was probably the most ambitious piece of equipment to be glider-borne but its rôle proved only to be subsidiary. The compact Welbike was imaginative but its potential was unfulfilled in wartime at least. More useful to the airborne troops was the cover provided by the 6-pounder A/Tk, although this, too, proved to be inadequate to its anti-tank task. The OML mortar and the Sten

machine carbine, on the other hand, were welcome and invaluable weapons that were used widely by airborne infantry. The 6-pounder anti-tank gun and the PIAT were the British parachute and glider infantrymen's forlorn hope of engaging enemy tanks. In September 1944 at Oosterbeek, during the Battle of Arnhem, Lance-Sergeant Baskeyfield of the South Staffords died earning a posthumous Victoria Cross manning a 6-pounder single-handed in the face of enemy armour

LIGHT TANK Mk VII TETRARCH

The British Tetrarch played a minor role in Normandy. Its tactical function was to act as an armoured recce vehicle, landed by glider and operated in support of Airborne Division HQ for a few days only before the main overland battle tanks were in the firing line. The 3-man

Tetrarch weighed 7 tons; its armour was 15 mm thick; and it had a 12-cylinder, 165-hp Meadows engine. Speed was 37 mph (59 km/h) and the tank was armed with one 37-mm or one 40-mm gun and one machine gun. The Hamilcar glider was designed with the Tetrarch in mind. Of the 171 Tetrarchs produced, 20 went to Russia

OML 4.2 MORTAR

The OML 2-inch, 3-inch and 4.2-inch mortars were invaluable weapons in the airborne infantry support role, for the British. They were quick into action and fired HE and smoke bombs with great accuracy over limited ranges. Mortars were conveniently stripped down for packing into equipment containers. The weight of the OML 4.2 mortar was 257 lb (115.6 kg). Its effective range was 4100 yd (3747 m)

WELBIKE

The Welbike two-stroke motorcycle conveniently fitted into an equipment container. Especially invented for the British paratrooper, it measured 4 ft 3 in (1.29 m) long and 15 in (0.38 m) broad. The handle-bars, steering column and saddle were arranged on a collapsible principle. Maximum speed was 30 mph (48 km/h) and maximum range was 90 miles (144 km). The machine weighed 70 lbs (31.5 kg). There is little evidence that the Welbike was of the slightest use to the paratroopers but it provided the post-war formula for lightweight, economy travel in busy towns and cities

STEN MK V

The Sten machine carbine was produced as a cheap expedient after the Dunkirk disaster. Designed and developed by R. V. Shepperd and A. J. Turpin at the Royal Small Arms Factory at Enfield, the name 'Sten' derived from the initial letters of the inventors' surnames and the first two letters of the place of origin. Altogether five versions were produced, starting with the Mk I in June 1941. The calibre was 9-mm. The Sten was made of sheet metal tubing. A 32-round box magazine was slotted into a receiver on the left side of the barrel. The version produced in greatest quantity was the Mk II, with its single tube shoulder stock. It fired 500 rpm. The Mk II weighed nearly 7 lb (3.15 kg) and was 30 inches long (0.76 m). Mks I, III and IV displayed triangular tube stocks but the Mk V, which was fitted with a bayonet, was equipped with a more solid wooden butt. The Sten gun proved effective up to 500 yd (457 m)

6-POUNDER A/TK

This weapon was designed in Britain in 1938 but not issued until September 1941. It was replaced in the Royal Artillery in 1943 by the 17-pounder but continued to serve as an infantry support weapon on all fronts. Calibre was 2.244 in, length of barrel 100 in and all-up weight approximately one ton (1016 kg). Rate of fire was 10 rpm and muzzle velocity 2700 fps. Effective armour-penetrating range was 1000 yd (914 m) but the 6-pounder could not cope with the frontal armour of the German Tiger tank. The 6-pounder was transported with its jeep tow-vehicle in a Horsa glider. Before loading the shield was removed .

Left to right: British 1st Glider Pilot Regt, 2nd Glider Pilot Regt, British SAS, British shoulder title, 3rd Parachute Btn, typical arm insignia arrangement

LZ was not under American control the tugs were diverted to a safer area. Even so, 37 of the C-47s were hit and the 75 gliders that reached the battlefield were widely scattered.

A further 100 tugs and gliders flew into the 82nd's sector just before midnight on 'D'-Day. These reinforcements included the sorely-needed gunners and their 75-mm and 105-mm howitzers, ammunition and stores. German anti-aircraft gunners sited on high ground near Neuville broke up the aerial formations and the Wacos and Horsas plunged earthwards into a cordon of fire from field and machine-gunners on the ground. Sixty-two gliders were totally destroyed: dead and wounded totalled nearly 200 but this time a fair proportion of the guns and jeeps were salvaged. A final glider lift was planned for the 82nd the following day. Two battalions of the 325th and one of the 401st Glider Infantry Regiments were airborne during the morning. The reception to the new arrivals, numbering almost 2,000 men, varied in intensity but the majority of them were soon in action in support of the hard-pressed paratroopers.

Whilst the US 82nd and 101st Airborne Divisions were assigned to hold the right flank of the Allied invasion forces on 6 June, the British 6th Airborne Division was to land 40 miles (64 km) east to secure the left between the Orne and Dives rivers. Major-General R N Gale's objectives were as follows: 5th Parachute Brigade (Poett) was to capture and hold the bridges over the Canal de Caen and the River Orne at Bénouville and Ranville; 3rd Parachute Brigade (Hill) was simultaneously to destroy the coastal battery at Merville and the bridges at Varaville, Robehomme, Bures and Troarn. The seizure of the 5th Brigade's bridge objectives was allocated to a *coup de main* party from Kindersley's 6th (Air-Landing) Brigade, landing from gliders five hours before the dawn. The importance of holding these bridges to assist the advance of the 3rd Division from 'Sword' beach was further emphasized by the plan to fly in the main glider force to this sector later in the day. The task of knocking out the Merville Battery, which had been strenuously rehearsed in great secrecy in the Newbury area, had been allocated to Lieutenant-Colonel Terence Otway's 9th Parachute Battalion.

Nos. 38 and 46 Groups RAF possessed about 300 converted bombers—Albemarles, Stirlings and Halifaxes plus 150 Dakota transports for the 6th Airborne operation. Six thousand parachute and glider assault troops were to be landed between midnight and first light on 'D'-Day, the aircraft returning to their airfields in southern England to lift 3,000 men of Brigadier the Hon Hugh Kindersley's Glider infantrymen.

At 23.03 hours on 5 June, six Albemarle aircraft bearing 60 Pathfinders of the 22nd Independent Parachute Company took off from Harwell. Almost as soon as the Pathfinders were in the air, six Horsas bearing a party of the Oxf. and Bucks. Light Infantry and Royal Engineers set off under tow for the Caen canal and Orne bridges. At three minutes to midnight, the two parachute brigades took off from their airfields and headed for the French coast. Later an assault party from 9th Parachute Battalion was launched in three gliders to make a pinpoint landing on the Merville battery. The take-off of the first lift was finally concluded when, shortly after midnight, 68 Horsas were hauled into the air supporting Gale and his HQ Staff, elements of 7th Parachute Battalion and equipment. Four Hamilcars also flew with this contingent.

The Pathfinders dropped at 00.20 hours on three separate dropping zones: DZ 'N' northeast of Ranville, DZ 'K' west of Troarn and DZ 'V' between the Merville battery and Varaville. At nine minutes to midnight, the first of the Halifax and Horsa combinations bearing the *coup de main* parties crossed the French coast. The first of the three gliders destined for the swing bridge over the Caen canal, having been released at 5,000 feet (1,524 m) near the mouth of the Orne, landed with amazing accuracy within 50 yards (48 m) of the objective. As the pilots, Staff Sergeants Wallwork and Ainsworth, and their passengers made for the bridge under fire, the other two gliders came in close behind. Several glider men were hit by Schmeisser fire before the bridge defenders were overwhelmed and a Piat was brought into action to repel an attack by tanks. Meanwhile, the remaining three assault gliders had landed intact near the Orne bridges.

'D'-Day was still only an hour old as 2,000 men of 5th Parachute Brigade (7th, 12th and 13th Parachute Battalions) tumbled out of their aircraft and floated earthwards. Brigadier Nigel Poett's 5th Brigade was fortunate in being able to assemble quickly on the ground. Whilst the 12th and 13th Battalions manned covering positions on high ground and along the roadways, after capturing Le Bas de Ranville and Ranville itself, the 7th Battalion raced in two main streams to hold the Caen canal and Orne bridges.

Elsewhere, the 9th Battalion and 1st Canadian Parachute Battalion of Brigadier James Hill's 3rd Brigade commenced jumping at 01.00 hours further east on DZ 'V' near Varaville; the 8th Battalion of the same formation landed well to the southwest with a view to capturing the Bures and Troarn bridges and advancing into the woodland area of the Bois de Bavent. The Merville battery, which was capable of creating havoc amongst the invasion fleet, was established in concrete emplacements. It had a main armament of four 150-mm guns and was defended by one 20-mm gun and several machine-guns. The battery was enclosed by a cattle fence, which was lined on its inner side by barbed wire entanglements. Having penetrated the wire, the attackers were faced with a minefield 100 yards (91.5 m) in depth. At the seaward side of the battery was an anti-tank ditch. The assault on the Merville guns by the 9th Battalion was the most critical of all the tasks assigned to 6th Airborne Division.

Lieutenant-Colonel Otway's 9th Battalion plan had all the elements of the 'forlorn hope' breach and assault tactics of medieval warfare. In this case the castle was the Merville battery but there would be no time for a leisurely siege. After an attack by Lancaster bombers, and ground reconnaissance after the drop, the outer fence and wire were to be breached and two lanes blown through the perimeter minefield with Bangalore torpedoes. Five gliders, carrying anti-tank guns, jeeps loaded with ammunition and scaling ladders, were due to land alongside the fence. Once through the breach, the main body of the battalion was to take on the garrison of 200 men while the sappers destroyed the guns.

The 3rd Brigade drop near Varaville was spread out over a wide area and many of the men landed in marshland flooded by the Germans. Otway found only 25 per cent of his battalion at the DZ rendezvous but resolved, as he put it, 'to advance' with less than 200 men. The time was then 02.00 hours and the gliders with the assault equipment were scheduled to descend on the Merville battery five miles (8 km) to the northwest of DZ 'V', two hours and 20 minutes later.

Top: Three Horsa gliders of the British 6th Airborne Division lie close to their objective – the 'Pegasus' lift-bridge over the Orne Canal, inland from the 'D'-Day beaches in Normandy. Bottom: Signallers instal land lines on the approach to the 'Pegasus' bridge

Public Records Office

Imperial War Museum

In the event, only three tug/glider pairs took off from base; one of the Horsas broke loose from its tow rope before crossing the English Coast. Of the two that made the journey to Normandy, Staff Sergeant Bone's glider crash-landed half-a-mile (800 m) from the objective and Staff Sergeant Kerr's burst into flames in an apple orchard only 200 yards (183 m) from the Merville wire. The party in the first Horsa was unaware of their whereabouts until daybreak but the second lot of troopers escaped from their burning fuselage only to meet head-on with a German patrol. The glider troops were instrumental in holding off German reinforcements while Otway's force made the main assault. As the dawn broke, the four heavy guns lay spiked as planned with Gammon bombs. Seventy of the airborne men were killed in the successful operation to silence the Merville battery.

Before dawn on 6 June, Naval Force 'S', carrying Major-General T G Rennie's 3rd Division, and its supporting units, were assembled off the mouth of the Orne. The daylight landing at 07.30 hours was preceded by a devastating, two-hour aerial and fleet bombardment concentrated on beaches west of Ouistreham and on heavy coastal batteries to the east. The sound of the guns, which included those of the battleships *Warspite* and *Ramillies*, was sweet music to 5th Parachute Brigade now fiercely engaged in the Ranville area. The 125th Panzer Grenadier Regiment was already in action and the 21st Panzer Division fast moving up. Behind the screen of gunfire, Nos. 1 and 4 Commando, 1st South Lancs and 2nd East Yorks, tanks of the 13th/18th Hussars and armoured assault teams streamed ashore on to 'Sword' beach exactly as

planned. Whilst the beaches were being cleared, Brigadier the Lord Lovat's No. 1 Commando strode ahead to rendezvous with General Gale and the airborne men hanging on grimly to the Caen canal bridge.

During the night, the paratroopers had been reinforced west of Ranville by glider troops deplaning from 47 Horsas and two Hamilcar gliders. The glider infantrymen quickly went to the assistance of 7th Parachute Battalion at Bénouville. As the morning developed, 'B' Company 7th Parachute Battalion, came under heavy attack at the Caen canal bridge. But at 10.00 hours General Gale himself was seen walking across the bridge with a staff officer at an unhurried pace. Three hours later the alert ears of the picquets at the bridge picked up the sound of bagpipes above the noise of battle. A solitary piper then hove into view followed by Lord Lovat marching at the head of No. 1 Commando. The sight of the green-bereted Commandos advancing in good cheer at a steady pace was a great moment in the history of airborne warfare. 6th Airborne's sector had still to be consolidated but all their 'D'-Day objectives had been taken. In less than five hours after the meeting with Lovat's Commandos, seaborne armour and infantry were across the Caen canal; the controversial 'airborne method' had been totally successful. Today this bridge, which lies east of Bénouville on the way to Ranville, bears the sign 'Pegasus Bridge', a permanent reminder of the part played by 6th Airborne.

The main glider landing on the afternoon of 'D'-Day, southeast of Ranville, involved 250 gliders, bringing the remainder of the 2nd Btn Oxf. and Bucks, along with the 1st Btn RUR. Flying in also with the afternoon lift were the Armoured Reconnaissance Regiment, which was equipped with Tetrarch tanks, Bren carriers and motor cycles, and the sorely needed anti-tank guns of the 53rd (Air-Landing) Light Regiment, Royal Artillery.

6th Airborne Division served as infantry of the line until withdrawn on 9 September from Normandy to the United Kingdom. Total casualties numbered 4,557 all ranks: 821 killed, 2,709 seriously wounded and 907 posted as missing.

The Special Air Service Brigade operations in France after 'D'-Day in the summer of 1944 were too numerous to discuss in this brief history. In execution however, these clandestine missions deep into enemy-held territory provided perhaps the classic example in the story of airborne forces of inspired co-operation between the Air arm and the parachute soldier. The SAS Brigade, which was commanded from the SAS cell at General Browning's Airborne HQ at Moor Park, in Hertfordshire, by Brigadier R W McLeod, carried out 43 operations in North West Europe. The key instrument of intelligence in the hands of the SAS teams and their Resistance comrades on the ground was the Jedburgh wireless set.

Before the war moved into Holland in autumn 1944, the SAS deployed its tentacles into central and eastern France after the French and Belgian elements had created mayhem amongst the German garrisons in the Cherbourg and Brest peninsulas. The code-names for the SAS operations of this period seem strangely inappropriate for such grim assignments. Here are some good examples: 'Barker', 'Harrods', 'Marshall', 'Snelgrove', 'Laurel', 'Hardy'; they were on the contrary no mere shopping trips or visits to the cinema. SAS soldiers who were unfortunate enough to be captured were shot by the Gestapo.

OPERATION 'MARKET GARDEN'

On 20 June 1944, General Eisenhower approved the organization of the First Allied Airborne Army. This army was composed of the British 1st Airborne Corps, consisting of 1st and 6th Airborne Divisions, 1st Special Air Service Brigade and 1st Polish Independent Parachute Brigade Group; the US 18th Airborne Corps, made up of the 17th, 82nd and 101st Airborne Divisions (and later the 13th) and several Airborne Aviation Battalions; the British 52nd (Lowland) Division re-assigned from a mountain rôle to fly in transport planes; 9th US Troop Carrier Command, and Nos. 38 and 46 Groups RAF. Lieutenant-General Lewis H Brereton USAAF was selected to lead the new Airborne army with 'Boy' Browning and Matthew B Ridgway as the two Corps commanders.

Many new tasks were discussed, even before the breakout from Normandy, for the employment of airborne troops as the battle for France developed but, apart from the SAS drops, none of the major plans materialized. Parachute and glider troops were, however, used in August 1944 for the invasion of the south of France. The 1st Airborne Task Force, which was not drawn from Brereton's command, consisted of five US parachute battalions and one US air-landing brigade and the 2nd British Independent Parachute Brigade Group. The fly-in from Rome of 1st Airborne Task Force, which landed ahead of the US Seventh Army, was handled by 51 US Troop Carrier Wing; the glider force numbered 61 Wacos and Horsas. Operation 'Anvil', which commenced on 15 August, was completely successful and the airborne troops were withdrawn from their sectors in the Cannes-Toulon-St Tropez area, leaving the south of France before the end of the month.

In late August 1944, after breaking the deadlock in Normandy, the Allies did not have the supplies to keep pace with the rapid advances that had been made in several directions. After enveloping the German Seventh and Fifth Panzer Armies, General Patton and the US Third Army spearheaded a swift Allied drive eastwards. At this time, General Dempsey's British Second Army was surging through Belgium to the Dutch frontier. The problem was lack of petrol: General Montgomery at 21st Army Group in the north demanded all the resources at the disposal of the Allies to plunge through Holland and outflank the Siegfried Line; General Patton similarly insisted on the same weight of support to breach the German fortifications from the front. Montgomery and Patton had only two things in common: each believed that he was the only commander capable of exploiting the German deterioration and both wanted to be first into Berlin.

Although Montgomery's reputation for caution was about as extreme as Patton's was for instant manoeuvre, the former bargained more successfully with Eisenhower and plans were immediately formulated for an almighty Allied offensive mounted with all available resources into Holland. We may wonder what might have happened if Patton, instead, had had his way; Operation 'Market-Garden', as it was christened, was in any case doomed to failure. The main drive from forward of the Albert canal would come from Horrocks' XXX Corps (the Guards Armoured Division, 43rd [Wessex] Division, Princess Irene Dutch Brigade, 50th Division and 8th Armoured Brigade) with XII and VIII Corps on its flanks. The line of advance was described by a single highway extending northwards for just over 60 miles (98 km) to Arnhem on the Lower Rhine. Once over the bridge at Arnhem, Montgomery

believed that, having turned the flank of the Siegfried Line, he would be free to wheel eastwards into the North German Plain.

Three airborne divisions – the British 1st and US 82nd and 101st – forming the *ad hoc* 1st Allied Airborne Corps – were assigned to drop ahead of XXX Corps to capture the bridges over a number of lateral water obstacles and so secure the on-going path of the Second Army. The 101st Airborne Division (Taylor) was ordered to drop north of Eindhoven to capture the bridge over the Wilhelmina Canal at Zon and another bridge over the Zuid Willems Canal at Veghel. The US 82nd Airborne Division (Gavin) was to land south of Nijmegen on both sides of the highway near Grave. In this locality, General Gavin's objectives were the bridge over the Maas River at Grave, the road and rail bridges over the Waal River at Nijmegen and the Maas-Waal Canal bridge on the southern approach to Nijmegen. Furthest away, Urquhart's 1st Airborne Division, with Sosabowski's Polish Parachute Brigade under command, was to seize the road bridge at Arnhem. 52nd (Lowland) Division was scheduled to fly into Deelen airfield after consolidation in the Arnhem area. The command of the 1st Allied Airborne Corps, much to the disapproval of the Americans, was given to Lieutenant-General Browning.

Sunday 17 September 1944 marked the commencement of Operation 'Market-Garden': 'Market' referred to the airborne assault and 'Garden' the land offensive. It was a beautiful day. The sky was clear and it was sunny and moderately warm. Twenty-four airfields in England throbbed to the noise of aircraft engines as the greatest sky armada thus far in Airborne history took off. On the Dutch frontier, more than 20,000 vehicles were waiting for the signal to advance. General Horrocks was confident of his ability to relieve the Americans at Eindhoven and Nijmegen but with General Student's First Parachute Army and other formidable units entrenched across his path it was looking a long way to Arnhem. 'We can hold the Arnhem bridge for four days,' Browning had said, 'but I think we might be going a bridge too far!'

In spite of intense flak, 6,669 Americans of the 101st made an almost perfect jump around mid-day at Zon, north of Eindhoven. The 'Screaming Eagles' were situated 15 miles (24 km) ahead of the British ground forces and no time was to be lost in seizing their objectives. In every way, General Maxwell D Taylor had the easiest of the three divisional assignments: he was nearest to the oncoming British tanks and initial opposition to the 101st was slight.

Further north, General Gavin's 82nd received a hot reception from the German AA guns. The 'All Americans' positions south of Nijmegen lay nearly 40 miles (64 km) to the north of Eindhoven and Jim Gavin's commitments were more extensive than those of Maxwell D Taylor. Two of the 82nd's Parachute Regiments were to drop close to the Groesbeek ridge, near the German border, and 50 Waco gliders accompanied by 38 Horsas and Wacos belonging to General Browning's Corps HQ were to land in the same area. A few miles to the north lay another drop zone, near Overasselt, assigned to Gavin's third Parachute Regiment.

In the woodland area near the village of Oosterbeek, west of Arnhem, the reception to the first elements of 1st Airborne Division was mild by comparison with the experience of the

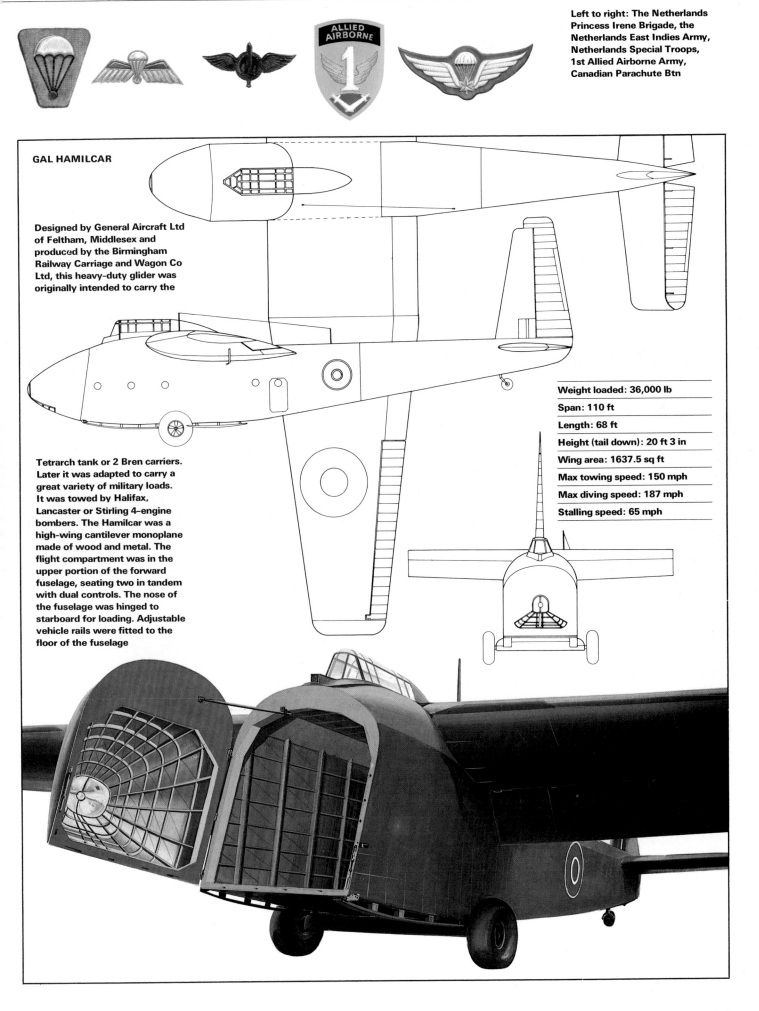

Left to right: The Netherlands
Princess Irene Brigade, the
Netherlands East Indies Army,
Netherlands Special Troops,
1st Allied Airborne Army,
Canadian Parachute Btn

GAL HAMILCAR

Designed by General Aircraft Ltd
of Feltham, Middlesex and
produced by the Birmingham
Railway Carriage and Wagon Co
Ltd, this heavy-duty glider was
originally intended to carry the

Tetrarch tank or 2 Bren carriers.
Later it was adapted to carry a
great variety of military loads.
It was towed by Halifax,
Lancaster or Stirling 4-engine
bombers. The Hamilcar was a
high-wing cantilever monoplane
made of wood and metal. The
flight compartment was in the
upper portion of the forward
fuselage, seating two in tandem
with dual controls. The nose of
the fuselage was hinged to
starboard for loading. Adjustable
vehicle rails were fitted to the
floor of the fuselage

Weight loaded: 36,000 lb

Span: 110 ft

Length: 68 ft

Height (tail down): 20 ft 3 in

Wing area: 1637.5 sq ft

Max towing speed: 150 mph

Max diving speed: 187 mph

Stalling speed: 65 mph

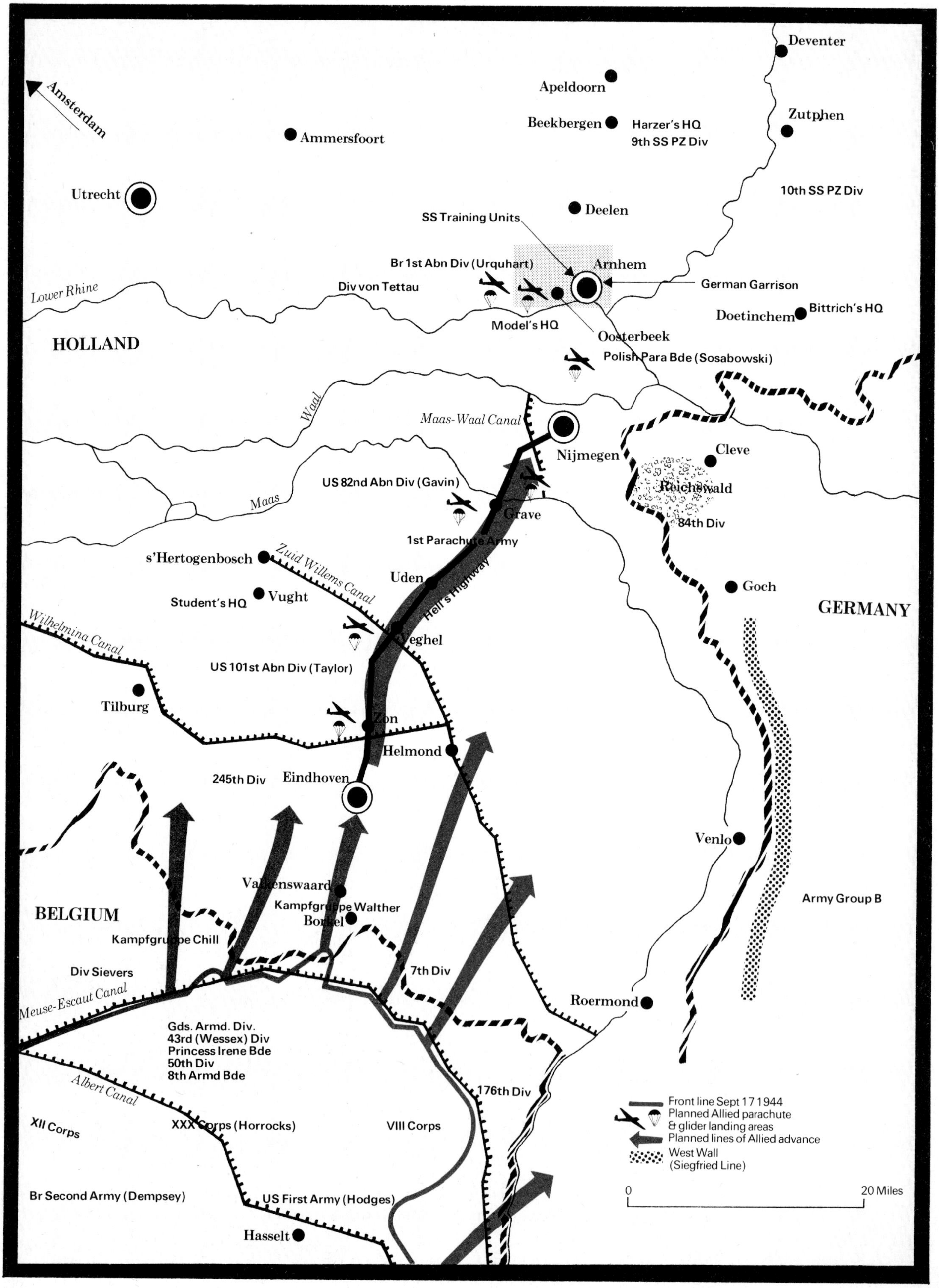

Deventer

Apeldoorn

Ammersfoort

Beekbergen

Harzer's HQ
9th SS PZ Div

Zutphen

10th SS PZ Div

Utrecht

Deelen

SS Training Units

Br 1st Abn Div (Urquhart)

Arnhem

Div von Tettau

German Garrison

Doetinchem

Bittrich's HQ

Lower Rhine

HOLLAND

Model's HQ

Oosterbeek

Polish Para Bde (Sosabowski)

Waal

Maas-Waal Canal

Nijmegen

Cleve

Maas

US 82nd Abn Div (Gavin)

Grave

Reichswald

84th Div

1st Parachute Army

s'Hertogenbosch

Zuid Willems Canal

Uden

Goch

Student's HQ

Vught

Hell's Highway

GERMANY

Wilhelmina Canal

Veghel

US 101st Abn Div (Taylor)

Tilburg

Zon

Helmond

245th Div

Eindhoven

Venlo

Valkenswaard

Kampfgruppe Walther

Borkel

Army Group B

BELGIUM

Kampfgruppe Chill

Div Sievers

7th Div

Meuse-Escaut Canal

Roermond

Gds. Armd. Div.
43rd (Wessex) Div
Princess Irene Bde
50th Div
8th Armd Bde

Albert Canal

176th Div

XII Corps

XXX Corps (Horrocks)

VIII Corps

Front line Sept 17 1944
Planned Allied parachute
& glider landing areas
Planned lines of Allied advance
West Wall
(Siegfried Line)

Br Second Army (Dempsey)

US First Army (Hodges)

0   20 Miles

Hasselt

Amsterdam

Peter Sarson and Tony Bryan

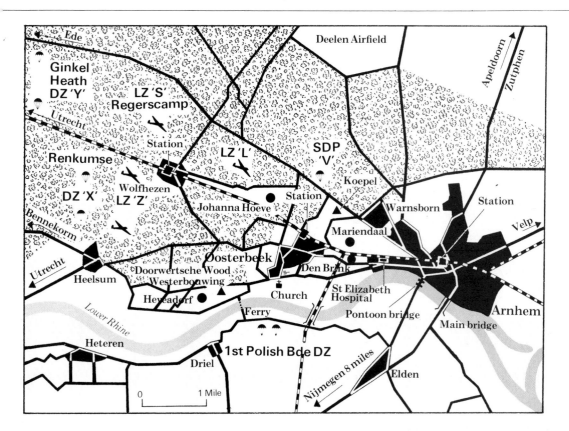

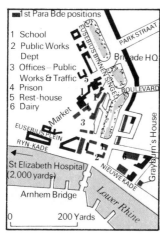

St Elizabeth Hospital (2,000 yards)

Arnhem Bridge

0   200 Yards

OPERATION 'MARKET GARDEN'

**Far left: The objectives, line of advance from the Dutch frontier to the Lower Rhine at Arnhem, and the dispositions of the German forces in Holland.
Left: Arnhem. The dropping and landing zones. Above: The positions at the Arnhem bridge.**

American divisions. The main parachute and glider landings, involving Brigadier Lathbury's 1st Parachute Brigade and 345 Horsas and 13 Hamilcars allotted to the air-landing battalions as well as support and service troops, were the most successful made by either side during the war. One problem immediately facing General Urquhart, however, was that 35 gliders containing the reconnaissance squadron's armoured jeeps had failed to arrive. It was to have been the recce troops' job to seize the Arnhem bridge; Frost's 2nd Parachute Battalion was accordingly ordered to lead the way to the objective. Meanwhile, the three glider battalions (7th King's Own Scottish Borderers, 2nd South Staffords and 1st Borders) took up defensive positions for the arrival of the second lift the following day.

Within two hours of landing in Holland, General Taylor's 101st seized Veghel at the northernmost tip of its 15-mile (24 km) sector of the corridor, along with four crossings of the River Aa and the Willems Canal. Several objectives further south between Veghel and Zon were also taken with relative ease but before nightfall on the 17th the Americans knew that they would have to fight hard to hold their ground. Taylor's priority was the highway bridge at Zon, approximately five miles (8 km) north of Eindhoven but as he directed his attacks in the area he already felt a sense of foreboding. The British tanks were nowhere in sight and at that time were barely beyond their start-line. Plans were immediately launched to co-ordinate the assault on the Zon bridge with a secondary attack to seize the bridge over the canal at Best, a few miles to the west. German resistance mounted as the 506th Regiment fought its way through Zon and the first set-back of Operation 'Market-Garden' occurred when the bridge was blown up by German engineers. Seizing boats, the 506th crossed to the south to take their objectives at Eindhoven but, although a light wooden bridge was erected, no crossing by XXX Corps would be possible until a more substantial bridge could be erected. Meanwhile, the 502nd Regiment was involved at the Best bridge in an action which was to last 48 hours.

As the German forces concentrated in strength at Best and that bridge was also blown up, the Zon crossing became a

British parachutists carrying a container to load into their   *aircraft prior to Operation 'Market Garden'*

critical factor. The central column remained standing, so the British engineers now arriving on the scene worked feverishly with the American paratroopers to provide a solid mounting for the advancing armour. The German Fifteenth Army planned to use Best as its base to drive across the main road, which had already been named 'Hell's Highway' by the Americans, but General Taylor countered this threat by renewing his assault at Best, this time with the support of British tanks. This battle was won by the Anglo-American units. With the capture of Eindhoven by the 101st, the Guards Armoured Division advanced over the resurrected bridge at Zon on the night of the 18th.

During the night of the 17th, all three parachute regiments of the 82nd Airborne Division reported to General Jim Gavin that they had the situation well in hand and that Colonel Reuben Tucker's 504th Parachute Infantry Regiment had captured the big Grave bridge and another at Molenhoek. A report received by the General at 06.55 hours on the 18th, that the 508th PIR had a patrol on the Waal bridge, gave him every confidence that his division would quickly secure the southern approaches to the town. Although Gavin was preoccupied with holding his primary objectives, including the dominant Groesbeek heights, and concerned for the fortunes of a delayed Glider lift, he set about his tasks to clear the path for Horrocks's now fast-approaching tanks. The principal objective was the huge highway bridge spanning the 400-yard (366 m) wide Waal River. After making a personal reconnaissance, Gavin was alarmed to discover that earlier reports that the 508th had reached the bridge were in error. Based on the

principle that the way to seize a bridge was by taking it at both ends at the same time, the 82nd's commander ordered up the 504th from the Grave area and informed Colonel Tucker that it was his 3rd Battalion that would launch an attack on the far end by means of an amphibious operation.

On the 20th, Major Julian Cook, the officer commanding the 3rd Battalion, was briefed to take his men across the river in broad daylight. Despite a strike by Typhoon aircraft and support by the guns of 30 Sherman tanks of the Irish Guards, the fleet of fragile boats was subjected to a devastating barrage of fire from the far bank. Major Cook's losses on the crossing were appalling and those who reached the other side advanced in the face of point-blank machine-gun and rifle fire. The paratroopers clambered on to the bridge just as a troop of four tanks of the Guards Armoured Division arrived at the other end. German General Harmel ordered the bridge to be blown but the explosion failed: to this day nobody knows who cut the wires. At that moment, Harmel was firmly of the opinion that nothing could stop the Second Army from reaching Arnhem.

Field Marshal Model, who held the command of all the German forces in Holland, had Student's First Parachute Army and von Zangen's Fifteenth Army plus a number of other units at his disposal for fending off the Second Army. Although Major General Allan Adair's Guards Armoured Division was on the south bank of the Waal within three days of the opening of the offensive, Model had ample forces to deal with Horrocks's XXX Corps advancing on a 'one-tank' front. The tenure of the highway was by no means secure:

Left: Airborne troops dug in at Arnhem to hold a Brigade HQ, 18 September 1944. Below: Men of the 1st Parachute Battalion take cover in a shell hole at Arnhem

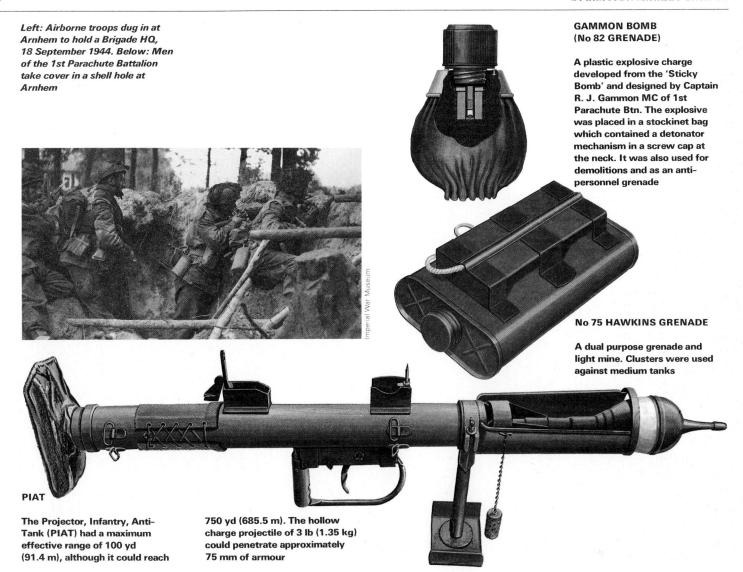

Imperial War Museum

GAMMON BOMB (No 82 GRENADE)

A plastic explosive charge developed from the 'Sticky Bomb' and designed by Captain R. J. Gammon MC of 1st Parachute Btn. The explosive was placed in a stockinet bag which contained a detonator mechanism in a screw cap at the neck. It was also used for demolitions and as an anti-personnel grenade

No 75 HAWKINS GRENADE

A dual purpose grenade and light mine. Clusters were used against medium tanks

PIAT

The Projector, Infantry, Anti-Tank (PIAT) had a maximum effective range of 100 yd (91.4 m), although it could reach 750 yd (685.5 m). The hollow charge projectile of 3 lb (1.35 kg) could penetrate approximately 75 mm of armour

stretches of the road were lost and recovered in the ensuing days in a welter of attacks and counter-attacks by both sides along the entire length of the road from Nijmegen south to Eindhoven. Montgomery's plan to send Dempsey's Second Army racing through Holland was fast losing its credibility. Model had in addition two armoured divisions near Arnhem: Bittrich's 9th SS (Hohenstaufen) and 10th SS (Frundsberg) Divisions – *embarras de richesse* in dealing with the lightly armed 1st Airborne Division which, within a few days, was fighting desperately for its very survival only half-an-hour's drive from Nijmegen.

In England, on the morning of the 18th, the take-off of the second lift due at Arnhem at 10.00 hours had been delayed by fog and it was 15.00 hours before the landings commenced. Both the 7th KOSB and 2nd South Staffords had been in action since early morning and the woodland abutting the reception zones was ablaze. One Dakota, hit by flak over the DZ, burst into flames but the troops jumped clear before the aircraft plunged helplessly to the ground.

'A' Company, 2nd Parachute Battalion, had entered Arnhem the previous evening but failed in an attempt to cross the bridge from the north end. During the night, both the 1st and 3rd Parachute Battalions were forced to entrench in positions near Wolfhezen station and west of Oosterbeek; the nearest units were at least four miles (6.5 km) from Arnhem. At 1st Airborne Div HQ on the first afternoon, General Urquhart found it impossible to make contact with Lathbury's 1st Parachute Brigade, moving into the town. Urquhart jumped into a jeep to find out what was going on and, as a

result of a series of adventures inside Arnhem, was not in command of his division for 48 hours.

Brigadier Hicks of the Air-Landing Brigade, who in Urquhart's temporary absence assumed command of 1st Airborne Division, decided, with the arrival of Brigadier J H 'Shan' Hackett's 4th Parachute Brigade, that his first concern was to direct as many troops as possible to the bridge. The Battle of Arnhem was now assuming a definite pattern. Frost's force, which had grown to an enlarged battalion group, was engaged in a desperate struggle with the Panzer forces. Four battalions, the 1st, 3rd, the South Staffords and 11th (4th Brigade) were fighting their way yard-by-yard into the town. The remainder of the 4th Brigade, with the 156th Battalion leading the 10th, were advancing on the left flank, with the 1st Borders, while the 7th KOSB were moving forward to secure a landing zone for the Polish glider troops.

Bittrich, having detached his 10th Panzer Division on the 17th to proceed south to Nijmegen, ordered Harzer's 9th Panzer Division to occupy the Arnhem area. With the Panzers in control of the Arnhem-Ede road to the north, Harzer immediately saw the possibility of encircling 1st Airborne Division. Brinkmann was ordered to patrol the town with armour and infantry and to clear the houses of British parachutists. Spindler's *Sperrgruppe* (blocking-group) was assigned to create a wall of armour and infantry on the outskirts of Arnhem and to patrol forward along the three 'approach' routes into the town.

'Black Tuesday' (the 19th) was really the day that set the seal on 1st Airborne's misfortunes. Inside Arnhem, Frost's

Imperial War Museum

Left: A German photograph of German troops on the alert during the attack on Arnhem
Below: A German soldier lies where he fell on the bridge at Nijmegen, Holland. The bridge was captured intact by American paratroopers of the 1st Allied Airborne Army landing behind German lines in Holland, 17 September 1944

Imperial War Museum

The vital bridge at Arnhem, showing British troops at the top end. Whilst part of the 1st Parachute Brigade was holding the north end during the early stages of the operation, the Germans rushed a large number of armoured vehicles across the bridge from the south side.

These were promptly destroyed by the paratroops at the north end

force occupied about 40 houses and were grimly defending their positions on the north-west side of the bridge. The whole of Arnhem was burning fiercely and Tiger tanks rumbled through the streets shelling each suspected hiding place. All hope of capturing the southern end of the bridge was abandoned; ammunition was running low and conditions generally grew worse and worse. At dusk on the 20th, the Germans were moving in on the last remaining strongholds with flamethrowers. Frost, who himself had been hit in the leg when running the gauntlet to one of his outposts, gave instructions for the fit men to make their way to Oosterbeek. It was the end of the war for the wounded men at the Arnhem bridge.

The story of the Battle of Arnhem is often only associated with the fight at the bridge but for courage and self-sacrifice the drive on the 19th by the South Staffords and the 1st, 3rd and 11th Parachute Battalions moving into the town from the north has seldom been equalled in the annals of military history. Sandwiched between a railway marshalling yard and the Lower Rhine, the 3rd Battalion shortly advanced along two adjacent roads and began the race from the St Elizabeth Hospital to relieve Frost's isolated troops. Fitch, commanding the 3rd Battalion, was killed, as were a majority of his men, while McCardie, Dobie and Lea, leading the South Staffords, 1st and 11th Battalions, followed up with attacks along the same two routes. Machine-gun fire plunged downwards from the upstairs windows of houses on to the troops until German tanks, forming an impenetrable barricade, swung into gear and moved forwards to decimate the ranks of the oncoming battalions.

Although 4th Parachute Brigade started strongly on the 19th along the northern route into Arnhem, the 156th and 10th Battalions were driven back with heavy losses. Both battalions successfully entrenched but their positions were pounded throughout the day by a systematic fire plan mounted by tanks, SPs, mobile flak guns and mortars. Machine-gun and rifle fire was aimed at the airborne men at close range and each platoon was left to fend for itself in a fight against impossible odds. At the end of the day 4th Parachute Brigade had ceased to exist as an organized fighting formation.

General Urquhart's headquarters had been established in his absence at the Hartenstein Hotel in Oosterbeek. When, later on 'Black Tuesday', the general arrived at the hotel, he was faced with several unpleasant decisions. The 4th Brigade had been savaged and those elements of the 1st and Air-

Landing Brigades that had attempted to relieve Frost's men at the bridge were in full retreat. Moreover, the collapse of resistance at the bridge was clearly imminent. But his assignment was to capture the Arnhem road bridge and to form a bridgehead for the Second Army to cross the Lower Rhine! Urquhart now ordered his division to concentrate in a perimeter measuring four miles square, based on Oosterbeek. This decision, taken two days before Frost's surrender, meant of course the abandonment of the paratroopers in Arnhem. In theory the Oosterbeek perimeter formed a reception area if the Second Army attempted to cross the Lower Rhine; in practice, although the Waal bridge had been taken by the US 82nd Division, the main body of General Horrocks' tanks had not crossed the river. The American paratroopers pleaded with the tank men to advance but Montgomery's offensive had ground to a halt and 1st Airborne faced extinction at the hands of the 9th SS Panzer Division.

The remainder of the story of the Battle of Arnhem was one of a steadily eroding stronghold at Oosterbeek, desperate air supply missions and incredible bravery by the parachute and glider troops. On the 23rd, General Urquhart was informed of the Second Army's decision to withdraw the airborne troops from north of the Lower Rhine. An attempt to facilitate the withdrawal by sending troops across the river to bolster the perimeter had, however, ended in failure. Polish troops, who had dropped with Sosabowski's Brigade on the afternoon of the 21st, and 5th Btn the Dorset Regiment attempted the crossing near the Heavadorp Ferry the previous night but murderous enemy machine-gun fire raked the boats and wounded men were carried screaming down the swiftly-flowing river. The fighting around Oosterbeek nevertheless continued unabated until the 25th when at 18.30 the order was given to prepare to move.

It was raining fairly heavily when at 22.00 hours the first men left their posts. At the river bank, British sappers awaited the survivors. When the last boat had gone, about 500 men were left behind; some plunged into the river and others went off in a hopeless search for other crossing points. Urquhart's Division had been virtually destroyed. Of his Brigadiers, Lathbury and Hackett were held prisoner: three battalion commanders (Fitch, des Voeux and Smyth) were dead; four (McCardie, Lea, Frost and Hadden) were in captivity. As to those men who were never to return, the cemetery at Oosterbeek, which over the years has been cared for with great devotion by the Dutch people, displays 1,500 white crosses.

Readers may draw their own conclusions about the failure of Operation 'Market-Garden'. Montgomery's offensive did not turn the flank of Hitler's West Wall. The big pursuit from the Seine was over and four months went by before the Canadian First Army attacked at Nijmegen and advanced up the west bank of the Rhine. American airborne losses, including glider pilots and IX Troop Carrier Command, were put at nearly 4,000 men. General Maxwell D. Taylor's 101st Airborne Division suffered 2,118 casualties; General Jim Gavin's 82nd Airborne Division 1,432; the USAAF lost 424 aircrew. Urquhart's 1st Airborne Division casualties, including glider pilots and Polish troops, totalled 7,578; only 2,427 out of the original force of 10,005 landing at Arnhem reached the Divisional lines at Nijmegen. In addition, the RAF lost 294 of their own men.

BEYOND THE RHINE

The reputation gained in Italy by *Fallschirm-Korps I* for dogged resistance was to be more than matched in tenacity by *Fallschirm-Korps II* after D-Day in France. Formed in eastern France, *Generalleutnant* Eugen Meindl's 2nd Parachute Corps (3rd and 5th Parachute Divisions) was committed to the Normandy beach-head in June 1944 but later fared badly at the hands of British and Canadian troops in the Falaise pocket. Ramcke's *Fallschirm-Division 2* also saw action on the north-west coast of France, fighting for several weeks to defend the Brest fortress, which did not surrender until 20 September. Plocher's *Fallschirm-Division 6*, formed in the Amiens area in June 1944, suffered heavy losses in operations to hold back the Allies after the Normandy breakout in July. During the pursuit to the Seine, the German parachute units in France were reassembled under *Generaloberst* Kurt Student for the defence of Holland as *Fallschirm-Armee 1*, which had been in existence since March 1944 for the purpose of training new parachute divisions. Student's *Fallschirmjäger*, having provided the hard core of the successful resistance to the British Second Army during Operation 'Market-Garden', were later (during November and December 1944 and the early months of 1945) involved under *Generaloberst* Schlemm in preventing the Allies from breaking through to the Rhine.

On 16 December 1944, Hitler launched his great counter-offensive in the Ardennes. Hitler's ambitious plan was to strike with three armies through the Ardennes forest, cross the Meuse River and recapture Antwerp, thereby sealing off four Allied armies in the north. Schimpf's *Fallschirm-Division 3* was in the thick of the assault in the Malmédy sector and it was in this vicinity that *Oberst* Freiherr von der Heydte's parachute battle group made the last German parachute assault drop of the war.

The Battle of the Bulge was the greatest pitched battle on the Western Front in the Second World War. A total of 29 German and 33 Allied divisions (mainly American) participated. General Matthew B Ridgway's US XVIII Airborne Corps, which on 16 December was resting in the Rheims area, was immediately alerted and the 82nd and 101st Divisions raced north in trucks into Belgium. The 101st, under the temporary command of Brigadier-General Anthony McAuliffe, was routed through the snow-covered countryside to Bastogne, the key to the southern flank; Gavin's 82nd was sent to Werbomont, near the L'Ambleve river. On the 19th, McAuliffe, a thick-set, diminutive, cigar-smoking General, received his orders (from Gavin) 'to organize the city for all-round defense and to stay there until he got further orders, reporting to the Commander of XVIII Corps'. General Troy Middleton, the US VII Corps' Commander, who was effectively the senior American officer in the area, similarly visited McAuliffe on the 19th and said 'Hold Bastogne'. 'Bastogne', which was relieved on 26 December, may not have been the longest siege in the history of land warfare but its name does cite a foremost battle honour in the story of the United States Army as well as its most celebrated remark. When *Generalleutnant* Lüttwitz, commanding XLVII Panzer Corps, considered the 'Screaming Eagles's' position to be untenable, the German General sent his emissaries through the lines with the

Generaloberst *Kurt Student* inspects von der Heydte's Fallschirmjäger *on 16 December 1944 before their final drop of the war*

CURTISS C-46 COMMANDO

Designed by Curtiss-Wright in 1936 as a 36-seat commercial airliner, designated CW-20 – prototype (NX 19436) first flew on 26 March 1940. Originally named Condor, the C-46 was later renamed Commando and was produced in substantial numbers for the USAAF, the US Navy and Marine Corps. The Army aircraft, used predominantly in the Far East, became famous for their round-the-clock flights across the Himalayas to keep open the supply routes between Burma and China. They first appeared in Europe in March 1945, when they were used to drop paratroops during the Rhine crossing. The freight-loading doors in the fuselage sides were used for the despatch of the airborne troops (C-46F) – the first time that troops jumped simultaneously from both sides of an aircraft. The aircraft proved very vulnerable to incendiary shells. 22 were lost in the Rhine crossing. They could carry 30 airborne troops or up to 40 airlifted troops or 33 stretcher cases or a 10,000 lb (4536 kg) payload of freight or military equipment

Engines (Army version): 2 x 2000 hp Pratt & Whitney R-2800-51 Double Wasp Radials

Span: 108 ft 1 in

Length: 76 ft 4 in

Height: 21 ft 9 in

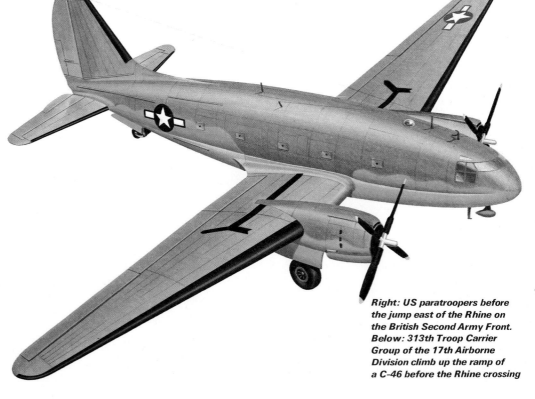

Right: US paratroopers before the jump east of the Rhine on the British Second Army Front. Below: 313th Troop Carrier Group of the 17th Airborne Division climb up the ramp of a C-46 before the Rhine crossing

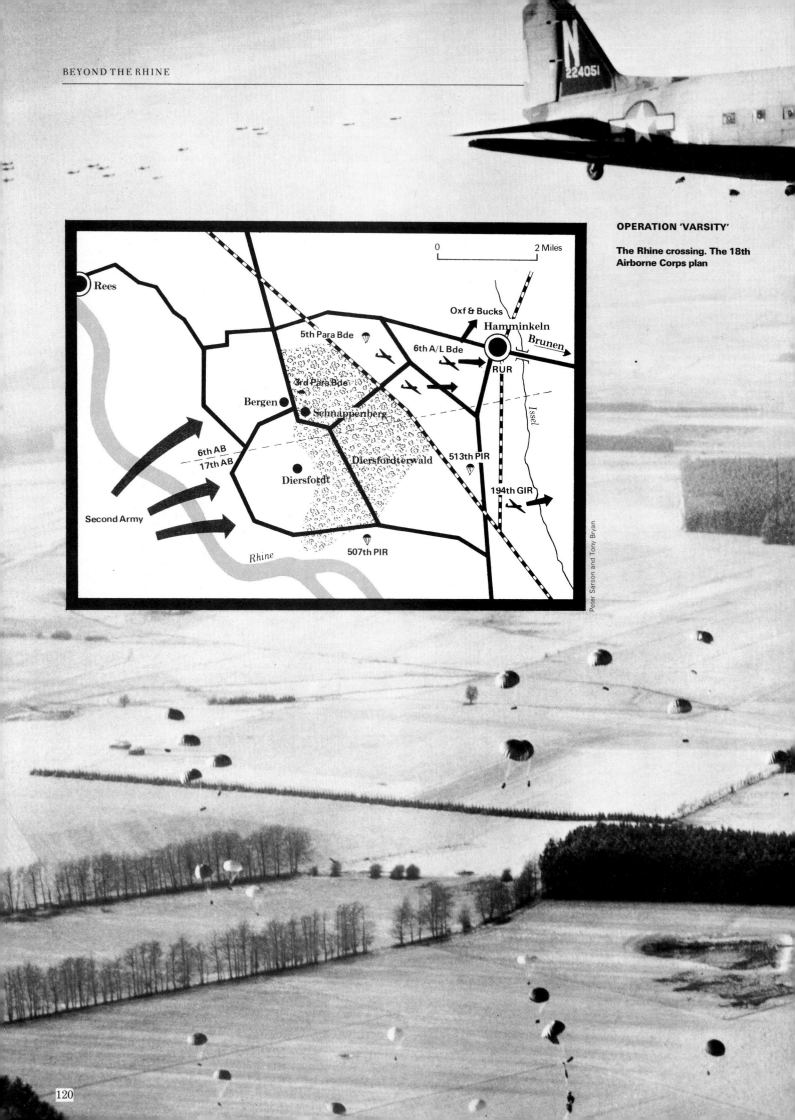

OPERATION 'VARSITY'

The Rhine crossing. The 18th Airborne Corps plan

Rees

0   2 Miles

Oxf & Bucks

Hamminkeln

5th Para Bde

Brunen

6th A/L Bde

RUR

3rd Para Bde

Issel

Bergen

Schnappenberg

6th AB

513th PIR

17th AB

Diersfordterwald

Diersfordt

194th GIR

Second Army

507th PIR

Rhine

Peter Sarson and Tony Bryan

N
224051

C-47 Dakotas of the 9th Troop Carrier Command dropping supplies to the defenders of Bastogne, Belgium, 23 December 1944

The 18th Airborne Corps lands east of the Rhine. US paratroopers dig in under the slight cover of an orchard, draped with parachutes, to set up their guns

Imperial War Museum

40-MM BOFORS

The universal 40-mm Bofors, used by almost every combatant during The Second World War, was adapted for use by airborne forces as a lightweight AA weapon. The Bofors fired a 2-lb (0.9 kg) shell at the rate of 120 rpm. The barrel could be removed for stowing in a glider. The jeep was used to deploy the Bofors and bring it into action

M22 LIGHT TANK

Known as the Locust by the British, this was designed as an airborne light tank. 830 were built by February 1944 and production then stopped. The illustration here shows the T9E1, a prototype of the standard M22.

A very small number were used on the Rhine crossing, in March 1945, by the British 6th Airborne Division. The Locust's gun was fitted with a Littlejohn adaptor. There was a 1-inch (2.5 cm) armour protection

Engine: Lycoming 162 bhp, with four-speed gearbox

Max speed: 40 mph

Armament: 37-mm gun co-axial with 0.30 Browning machine-gun

threat that, unless the 101st surrendered, the Americans in Bastogne would be annihilated by his Corps artillery fire – McAuliffe's answer was 'Nuts!'

Meanwhile, on 12 October 1944, the British 2nd Independent Parachute Brigade launched Operation 'Manna', an airborne landing in Greece. Flying from Brindisi, Coxen's 4th Parachute Battalion Group was quickly followed into Megara by the 5th and 6th Battalions. Megara airfield lies a short distance from Athens and Brigadier Pritchard led his men into the Greek capital a few days later. The parachute troops, who formed part of Arkforce with 23rd Armoured Brigade, were at first involved in pursuing German units northwards but in December were in the thick of the fighting against the Elas faction in Athens. After four weeks of vicious street fighting, the insurgents were driven from the Greek capital and the red berets returned to Italy. Thirty airborne operations were planned by the 2nd Brigade to support the Eighth Army in northern Italy but all were cancelled.

Following the Battle of the Ardennes, 6th Airborne Division took up positions on the River Maas (Meuse) between Roermond and Venlo but returned to England in February 1945 to prepare for airborne operations. At this time, the Allies, after a hard winter war in north-west Europe, were ready to cross the Rhine and advance into the heart of Germany. In the north, Montgomery's 21st Army Group was to send the Second Army, on the night of 23 March, across the river between Xanten and Rees to capture Wesel. The assault, spearheaded by Commandos, went smoothly and at daybreak General Matthew B Ridgway's XVIII Airborne Corps flew in

to seize high ground in the Hamminkeln area. The skytrain carrying the US 17th and British 6th Airborne Divisions (Miley and Bols) consisted of 1,696 transport planes and 1,348 gliders, which were escorted by nearly 1,000 fighters. Ridgway's XVIII Airborne Corps arrived successfully in spite of heavy AA fire and quickly seized their objectives in woodland – the Diesfordter Wald – overlooking the river. Late on the 24th, Dempsey's Second Army was streaming unopposed across the Rhine.

After the Rhine-crossing, the British 6th and the US 17th, 82nd and 101st Airborne Divisions all took part in the rapid Allied advance into Germany. Apart from some SAS drops (the British, French and Belgian elements were mainly assigned to jeep reconnaissance) there were no more airborne operations in Europe. Spearheading the race of Dempsey's Second Army to the Baltic, Ridgway's XVIII Airborne Corps crossed the Ems, Weser and Elbe; the Canadians of 6th Airborne Division were the first to meet the Russians on 1 May at the port of Wismar. The US 7th Armored Division should have reached the Baltic first but, as a gesture to General Dempsey, Ridgway held open the Elbe bridges at Artlenburg and Lauenburg for tanks of the British 11th Armoured Division. General Gavin, whose 82nd Division in the latter stages advanced in concert with XVIII Corps, first met the Russians in the small town of Grabow in Mecklenburg. Away to the south, the 101st Airborne Division finally came to a halt after capturing Hitler's mountain lair at Berchtesgaden in the Obersalzberg, a fitting end to the story of airborne warfare in Europe 1940–45.

PACIFIC AND SOUTH EAST ASIA

urning, lastly, to the Pacific and SE Asia theatres, the US 503rd Parachute Infantry Regiment was fast taking shape in Australia in early 1942. During the New Guinea campaign, General MacArthur landed on the Huon peninsula using the Australian 9th Division. A day later (6 September 1943), the 503rd made the first American airborne drop of the Pacific War at Nadzab airfield northwest of Lae; the Australian 7th Division air-landed in Dakotas as soon as the drop zone was cleared. The Airborne involvement greatly assisted the Allied advance on Salamaua.

The 503rd carried out its second airborne operation on 3 July 1944 on Noemfoor Island but its final and most spectacular jump occurred on 16 February 1945 on Corregidor Island in the Philippines. At dawn on the 16th, the men of the

3rd Battalion, Battery 'C' of the 462nd Parachute Field Artillery, Company 'C' 161st Airborne Engineers and most of the 503rd's regimental headquarters, took off in C-47s from Mindora for Corregidor. Two more lifts followed and heavy fighting against a strong Japanese garrison continued until the island was overrun two weeks later. On 2 March, a guard of honour of the 503rd presented 'Fortress Corregidor' to General MacArthur.

The US 11th Airborne Division was first committed to battle in the Pacific in November 1944, on Leyte Island, where the 457th Parachute Artillery was dropped into a jungle clearing. The 11th's main scene of operations was Luzon island, during February–June 1945. On 3 February, the 511th Regiment mounted a wholly successful parachute operation

US Airforce

Left to right: Japanese airborne, Navy (summer), Navy (winter), Army, Army, 44th Indian Airborne Division

to rescue 2,200 American prisoners of war near Tagaytay ridge. On 23 June, the 511th was again landed (this time from 54 C-47s, 13 C-46s and seven Waco CG-4As) on the most northerly tip of Luzon, to cut off Japanese troops retreating to the port of Aparri. The action by the 511th continued for three days until the airborne troops were relieved by the US 37th Division.

Japanese airborne forces had existed since 1940. Both the Army and Navy were to support airborne formations and, before the end of 1941, Germany had a team of instructors in Japan. The Army's airborne force, consisting of a parachute brigade, a glider brigade and support units, was to be used as a raiding force; the naval parachutists formed two landing units and were similarly used as air commandos.

9th Troop Carrier Command Dakota 'hooks' a Waco glider in training. This technique was used to recover gliders in Burma with the 2nd Chindit expedition

Early in the war, the Japanese mounted an airborne operation from Davao in the Philippines on Menado airfield at the northern tip of Celebes island, in the Dutch East Indies. On 11 January 1942, naval parachutists of the Yokosuka 1st Special Landing Unit captured the airfield with little difficulty, thus providing a useful base for Zero fighters. The most important Japanese airborne operation of the war took place shortly afterwards on Sumatra. On 9 February 1942, Colonel Kume's Army Parachute Brigade dropped ahead of the Japanese 38th Division, landing from the beaches to capture Palembang airfield and a nearby oil refinery. Dutch, British and Australian troops resisted the invasion strongly but the Japanese paratroopers, split into two groups, had a sufficient hold on their objectives by mid-February to allow the 38th Division to consolidate its positions. The Yokosuka 1st Special Landing Unit also made a minor drop in early 1942 on Koepang, the capital of Dutch Timor. The Japanese thereafter were unable to make much use of their airborne troops but small parachute units made a few disruptive raids in the Philippines after MacArthur's return to these islands. Japanese Army and Naval parachutists wore combat dress based on the German model. The Army jumpers wore a wing designed in the form of the legendary 'Golden Kite'; the Navy wore a crossed parachute and anchor emblem.

In the SE Asian sphere, the Air-Landing School at Willingdon Airport near New Delhi, in India, was moved in 1942 to Chaklala, near Rawalpindi, where No. 3 Parachute Training School was established by Ringway instructors. In early 1944, Major-General E E Down formed 44th Indian Airborne Division from the 50th Indian Parachute Brigade. On 1 May 1945, an improvised battalion group, made up from 1st Indian and 2nd and 3rd Gurkha Parachute Battalions, was dropped on a successful operation ('Dracula') to destroy Japanese gun positions at Elephant Point, at the mouth of the Rangoon River. Plans existed for the formation of an airborne corps comprising 44th Indian and 6th Airborne Divisions but only 5th Parachute Brigade arrived in India (July 1945).

Some mention must be made of the strategic use of air-landed troops during Major-General Orde Wingate's Chindit operations in Burma. The Fourteenth Army's second offensive in 1943 against the Japanese on this front was launched by Wingate's 77th Infantry Brigade. The Brigade formed columns for a deep-penetration raid; the British and

Indian troops, called the 'Chindits' after the legendary lion 'Chinthé' (the 'Protector of the Pagodas'), took part in an expedition lasting four months behind the enemy lines. No troops were flown into action but air supply played an important rôle in the operation.

The Second Chindit Operation commenced in February 1944. Wingate's objective was to draw off Japanese forces on the Salween River by forming a series of jungle strongholds south of Mogaung in the area of Indaw. His forces of '3rd Indian Division' consisted of six brigades plus support and service troops. On 5 February, the 16th British Brigade (Fergusson) began a strenuous approach march from Ledo in the Brahmaputra Valley to Indaw, a distance of 360 miles (576 km) across the Upper Chindwin River and over the Patkai ranges. When Fergusson's brigade reached the Chindwin, four Waco gliders of No. 1 Air Commando flew in with equipment to assist the crossing. At the same time, two gliders landed on the far bank to secure a bridgehead.

On 5 March, Brigadier Calvert's 77th Indian Brigade took off in the first wave of Wacos from airfields in Assam and headed for the Irrawaddy River. Thirty-seven gliders were successfully landed on a jungle clearing, code-named 'Broadway'. The troops immediately set about making a safe runway and over 100 Dakotas were landed by night over the next few days. Brigadier Lentaigne's 11th Indian Brigade also flew in to 'Broadway' after another jungle clearing at 'Chowringhee' was closed down on Wingate's orders. Six hundred and fifty Dakota and glider sorties were flown during the first seven nights of the operation. During that time 9,000 men, 1,350 mules, field and anti-aircraft guns were deposited behind the Japanese lines without loss and without the enemy being aware. All the Chindit airlifts and re-supply missions were handled by Colonel Phil. Cochrane of the USAAF and his No. 1 Air Commando.

The next airborne phase involved the fly-in on 22 March of Brodie's 14th British Brigade and Gilmore's 3rd West

KOKUSAI KU-8

The Ku-8 (left and below) was less interesting than the Ku-7 but nonetheless successful. It stemmed originally from a twin-engined, high-wing, light transport plane. The second version of the Ku-8 was produced early in 1944. The fuselage was of steel tube, fabric-covered, and the nose was hinged sideways for loading. Wings and tail were of wood. The crew of two sat in the hinging nose section and the hold accommodated 20 troops or a jeep and light gun. The Ku-8 was the only Japanese glider to be used on operations

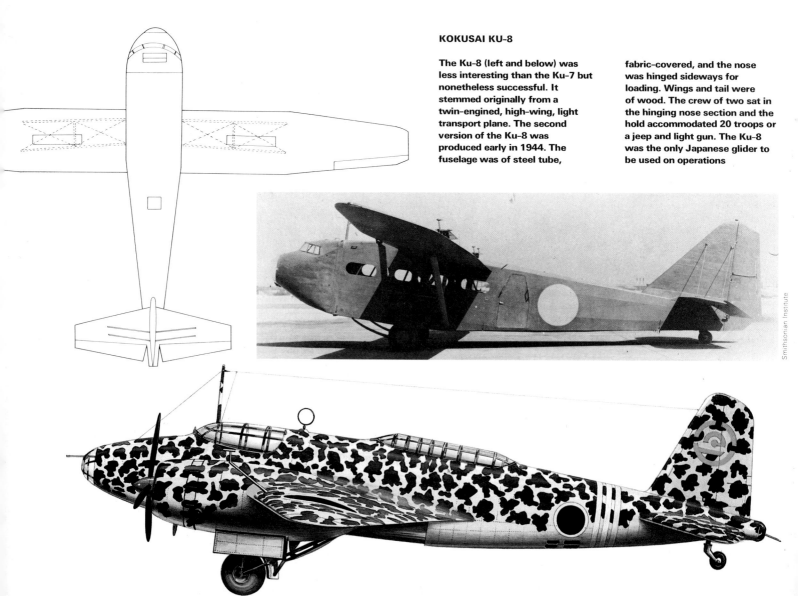

Smithsonian Institute

African Brigade at 'Aberdeen', situated north-west of Indaw in the Meza Valley. By this time Fergusson's 16th Brigade had reached the same area; the 23rd British Brigade were re-allocated from Wingate's Special Force to a short penetration raid across the Chindwin. By early May, two more strongholds had been formed between Indaw and Mogaung at 'White City', which was thus named because of the parachutes that draped the trees, and 'Blackpool' in the Mogaung valley. When the last Chindit Brigade was pulled out of Burma in August, the tide had turned on the Burma front and the Japanese Army was in full retreat across the Chindwin River. Opinions vary as to the success of Orde Wingate's deep penetration concept. He himself lost his life in a plane crash on 24 March but the record clearly demonstrates that the Chindits under Lentaigne, following Wingate's tragic death, pinned down three Japanese divisions whilst the Fourteenth Army made its victorious advance through the jungles of Burma.

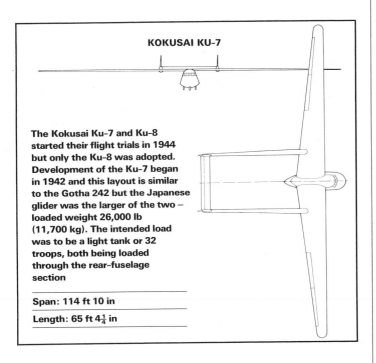

KOKUSAI KU-7

The Kokusai Ku-7 and Ku-8 started their flight trials in 1944 but only the Ku-8 was adopted. Development of the Ku-7 began in 1942 and this layout is similar to the Gotha 242 but the Japanese glider was the larger of the two – loaded weight 26,000 lb (11,700 kg). The intended load was to be a light tank or 32 troops, both being loaded through the rear-fuselage section

Span:	114 ft 10 in
Length:	65 ft 4¼ in

MITSUBISHI Ki-21

The Ki-21, known as 'Sally', was a standard Japanese Army bomber at the time of Pearl Harbor. With the appearance of the Model 2B, the original Ki-21s were withdrawn for conversion to HC-21 transports or training aircraft, and were used later in the war for air-landing assault troops and special missions. Nine men could be carried with some cargo, much of it hung on the wings. The payload of just over a ton (1016 kg) could be increased for short-range missions

Engines:	2 x 1500 hp Mitsubishi Ha 101 radials
Max speed:	302 mph
Normal range:	1678 miles
Span:	73 ft 9⅞ in
Length:	52 ft 6 in

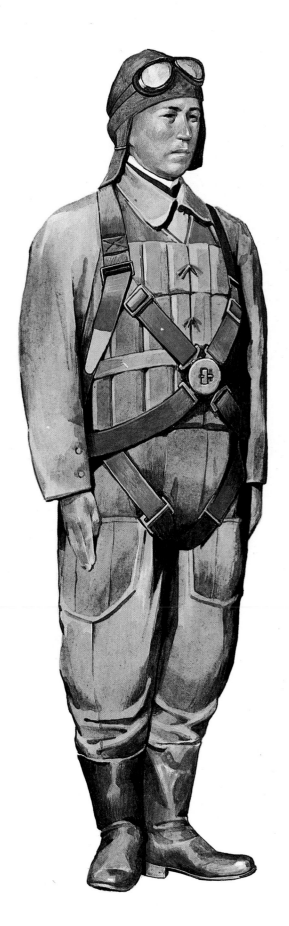

John Fraser

Artwork Index